The Relentless Pursuit of Mediocrity

Endurance Triathlons For The Recreational Athlete

by
Brian Goodyear

Ironman® is a registered trademark of the World Triathlon Corporation.

Copyright © 2012 Brian Goodyear
All rights reserved.

This book may not be reproduced in any form without the written permission of the author

ISBN: 0615599761
ISBN 13: 9780615599762

Library of Congress Control Number: 2012902464
Brian\Goodyear, Honolulu, HI

Contents

Acknowledgements	v
Introduction	vii
Part 1: In Defense of Mediocrity	1
Chapter 1: Mediocrity as a Reality for Most of Us	3
Chapter 2: A Little Philosophizing	7
Chapter 3: How We Stack Up Against Others	11
Chapter 4: Learning to Accept our Mediocrity	15
Chapter 5: Transcending Our Mediocrity	21
Chapter 6: Keeping it Simple	27
Chapter 7: Taking on the Challenge	31
Part 2: My Own Journey	35
Chapter 8: Preliminary Steps	37
Chapter 9: My First Triathlon	45
Chapter 10: On to the Tinman	53
Chapter 11: Upping the Intensity	63
Chapter 12: Endurance Starts to Call	69
Chapter 13: Halfway There	79
Chapter 14: Let's Go for the Iron!	91
Chapter 15: Disappointment...Big Time!	103
Chapter 16: Opportunity Knocks	119
Chapter 17: The BIG Day	131

Chapter 18: More Challenges 145
Chapter 19: Second Time Around 159
Chapter 20: A Change in Focus 177

Part 3: Endurance Training For The Recreational Athlete 195

Chapter 21: A Brief Background 197
Chapter 22: Setting Priorities and Goals 201
Chapter 23: A Simple Conceptual Framework 209
Chapter 24: From Conceptual Framework to Specific Plan 239

Appendix

Appendix A: Kona 2006: Weekly Training Schedule 255
Appendix B: Kona 2006: Training Summary 267

Acknowledgements

As you will see, one of the themes within this book is simplicity, so I decided to keep the acknowledgements simple too. It is true that a triathlon is ultimately an individual sport. It is also a simple fact of life, however, that a web of interdependent relationships inevitably links each individual person to many others. Without that web of relationships, our individual lives would not amount to much. I am very much aware that I would not have anything significant to write about if it were not for all those others to whom I have had the fortune to be linked. There are so many people who have provided the love, support, inspiration, encouragement, advice, and friendship that have contributed to my admittedly mediocre athletic accomplishments, and therefore to the writing of this book, that it would truly be impractical to attempt to list every single person here. Instead, I have attempted to acknowledge many of the people who have played important roles by mentioning their names in various places within the body of the book. Many of these friends have stories of their own that are worth telling, and I hope this book motivates them to tell those stories. I know there are numerous other friends and acquaintances whose names could have been mentioned, and I regret that I have not been able to include them all.

I must, however, directly acknowledge those whose love and support have been most important throughout my life, particularly my late parents, Stanley and Marjorie Goodyear, as well as my two daughters, Jennifer (a.k.a. Jen, a.k.a. Noelani) and Vanessa (a.k.a. Nes, a.k.a. Kulamanu), and my two granddaughters, Hina and La'i, who have all provided me with much joy and an ongoing *raison d'etre* for so many years. Special thanks goes out to Jen for taking the time to review drafts of this manuscript and providing helpful feedback that contributed to the final version of the book.

In addition, I want to thank my training buddy, Andrea Huston, for taking the time to read and comment on an early draft of the first part of the book. Mahalo also to Dee Dee Lum, a great friend for over 25 years since our days in graduate school, who provided some helpful suggestions about the organization of the beginning of the book. Life is not always a cabaret, old chum, but it is without a doubt the biggest endurance event that we will ever have the opportunity to participate in. Let's make sure we make the most of it! I would also like to acknowledge the professional editorial expertise of Karyl Reynolds who reviewed the entire manuscript, assisted in the preparation of the final draft of the book, and patiently tolerated my reluctance to make necessary changes.

Introduction

I begin this book with a simple statement of fact about myself. I am an ordinary recreational athlete who has not been endowed with any outstanding athletic talent or ability. To put it more bluntly, I am a mediocre athlete. Yes, that's right. I said mediocre.

Now, you may be wondering why I would ever want to begin a book with a statement like that. Is that really the best I can say about myself? Let me explain by telling you a little story.

Back in 1982, at the age of 37, I decided to enter a 5-mile run. At the time, I was in the process of trying to make some healthy changes to my lifestyle. I had quit smoking the previous year, and was trying to make a point of eating less junk food. In addition, the run was a fundraiser for what I considered to be a worthy cause, so it seemed like a good idea to give it a shot. I had not done any running to speak of for years, and I had not consistently exercised on a regular basis since some time in my teens. However, I had not been a complete couch potato either, as you could find me bodysurfing and hiking on at least an occasional basis. I stand 6 feet tall and typically weigh around 170 pounds. At that time, I may have been a few pounds heavier, but I liked to think of myself as being in relatively decent shape. Plus, I recalled having done quite well in a cross-country meet when I was only 12 years old, so why couldn't I do that now? With supreme hubris, I thought that running 5 miles, despite virtually no training at all, would be a breeze. I went into the event with a totally unrealistic expectation of how long it would take me to finish—I was thinking 30 minutes or so. I guess I was assuming that I still actually possessed whatever athletic ability I imagined I had when I was younger.

As it turned out, I was in for a major wake up call. I went out as fast as I could, but after less than a mile, running was already beginning to feel like hard work. I knew I wasn't going anywhere near as fast as I thought I would have been able to. As my pace got slower and slower, I found that I was even being passed by people who looked like their training had involved nothing more than the consumption of large quantities of doughnuts. Before I even got to the halfway mark, I was struggling just to keep going and asking myself how much longer this torture would last. Every few hundred meters I had to stop running and walk for a while. By the time I passed the 3-mile mark, I just couldn't motivate myself to run any more. After that, I was down to a slow, painful walk. I have no idea what my finish time was, but I'm sure it was at least twice as long as I had assumed it would be. To say the least, that first 5-mile run was a humbling experience.

How's that for mediocre? Actually, when I think about it, it would be overly generous to even call my performance "mediocre"— "pitiful" would probably be a more accurate description.

Fast-forward a little over 24 years. In October of 2006, at the ripe old age of 61, I was able to successfully finish my first Ironman® triathlon. I expect that most people who will read this book will be familiar with what is involved in such an event. For those who are not, it consists of the following: a 2.4-mile swim, followed by a 112-mile bike ride, and then a 26.2-mile run, for a total distance of 140.6 miles, all needing to be completed within a 17-hour time limit. I was fortunate to have the opportunity to participate in the Ford Ironman World Championship in Kona, in my home state of Hawai'i, and I'm happy and proud to say that I was able to make the most of the experience. When I crossed the finish line, the race announcer, Mike Reilly, made it official, "Brian Goodyear, you are an Ironman!" Could this possibly be the same person who couldn't even make it through a 5-mile fun run without running out of gas when he was 24 years younger? Yes, indeed it could.

In this book, I tell the story of how it all happened, and also show how you can do it too. One of the essential points is that I did not somehow manage to qualitatively transform my ability level over the course of those 24 years. Although I was certainly in much better physical shape in 2006, my athletic ability was essentially still just as "mediocre" as it was in 1982.

Introduction

I initially decided to write this book because preparing for and participating in my first iron-distance race was so extraordinarily rewarding that I felt compelled to share the experience with others. My hope was that my experience could be of at least some small benefit to people other than myself. I started to write the book not long after my Kona experience in 2006, but life got in the way before I got very far with it. Work and family responsibilities required my time and energy, so I had to put my manuscript on the shelf for over 4 years before I was able to get back to working on it consistently.

It turns out that those years away from my writing were a good thing. There were times when I wasn't sure that I had something worthwhile to put in print. I was proud of what was, for me, an extraordinary personal accomplishment. However, if I were going to write a book, I wanted it to be more than just an account of what I had accomplished. The intervening time has given me an opportunity to reflect more deeply on some of the lessons I learned from my experiences in endurance triathlons. Along with the story of that experience, I have also incorporated some of the ideas that have emerged from my reflections—ideas about what participation in athletics can mean in the larger context of one's life.

Primarily, this book is aimed at recreational athletes, like me, who do not possess exceptional natural ability but who nevertheless do have the desire to take on the challenge of doing something out of the ordinary. In addition, I hope that it will be of some interest to anyone who can relate in a more general way to the reality of being mediocre. One of the ideas that I propose is that we should not only accept our mediocrity but also celebrate it. Since 2006, I have developed a much deeper acceptance of my own inherent mediocrity as an athlete, along with an understanding that coming to terms with that mediocrity doesn't mean I can't sometimes accomplish extraordinary things. The phrase "anything is possible" (or its converse, "nothing is impossible") has been tossed around so much that it has become something of a hyperbolic and essentially meaningless cliché, not to mention the fact that that phrase is patently untrue. For example, try flapping your arms and flying up to top of the nearest tree and see how possible that is. It is simply a truism that none of us will ever be able to do what is really impossible. However, if we set realistic goals and make a firm commitment to the attainment of those goals, we are, at least on a personal level, all capable doing something extraordinary. So, if you happen to be an ordinary recreational athlete who has thought or dreamed about the possibility of doing an iron-distance triathlon but wondered, just like I did, if you really have what it takes to accomplish such a seemingly enormous and daunting challenge, then I hope this book can in some way serve as both an incentive and a guide for you.

Before I proceed with my story, I do need to make a few disclaimers right up front. First of all, I am eminently unqualified as an athletic coach. I have had no formal training whatsoever as a coach, and I certainly do not present myself as having any particular coaching expertise. If you are looking for someone to help you fine tune your training so you can finally beat that nemesis or achieve that personal record (PR), I probably can't be of much help. In the words of one of my favorite singers, Bob Dylan, "It ain't me, babe."

Second, in my athletic endeavors, I am not primarily focused on competition and improving my performance. I am a "recreational athlete," as opposed to a "competitive athlete." I define a recreational athlete as someone whose primary goal is something other than winning or placing as high as possible in every race. That is not to say that I don't try to do my best when I enter a race. Once in a while, I'll participate in an event just for fun, with a good deal of lollygagging and socializing along the way, but I usually do try to perform to the best of my ability, no matter how mediocre that may be. In fact, if I pick and choose my races carefully, I can occasionally find a small event in which, if I work really hard at it, I am able to place in the top three in my age group. For a recreational athlete like me, that's real thick icing on the cake! It just goes to show that if you find a small enough pond, even the most mediocre athlete can aspire to be a big fish once in a while. Although I do not consider myself to be a competitive athlete, I must admit that it is great to occasionally be able to experience this kind of competitive success. I do want to emphasize clearly, however, that competition is not the primary reason why I do what I do.

Third, as a recreational athlete, despite years of rigorous, and sometimes positively grueling, training, my ability level is still just about as mediocre as it has ever been. For a long time, in fact, I had some real difficulty defining myself as an "athlete." I mean, aren't athletes people who can do things like running the marathon in just over two hours, and crazy stuff like that? Can a guy who would take two to three times longer than that really be considered an athlete? I finally told myself, if I keep putting all of this effort into participation in athletic activities, why shouldn't I call myself an athlete? I still can't deny the fact that I'm mediocre, but that doesn't mean I can't be an athlete.

Fourth, I have absolutely no association or affiliation with the World Triathlon Corporation, of which the term "Ironman" is a registered trademark. My story is simply about the process of learning to make full use of my mediocre athletic ability, to the point at which I, as an individual, was capable of finishing an iron-distance triathlon.

The rest of the book is organized into three parts. In the first part, I explore the concept of mediocrity, and suggest that, far from being negative, it is actually something we can embrace and celebrate. The second part takes the form of a narrative that simply tells the story of my journey from naive novice triathlete to two-time iron-distance triathlon finisher. In accordance with two of the main themes of the book, I have described the process that I went through in learning to make full use of my mediocre athletic ability while, at the same time, emphasizing the value of keeping that process as simple as possible. The third part of the book takes a slightly more didactic approach in describing a simple conceptual framework that evolved when I was thinking about how to develop a training program for myself. I want to emphasize, however, that it is not intended as a comprehensive training manual. There are already many such books on the market. I have merely described in simple terms how I have come to conceptualize the principles involved in the training process. At the end of the book, there are also two appendices that include more specific details of my training schedule for Kona in 2006. When taken as a whole, the book is intended to provide an example of how, through the vehicle of an iron-distance triathlon, ordinary individuals like you and I can learn to come to terms with and, in some small way, ultimately transcend our inherent mediocrity.

Part One: In Defense Of Mediocrity

Chapter 1

Mediocrity as a Reality for Most of Us

One of the main themes of this book is that, for the vast majority of us, mediocrity is an inevitable reality that we have to come to terms with, particularly in the field of athletics, but also in other areas of our lives. At the same time, the message that I want to send is that we are all capable of finding ways of transcending our inherent mediocrity and accomplishing extraordinary things.

At this point in my own life, I think I can finally say in all honesty that I am fully able to accept and embrace my mediocrity as an athlete. I have to admit, however, that it has taken me a long time to get to this point. After the fiasco of that 5-mile run in 1982, I was somewhat grudgingly forced to face the reality that I didn't have anywhere near the athletic ability that I would have liked to have. But, at that time, I'm sure I could not have brought myself to actually utter the word "mediocre" about myself. Being forced to face a particular reality is not the same as really coming to a full acceptance of that reality. Back in those days, frankly, my pride was still significantly higher than my ability level.

It was not until many years later that I could consciously begin to think of myself as mediocre and feel okay about it. I recall that I went to a training session one day and someone asked me how my training was going. It happened to be one of those days when I was feeling a little frustrated because I wasn't making as much progress as I would have liked. So I replied, perhaps a little sarcastically, "For me, training seems to be the relentless pursuit of mediocrity." Although I said it in jest at the time, those words stuck in my mind, and ultimately became part of the title of this book. In many ways, the phrase truly captured the essence of what my training was all about. On the one hand, I had come a long way since 1982. On the other hand, the reality was that my athletic ability was still profoundly mediocre and would inevitably continue to be no matter how much effort I put into my training.

Definitions for the word "mediocre" may include words or phrases such as "unexceptional," "unremarkable," or "not outstanding." When you first think about the word in those terms, mediocrity certainly doesn't really sound like the stuff of which particularly lofty aspirations should be made. For example, as kids, we don't usually say things like, "I really want to be a mediocre athlete when I grow up!" On the contrary, being mediocre often carries those negative connotations about being "inferior" or "not good enough" that many of us carry in the back of our minds, often as the result of experiences that go back to childhood. Out of necessity, however, I have gradually come to embrace the concept of mediocrity as part of my reality. In fact, at this point in my life, I can honestly say that I think the word actually has a nice ring to it.

When I look back over the course of my athletic endeavors, I recognize that the first step in coming to terms with my own mediocrity involved a somewhat belated recognition that "mediocre" can be regarded as a relative term. Simply put, what may seem quite outstanding or extraordinary in one context is likely to be perceived as being glaringly mediocre in another. In that sense, the quality of mediocrity basically depends on the particular comparison group that you happen to choose. For example, after I became a regular runner, I once actually came in first in my age group in a relatively obscure and very sparsely attended 5K fun run. On the other hand, I routinely put in what can only be described as indubitably mediocre performances in bigger events in which the number of participants exceeded the number of fingers on my hands. You could say that it's essentially the "big fish in a small pond" effect. One seemingly obvious lesson here—choose your comparison group carefully.

There is, however, much more involved in coming to terms with our mediocrity than just being careful about which comparison group we choose. If that were all that was involved, we would just end up limiting ourselves to some pretty small ponds. At some level, we will inevitably have a tendency to compare our abilities not only to a small, carefully selected group of people but also to the larger group—ultimately to everyone else out there. It is human nature to make that larger comparison. There seems to be an inherent wish in many individuals to be the best at something. This can be seen, for example, by the rather bizarre things that some people will do to get their names in the Guinness Book of World Records. In addition, that natural tendency to compare ourselves with everyone else is reinforced by cultural and societal pressures to succeed and excel, particularly for those of us raised in cultural environments that emphasize competition and the pursuit of excellence. For example, from a relatively early age, our academic skills are repeatedly tested in school, and our performances on tests are usually assigned percentile rankings based on how we compare with other kids, not only on our own little local level but also on state and national levels.

The problem is that, when we make these broader comparisons, it is easy to get discouraged about being not good enough. The chances are that we are not going to measure up particularly well in comparison to the few outstanding individuals among us. Some of us may try to console ourselves by noting that our ability in some area or another is considered "well above average" or even "excellent."

But, even then, the reality is that in a large population there are still a heck of a lot of people who are significantly better than we are at that particular ability. In other words, we're still pretty mediocre. Consequently, unless we happen to be one of those fortunate few individuals who are truly outstanding—"world-class," "the best of the best," "the cream of the crop"—we need to go beyond making comparisons to other people if we are ever going to fully come to terms with our mediocrity.

Chapter 2

A Little Philosophizing

I propose that the next step involves the development of a somewhat more philosophical perspective on the concept of mediocrity.

This philosophical perspective involves the recognition that there is a sense in which all of humanity can be seen as profoundly mediocre. (Incidentally, I'm not sure that we humans, as a species, have really even begun to come to terms with this fact, as our rather checkered history to date, replete with our repeated collective tendencies toward hubris, arrogance and narcissism, would seem to indicate. Just look virtually anywhere on the world political stage and I think you'll get my drift!) In the field of cosmology, there is actually a concept that is known as the Principle of Mediocrity. This principle basically stems from a series of revolutionary scientific discoveries that have taken place over the last few hundred years. First, pioneering thinkers like Copernicus and Galileo in the 16th and 17th centuries challenged the prevailing religious dogma of their time and conclusively demonstrated that the earth revolves around the sun, rather than the other way round, as most people had previously believed for many millennia. (It should be noted, however, that at least some of the ancient Greeks, most notably Aristarchus of Samos, actually had the insight to propose a heliocentric model of the solar system almost 2,000 years earlier. Talk about re-inventing the wheel! This just goes to show what slow learners we humans tend to be in many ways—another sure sign of our mediocrity.) Later, we found out that our sun is nothing more than an average sized star that is just one of many billions of stars in our galaxy, the Milky Way. In turn, we learned, only within the last century, that our apparently rather ordinary galaxy is just one of hundreds of billions of galaxies in our universe. Furthermore, despite the already almost incomprehensible vastness of this universe, as we move into the second decade of the 21st century, many cosmological theorists now subscribe to the mind-boggling hypothesis that there may even be billions of other universes out there beyond the cosmos as we know it, even though there is no way that we are currently able to acquire any direct knowledge of them.

In addition to these astonishing developments in the field of cosmology, throughout the past century and a half since the initial pioneering works of Darwin and Wallace were first published, remarkable advances have taken place in our understanding of the evolution of life on Earth. These findings have conclusively shown that we humans can no longer view ourselves as being the ultimate crown of creation in a world that was designed especially for our benefit. The most that can be said is that human life in its present form appears to be the current high point, and not necessarily the ultimate end point, in an evolutionary history of life forms that dates back, on this planet at least, for over 3.5 billion years. Furthermore, even the notion that human life represents a current high point in this process might reasonably be considered debatable, especially in light of the behavioral atrocities that members of our species have frequently shown themselves to be capable of committing, as the world news continues to show on an almost daily basis.

In relation to the concept of mediocrity, the essential philosophical implication of all these remarkable scientific discoveries is that, in the greater scheme of things, there does not appear to be anything particularly outstanding or extraordinary about this planet that we live on. It logically follows, furthermore, that there is probably nothing particularly outstanding or extraordinary about any of its inhabitants either. Yes, that includes us—all of us—even the most outstanding and extraordinary ones amongst us. From that perspective, we can probably all be thought of as being relatively mediocre in relation to what is potentially out there somewhere in the multiverse.

It seems to me that this philosophical perspective can help to provide us with a different connotation to the concept of mediocrity. On the one hand, by putting all of us more firmly in our place in our tiny little corner of the cosmos, it can hopefully lead us to a much greater sense of humility, which is something that I believe our global society desperately needs in order for us to face the enormous challenges that lie ahead for our species. On the other hand, when we adopt this type of perspective, mediocrity becomes something that we can see as an inherent quality of all humanity, and therefore something that we all can, and perhaps should, more wholeheartedly embrace. On that basis, mediocrity somehow doesn't sound nearly as negative to me as it used to. Indeed, I've come to think that it can actually be seen as a rather positive concept. From this perspective, mediocrity, can, in fact become something that we can even celebrate as part of what it means to be human.

Chapter 3

How We Stack Up Against Others

Now, let us return to the more mundane issue of making comparisons with other members of our species, because this is how we, as individuals, are usually first confronted with the reality of our own mediocrity. When we stop to consider any particular human ability, it is evident that there are usually a very small number of individuals who can be regarded as outstanding in comparison to everyone else—the best of the best, if you will. (I have sometimes thought that it might sound better to those of us who are not outstanding if we just called such people "unmediocre" or maybe "non-mediocre.") One of the brutal facts of life, however, is that, when we compare ourselves to those few truly outstanding individuals, the vast majority of us are inevitably going to seem mediocre. We can, of course, try to console ourselves by thinking about degrees of mediocrity. Maybe it will make us feel a little better if we are able to say that some people are even more mediocre than we are. Nevertheless, the bottom line is that, in comparison to the best of the best, everyone else is mediocre to some degree. This is certainly the case when it comes to athletics, and the chances are that it is also true of most of the other things we do in life.

Let's take a look at how we are likely to stack up against others in statistical terms. Many studies have shown that human physical and mental abilities tend to be distributed throughout the population as a whole in a way that can be graphically represented in the form of the well known "bell curve." In statistical terminology, this is known in its pure form as a "normal distribution." It is from this type of distribution that statistics like state or national percentile rankings are derived. You don't need to be an expert in statistics to understand the significance of this type of distribution. For our purposes, all you really need to know is that, for any type of ability that can be represented in the form of a bell curve, the great majority of people are going to fall within a relatively narrow range within the distribution.

Now, let's look at some specific numbers. We know that athletic ability variables, such as swimming, biking, or running speed, or combinations thereof, are, roughly speaking, normally distributed in the population as a whole. For any normally distributed variable, 68.26% of the population that is being measured will, by definition, fall within the range of plus or minus one standard deviation from the mean. Furthermore, 95.46% of that population will fall within plus or minus two standard deviations. (Standard deviation is simply a statistical measure of the degree of variability of whatever is being measured—the precise definition is not important for our purposes.) That means that only 4.54% of the population will fall more than two standard deviations above or below the mean. When we look at the bell curve, we can easily see that half of that 4.54%, or 2.27% of the population, will fall more than two standard deviations below the mean, at the bottom end of the distribution. Consequently, only the remaining 2.27% of the population will fall more than two standard deviations above the mean, at the top end of the distribution. You don't have to be a statistical genius to see that the odds of any particular person being in that top 2.27% are not very good. To be more precise, the odds against it are about 44 to 1—not something you'd want to put a whole lot of money on.

Now, let's say that you happen to take some kind of athletic ability test, maybe a test of running speed. Let's further suppose that your performance on that test actually does happen to fall exactly two standard deviations above the mean in a large, representative national sample. In that case, statisticians might typically classify your ability level as "superior," because your performance is better than 97.73% of the population. In more colloquial terms, you might be considered "pretty damn good" as a runner. However, when we consider the size of the national population, the fact that 2.27% of the population scored higher than you means that there are still going to be an awful lot of people who can run faster than you. Specifically, in a population of about 300 million, we can expect that approximately 6,810,000 Americans are going to perform better than you on that test of running speed. On that basis, although a lot of people may consider your performance to be "pretty damn good," I'm going to suggest that it's still very firmly within the realm of the mediocre.

For most human abilities, the reality is that in order to have a chance of being considered "outstanding"—up there with the best of the best—you absolutely have to be well over two standard deviations above the mean. In other words, you've got to be at the very top end of that top 2.27%, maybe in the top 0.01%, although I don't think it's particularly helpful to try to put specific numbers on it. In the case of athletes, we are talking about the superstars, the hall-of-fame candidates. In the field of iron-distance triathlon, more specifically, we could certainly include pioneers of the sport like Dave Scott and Mark Allen, as well as more recent world champions like Chrissie Wellington and Chris McCormack. In addition to these famous athletes, a relatively small number of other elite triathletes might reasonably be considered to be among the best of the best. In statistical terms, these elite athletes are always going to be way out at the extreme high end of the bell curve. By definition, when you get that far out on the distribution, there are simply not going to be many of them, and the rest of us are inevitably destined to fall somewhere below that level, most of us far below.

Chapter 4

Learning to Accept our Mediocrity

Many of us have dreamed about the possibility of being a top notch, world-class athlete of some kind at some point in our lives. As I have already noted, there seems to be a natural human tendency to wish that we had what it takes to be up there with the best of the best. As a young kid growing up in England during the 1950s, my idols included famous professional football (soccer) players of the time—guys like Stanley Matthews, Tom Finney, and Nat Lofthouse. I also recall being enthralled by the accomplishments of world class runners like Roger Bannister, Chris Chataway, and Chris Brasher, who were, in those days, elite amateurs rather than professional athletes. I was not a bad young soccer player in those days, and I was actually considered one of the best runners among the kids at the little primary school that I attended in a small town in the south west of England. However, my childhood memories serve as a perfect example of the select comparison group issue again. In reality, I was nothing more than a not so big fish in a very small British pond. As I grew, I was inevitably forced to face the fact that I simply didn't even come close to having the level of ability to become what I now define as an outstanding athlete such as a professional soccer player or an elite runner. Those of you who have played sports can probably relate to the experience of getting trounced by an opposing team, and dejectedly realizing that some of your opponents were just in a whole different league than you.

Although we are inevitably going to be faced at some point with the reality of our mediocrity, it is not necessarily easy for us to accept that reality. One of the reasons may be that another universal aspect of human nature is to desire, and maybe even expect, fairness and to experience a deep emotional reaction to perceived unfairness. Some recent psychological and anthropological studies do seem to suggest that this is indeed the case. When it comes to abilities, athletic or otherwise, it somehow just doesn't seem fair that some people are so much better than we are. I wonder also if it has been difficult for me to accept this inevitable unfairness because of the fact that the values of fairness and equality are so deeply embedded in the cultures in which I have lived almost my entire life. For example, our entire political and legal systems in North America and Western Europe are based on the principle that all people are equal under the law, and that one person's vote is just as good as anyone else's. Those of us who live in the United States are presumably all familiar with the words of the Declaration of Independence: "We hold these truths to be self evident, that all men are created equal...." When it comes to athletic abilities, however, the reality is that the words of the great songwriter, Ira Gershwin, seem to be more applicable—"It ain't necessarily so." At some level, we are obviously very sensitive to that reality, as illustrated by the intense feelings that we have about outstanding athletes. These feelings vary from love and hero worship, on the one hand, to resentment or even hatred on the other. As a contemporary example, consider the range of emotions that world-class athletes such as Tiger Woods and Lance Armstrong have been capable of eliciting in people. At the same time, we do not usually acknowledge in explicit terms our own inevitable mediocrity in comparison to those few individuals who can legitimately be described as outstanding. Despite my pitiful performance in that first 5-mile run back in 1982, I still could not have brought myself to openly articulate the simple fact that I am mediocre as an athlete, let alone to honestly add that I can accept that fact with some degree of equanimity.

I think there is also, in many of us, a rather deep-seated desire to be thought of as special in some way. Again, this type of desire probably stems from a combination of human nature and cultural influences. There are certainly many ways in which our culture encourages us to think of ourselves as being special. We often make a point of teaching our children to think of themselves as special individuals. In the popular media, we are bombarded with commercials that convey the message, either directly or indirectly, that we should reward ourselves for being special by buying a particular product. In my work as a clinical psychologist, I have often been in the position of trying to help people get in touch with the ways in which they can be seen as special in order to help them to build their self esteem. It is certainly true that each of us is a unique, one-of-a-kind individual, and I believe it is good that we place a high value on that individuality. There is definitely a positive aspect to the desire to be special if it can be equated with wanting to be the best that one can be. On the negative side, however, it can be argued that this same desire may be one of the bases of the narcissism that many observers find to be so pervasive in modern American society. In any event, when we consider specific human abilities such as athletic ability, we are again inevitably faced with the harsh reality that the vast majority of us are not at all special. Reaching some resolution of that often-massive discrepancy between our wishes and the reality of our situation does not necessarily come easily. Along the way, there are likely to be numerous disappointments and disillusionments.

For one reason or another, I gradually drifted away from regular participation in athletic activities as I went through adolescence and into young adulthood. During that time, I actually fell into a rather unhealthy lifestyle for a number of years. Like many of my peers in those days, I took up smoking cigarettes and spent far too much time propping up the bar with the lads at the local pub instead of getting out on the track or the soccer field. Nevertheless, although I clearly knew by then I didn't come close to having what it took to be an outstanding, elite athlete, at the back of my mind I still liked to think that maybe I could at least have been a "pretty damn good" athlete of some type had I really wanted to be. Oh, how I deluded myself, as I would find out in that rude awakening of 1982.

As an adult, I was at least intermittently active with hiking and, after moving to Hawai'i in 1971, bodysurfing, but I didn't start participating regularly in athletic activities until I was in my late 30s, about a year after I finally quit smoking for good. After that initial humiliating experience in 1982, it didn't take me too long to realize that, in comparison to everyone else in my age group, no matter how much or how hard I trained, I was never even going to come close to getting up to the "pretty damn good" level, let alone to becoming outstanding. Initially, my reaction to this reality was not one of real acceptance but rather of reluctant resignation. As the years have gone by, however, I have gradually become more genuinely acceptant of the reality that, like the vast majority of people, I am a mediocre athlete—nothing more, nothing less.

Incidentally, I am a psychologist by profession, and it so happens that I have been giving some thought to developing a psychometrically reliable and valid test that would assess the extent to which you have accepted your mediocrity. I think I might call it the "Mediocrity Acceptance Test" (MAT). Although its reliability and validity are far from being substantiated, part of the procedure is as follows. Imagine that you are approaching the finish of a competitive athletic event. All your friends and family are there yelling out to you, "Mediocre job! Mediocre job!" If you can imagine that and not feel grossly offended by it, you are well on the way to acceptance of your mediocrity!

In summary, I am suggesting that ultimately we are all, in some way, mediocre, and that there are two ways in which we can come to terms with our mediocrity. First, because of the way that human ability cards get dealt, the great majority of us will inevitably be forced to face the fact that we are not holding an outstanding hand when it comes to athletic ability. Consequently, we might as well graciously learn to accept that we are inevitably going to seem mediocre in comparison to those lucky few who are endowed with truly outstanding ability. Second, from a more philosophical perspective, mediocrity can be seen as an inherent part of the human condition, even for those whom we consider outstanding. Accordingly, we might as well learn not only to accept our mediocrity but also to celebrate it as part of what makes us human.

Chapter 5

Transcending Our Mediocrity

We might then ask, if we are forced to accept these unavoidable facts of life, does that mean we are doomed forever to nothing more than mediocrity? I am going to argue that we are not, and that it is possible to find ways, at least on a personal level, to transcend our own mediocrity. The experiences that I recount in this book have taught me the important lesson that accepting and coming to terms with my mediocrity does not necessarily mean that I cannot do certain things or take on challenges that are, in some way or another, a little out of the ordinary.

I was recently introduced to a thought provoking, and also amusing, book entitled *The Black Swan: The Impact of the Highly Improbable*, by Nassim Nicholas Taleb. (No, it has nothing to do with the recent movie by the same name.) In the book, Taleb makes an important distinction between "scalable" and "non-scalable" variables, and explores the implications of those differences. Although Taleb is concerned primarily with economic, political, and social implications, it occurred to me that his ideas might have some relevance to my own. Non-scalable variables, on the one hand, often have a relatively limited and predictable range. In other words, they typically do not deviate more than a couple of standard deviations from the mean, and can therefore be reasonably well represented by the bell curve of the normal distribution. Scalable variables, on the other hand, are relatively limitless in range and can, on occasion, deviate wildly from the mean, sometimes in a highly improbable and unpredictable manner. As Taleb repeatedly emphasizes, the typical parameters and limits of the bell curve do not necessarily apply to scalable variables.

Taleb humorously calls the realm of non-scalable variables "Mediocristan." (I loved this name!) As we have already seen, most human physical attributes, including athletic abilities, are normally distributed and can, therefore, be regarded as non-scalable variables, falling squarely within the boundaries of Mediocristan. Running speed is a good example of an ability that has a relatively limited and predictable range. Thus, in the next Olympic marathon, we can reasonably predict that it will take every participant, even the most outstanding runners, at least 2 hours to finish the race. We can be extremely confident, to the point of certainty in fact, that no human participant is going to break 2 minutes. And even 2 minutes would be considered agonizingly slow in comparison to the speed of light, which takes about .00014 seconds to travel the distance of a marathon. From this perspective, outstanding athletes are outstanding only within the context of the relatively restricted parameters that are defined by the realities of human biology. Indeed, those individuals that we now consider outstanding might eventually turn out to be mediocre indeed in comparison to what is potentially out there somewhere in the multiverse.

In contrast to Mediocristan stands the realm of scalable variables, to which Taleb gives the name Extremistan. Many of the variables in this realm, which tend be social, economic, or even political, rather than physical, in nature, could theoretically be almost infinite in range. As a result of the potentially limitless nature of these variables, highly extraordinary and improbable events can occasionally happen. Taleb calls these extreme and rare events "Black Swans," because it was once thought that black colored swans did not even exist. Depending on the context, "Black Swans" can potentially be positive or negative, even catastrophic, in nature. I am going to ignore the negative and focus only on how we can potentially bring positive "Black Swans" into our lives. Although human athletic abilities undoubtedly fall within the realm of Mediocristan, I believe that even the most profoundly mediocre athletes among us have the potential to choose to use those abilities in extraordinary and improbable ways. From this perspective, our ability to choose how we make use of our athletic abilities, and all our other abilities for that matter, can be regarded as a scalable variable that potentially falls within the realm of Extremistan. We all, therefore, have the potential ability to bring positive "Black Swans" into our lives if we are willing to make the choice to take on challenges that seem, at least from our own point of view, extraordinary in nature.

At this point in my life, I am ready to openly admit that I am a flag-waving Mediocristani citizen, certainly in terms of my athletic abilities, and probably in terms of most of what I do in my life. At the same time, however, I like to be able to indulge myself in the idea that once in a while I can choose to make the challenging journey to my own personal Extremistan, where there is at least the possibility of bringing the occasional positive "Black Swan" into my life, provided that I am willing to commit myself to doing whatever is needed to make it happen. (Perhaps we could think of this as a form of "mediocre extremism," or should we say "extreme mediocreism.") I can now say that, despite my profoundly mediocre athletic abilities, or perhaps to a considerable extent even because of them, taking on the challenge of training for, participating in, and ultimately finishing two iron-distance triathlons has, without a doubt, been one of my personal "Black Swans." It has definitely qualified as an extraordinary and improbable event in my own life, and, I must say, an extremely positive one to boot.

I must acknowledge that, in the greater scheme of things, there are a number of perfectly valid reasons to believe that there is nothing particularly outstanding or extraordinary about simply participating in a long distance triathlon. First, the fact that I was able to make it to the finish line obviously does not necessarily mean that my performance was outstanding, particularly when seen in comparison to the performances of those elite athletes who are routinely able to finish in little more than half the time that it took me. Second, I know very well that lots of people participate in Iron-distance races these days, so I couldn't really argue if someone were to say that just participating in one of these events can't be that extraordinary any more. Third, I am also very much aware of the fact that the long, time-consuming process of training for endurance triathlons requires a rather intense and extended focus on oneself in many ways, which obviously doesn't directly contribute a great deal to the wellbeing of our society as a whole. Nevertheless, on a personal level, I can say without doubt that taking on the challenge of participating in an iron-distance triathlon was a truly wonderful experience that allowed me to transcend, at least for the moment, my own mediocrity, and to savor the accomplishment of doing something that was, by my own standards, quite extraordinary.

Triathlons in general, and iron-distance events in particular, have exploded in popularity since the late 1970s. From simple beginnings in 1978 when 15 intrepid souls on the island of Oʻahu set out to cover a total distance 140.6 miles under their own power with no organized support, participation in iron-distance events has grown to many tens of thousands of people every year in dozens of different events in countries all around the world. What is the reason for this spectacular growth? I think that one of the reasons for the exponential growth of this phenomenon has to do with the fact that it has come to be perceived by a significant number of recreational athletes like you and me as an extreme endurance event that is, nevertheless, potentially within our capabilities despite the inherent mediocrity of our athletic ability. Although we can never aspire to be world-class athletes, the achievement of claiming an iron-distance finish is within reach for many of us if we are simply willing and able to put all of the necessary time, energy, and commitment into training for it.

That is not to say that doing such an event is ever going to be easy by any means. If it were easy, it really wouldn't mean that much to anyone, and it wouldn't have the kind of appeal that it does. The iron-distance event presents us with a challenge that does, on one hand, require a great deal of very hard work. As the title of this book suggests, we must, in fact, be relentless in the pursuit of the goal that our mediocrity will ultimately allow us to accomplish.

For some of the athletes I have come to know during my training over the past several years, participating in iron-distance races has become a relatively routine part of life. But for me, Kona 2006 was truly the experience of a lifetime, simply because for most of my life I could never have even imagined myself doing such a thing. I have since been able to finish another full iron-distance race in Western Australia in 2009, and several half-iron-distance races, as well as numerous shorter distance athletic events of one kind or another along the way. Although I still get a great sense of accomplishment from participating in such events, even the shorter ones, I don't think that anything will ever fully compare to that first time experience at Kona in 2006. At that point, I had truly transcended my mediocrity.

Chapter 6

Keeping it Simple

Another important theme in the book is simplicity. I believe that part of the appeal of athletics lies in its fundamental simplicity. Despite the fact that the vast majority of us have nothing more than mediocre athletic abilities, there is something about athletics that resonates deeply with us at a basic and primal level. We can see this partly in the massive popularity of spectator sports such as football, soccer, baseball, and basketball. More importantly, we can also see it in the rapid growth of participation in sports and athletics by ordinary people in recent decades. In particular, millions of people worldwide have been drawn to various kinds of aerobic activities such as running, biking, and swimming. In my home state of Hawai'i, other activities such as surfing, outrigger canoe paddling, and standup paddle boarding attract literally tens of thousands of enthusiastic participants every week. The attraction of all these kinds of activities has to do with the essentially simple and uncomplicated challenge of exploring and testing the limits of the wonderful natural physical abilities that are the legacy of our long evolutionary journey as a species.

This may be particularly true for long distance endurance events like the marathon, the Molokaʻi to Oʻahu canoe races, and, of course, iron-distance triathlons. Although humans do not move particularly fast in comparison to many other animals, either on land or in the water, we do have the ability to develop a very high level of endurance, as long as we keep ourselves fit and healthy. A number of anthropologists now believe that this ability for endurance emerged during the course of our evolutionary history when, for hundreds of thousands of years, the tracking and hunting of prey over extended distances was a necessary survival activity. No matter how mediocre we are as athletes, thanks to our ancestors, we all still have that innate potential for endurance within us. Unfortunately, for many of us in this sedentary modern society, that potential may often remain dormant for long periods of time—until the challenge calls!

I have already emphasized the point that most of us are inevitably faced with the reality that we are not naturally endowed with the extraordinarily high level of ability that is needed to become an outstanding elite athlete. Furthermore, even for those lucky few who do have the right kind of natural endowment, it is evident that becoming an elite athlete is not a simple achievement. It also involves a high level of commitment and dedication to an enormous amount of hard work and skill development over a period of many years. Nevertheless, at the most basic level, there is a fundamental, and, I think, beautiful, simplicity to athletics that makes participation easily accessible not only to outstanding, elite individuals but also to those of us whose abilities are considerably more limited. Ultimately, all that participation in endurance-based athletic events requires of us is the simple ability, and of course the will, to keep moving forward under our own power toward the finish line, wherever that happens to be.

Athletics thus allows us all, recreational and competitive athletes alike, the opportunity to potentially transcend our mediocrity by taking on challenges that are potentially very tough but still, in essence, very simple in nature. As a result of this duality of being extremely challenging yet ultimately quite simple, the iron-distance triathlon has become a vehicle through which ordinary people of mediocre athletic ability can accomplish what we are likely to experience, on a personal level, as something quite extraordinary and outstanding.

Chapter 7

Taking on the Challenge

There are many reasons why people participate in athletic activities. One important reason that may be common to both competitive and recreational athletes is the feeling of accomplishment that comes from simply taking on the challenge of participating in a race and knowing that you have given it your best, even on those, hopefully rare, occasions when you don't make it all the way to the finish line. This sense of accomplishment is particularly powerful in the case of long distance endurance events. Moreover, one of the great things about athletics is that this sense of accomplishment can be just as real and just as meaningful for the mediocre recreational athlete as for the outstanding competitive athlete. In fact, perhaps one of the benefits of mediocrity is that the more mediocre you are, the greater the sense of accomplishment you can potentially get from just participating in the event. Maybe we should call that the first law of mediocrity.

I know that I do, without a doubt, get a great sense of accomplishment from the simple act of participating in athletic events, and that has certainly been one of the reasons I have continued to participate in such activities on an ongoing basis. Particularly when it comes to the longer distance triathlons, such as the half and full iron-distance races, I think that just being able to shuffle through those last few miles to the finish line will always feel hugely satisfying for me, no matter how far back in the pack that I am. However, that sense of accomplishment is by no means the only reason that I participate in athletic activities. Over the years, I have found, in fact, that I enjoy the training just as much, and sometimes even more, than the actual races. I train not just to get prepared for a race, but because I have made a commitment to stay physically fit and healthy for as long as I possibly can in my life. I train also because I enjoy the simple pleasure of being outdoors and doing something physically active. I train because it helps me to cope more effectively with stress. Last, but certainly not least, I train because I very much value the fun, friendship, and camaraderie that comes from getting together and working out with a solid group of training buddies, particularly if most of them are just as mediocre as I am! There are, therefore, many good reasons to participate in athletics. In many ways, the sense of accomplishment that comes from finishing a long distance endurance event is simply the icing on the cake. It can, nevertheless, serve as a very enticing carrot that can lead you to take on the challenge in the first place.

I have already commented on the exponential growth of the endurance triathlon phenomenon over the past couple of decades. I would guess that the total number of people who have participated in at least one iron-distance event probably runs into the low millions. Nevertheless, simple statistics tells me that this is still a small percentage of the population as a whole. There must, therefore, still be huge numbers of mediocre, recreational athletes just like me who have not yet entered an iron-distance triathlon, but who have, at some point, given it at least a fleeting thought. There must be people who have done a few sprint or Olympic-distance triathlons and who now wonder if they might be able to go longer. There must be people who have done some running or swimming or biking events and who now wonder what it would be like to do a triathlon. Above all, there must be a great number of people who haven't yet done much at all in the way of athletic activities but who now feel ready to make a determined effort to get in shape physically and take on some new challenges in their lives. If you are one of these people, I can confidently tell you, based on my own experience, that you are capable of taking on that challenge if you would just give yourself the chance to try.

When I first considered the possibility of doing an Iron-distance event, it would be a gross understatement to say that I had some real doubts about whether I had the strength, endurance, ability, and whatever else it might take to finish such a long and grueling event. I can look back now with pride and say that I have done it twice. If this mediocre athlete can do it, you can do it too!

Although the book is aimed particularly at recreational athletes who have some dream or desire to take on the challenge of an iron-distance event for the first time, I hope it will also be of some interest to others. Hopefully those of you who already have some experience doing similar events will be able to relate to, or maybe laugh at, some of my own experiences. In addition, I hope that it will be of some interest to those of you who may be considering taking on some other type of challenge in your life. Although the book is written specifically about the simple experience of doing an iron-distance triathlon, I would like to think that it could also be relevant to the more general issue of overcoming whatever challenges we face in our lives. Despite our inherent mediocrity, one of the ways in which we can grow as individuals is by making the choice to step out of our comfort zone and take on new challenges.

At certain times in our lives, challenges may not so much be chosen as thrust upon us. In many ways, endurance athletic events provide a wonderful metaphor for the process of confronting these other types of challenges in our lives. We learn from the endurance triathlon that if we simply keep moving ahead, stroke by stroke, step by step, just doing whatever we know we need to do at the time, even when we feel like quitting or giving up, eventually we will get to our personal finish line, wherever that may be. In the process, we may find that we are actually able to accomplish something extraordinary, at least on a personal level, no matter how mediocre our abilities are.

Part Two:
My Own Journey

Chapter 8

Preliminary Steps

"Do you think a guy like me could ever do an Ironman?" That was the question that I posed to Jay Paul, one of my coaches in the Boca Hawaii triathlon training program. If my memory serves me correctly, this was in the early summer of 2004, shortly after I had turned 59. At that time, I was training for my second Tinman Triathlon, an event that has been held annually in Honolulu since 1979. For those of you not yet familiar with the details of triathlon distances, the Tinman is similar to an Olympic-distance triathlon, which consists of a 1500-meter swim, a 40-kilometer bike, and a 10-kilometer run, for a total distance of 51.5 kilometers or approximately 32 miles. However, the Tinman swim was only 800 meters. It is often referred to locally as the "people's triathlon" because it attracts many different levels of athletes. In short, despite the presence of a few outstanding athletes, it is a veritable hotbed of athletic mediocrity. I can say that now, but I certainly didn't think of it in those terms back then. In the summer of 2004, it was still the longest triathlon that I had ever done, and I still regarded it as a major test of my endurance. Although my question to Jay represented the first signs of genuine curiosity on my part about the possibility of doing an iron-distance event, the fact of the matter was that the idea of actually participating in such an event seemed like nothing more than the stuff of fantasy at that time.

I'll get to Jay's answer to my question a little later. In the meantime, let me tell you how I got to the point of asking the question. After that first 5-mile run in 1982, there had been a rather prolonged period of time during which, I can now see, I was essentially taking the preliminary steps toward my later involvement in the sport of triathlon.

The humiliating experience of that first run had obviously made me painfully aware of the fact that I was never even going to come close to being outstanding as an athlete, but I certainly cannot say that I had completely come to terms with the reality of my mediocrity. At that time, I was not ready to fully accept and embrace it; instead, I rather grudgingly resigned myself to it. Nevertheless, I did manage to motivate myself to continue to put on my running shoes and get out on the road on a fairly regular basis. In the process, I gradually came to recognize and appreciate the value of exercising consistently. I read a great deal about the benefits of exercise in terms of both physical and mental heath, and I began to notice many of those benefits in my own life. Initially, I just took up running because it seemed to be the simplest and easiest form of exercise and because I liked being outdoors rather than in a gym. Within a year or so of running regularly, I was able to get back to at least a minimal level of physical fitness. Although I often deeply resented the fact that I couldn't run nearly as fast as I would have liked, I was at least able to successfully finish a few short running events without running out of gas like I had done in 1982.

By early 1985, I had built up my endurance considerably and had even participated in a few long distance running events, including my first half marathon. Later that same year, I managed to make it all the way to the finish line of the Honolulu Marathon in the unquestionably mediocre time of 5 hours 40 minutes. Over the following year or two, with the benefit of some fairly consistent training at a somewhat higher level of intensity, I found that I was able to pick up the pace in some shorter races and actually set what remain as my personal record (PR) times at a couple of distances—48 minutes for a 10K, 1 hour and 55 minutes for a half marathon. In terms of speed, that was about as good, or should I say "mediocre," as it was ever going to get.

Despite my incredibly poor technique at the time, I also started doing some swimming on a fairly regular basis, simply because I enjoyed being in the water so much. Over a period of a year or so, I managed to build my endurance to the point that I was able to struggle through a few long distance ocean swims, including the North Shore Challenge and the Waikiki Roughwater Swim (WRS), typically just managing to beat out a handful of other swimmers to avoid finishing in last place. I vividly recall one now defunct swimming event, the Blue Water Classic, which was held at Makapu'u Beach during the summer of 1985. After heading out through the shore break, I soon found myself almost at the back of the pack. My goggles, which I had never really gotten used to wearing, started leaking badly, so I eventually took them off and ended up swimming breast stroke much of the way in order to keep my eyes out of the water as much as possible. As we eventually neared the finish, I looked around and saw that there was just one other swimmer still in the water. He was slightly ahead of me. Not wanting to be last, I tried to put on some semblance of a sprint to get to the shore. With the help of a couple of waves, I barely managed to come out of the water ahead of the other guy, only to find that, by doing so, I missed out on the award that was given to him for being the swimmer who spent the longest time in the water. I should have just taken my time! As you can tell, even back then in somewhat younger years, my hypo— or should it be hyper–mediocrity was plainly evident.

In 1986, I entered graduate school on a full time basis, and for much of the next 15 years or so, I was busy with all the demands of my studies and then my work, together with the responsibilities of parenthood, so I simply did not have the time to enter many athletic events except for the occasional fun run. I had, however, very much come to value the benefits of regular exercise, so I did try to keep up at least a minimal training schedule in order to maintain a modicum of physical fitness. Over those years, my running was usually limited to 3 or 4 miles, two or three times a week, whenever I could fit it into my schedule. Swimming tended to be even less frequent—no more than 1000 meters at Ala Moana Beach or Kaimana Beach once, maybe twice, a week, except for a year or two in the mid 1990s when my younger daughter, Nes, was swimming with the Kaimuki-Waialae YMCA swim team. I was able to participate in a few long distance ocean swims with her at that time, although, at the age of 9 or 10, she was already a much better swimmer than I ever had been or was ever going to be. For fun, I also occasionally participated in some short distance biathlons, typically consisting of a run of up to 5K followed by an 800- to 1000-meter swim. About half a dozen of these biathlons are held each year in the Honolulu area, mostly during the period from December to April. Once in a while, I would do one of these biathlons as an individual, but usually it was as the runner in a team, with one of my daughters, Jen or Nes, or one of my friends, as the swimmer. I always enjoyed those events, particularly when I was able to do them with my daughters, and perhaps they served to keep alive in the back of my mind the idea of eventually doing a triathlon some day, although I never really thought about it consciously at the time—probably for good reason. I had hardly done any biking since I was a kid in England and had never participated in any type of bike race or even an organized ride.

During those years, despite the somewhat sporadic nature of my athletic activities, I became more and more committed to regular exercise as an integral part of my life style. I realized that I invariably felt better both physically and mentally when I made the time to exercise regularly. Even my relatively short runs and swims served as effective outlets for stress during a very challenging period in my life that saw me going through a divorce, completing a doctoral degree program and a post-doctoral fellowship in clinical psychology, and then embarking on a new career in private practice. I clearly recall running around the University of Hawai'i track one evening, while I was still working on my doctoral dissertation, and making the metaphorical connection between persisting with my run until I had completed the planned number of laps and continuing to work step by step on my dissertation until completion.

By 2002, I had been a regular recreational runner, and a somewhat less regular recreational swimmer, for almost 20 years. I'm not sure why, but during the early part of that year, for the first time in many years, I had actually not done much at all in the way of exercise. Ever since I started my private practice in 1991, I had been putting in a lot of time at the office, often up to 60 or 70 hours a week, which sometimes left me feeling tired and more than a little bit drained. Nevertheless, things in my life were looking pretty good for the most part. Although it was initially a struggle, I had been able to get back on my feet both emotionally and financially after the divorce and had bought a modest but very comfortable house in Honolulu. My career was successful—I consistently had as much work as I could realistically handle. My older daughter, Jen, was doing very well in graduate school, and my younger daughter, Nes, was getting ready to graduate from high school and go on to college. Despite all those positives in my life, I was losing the motivation to get out and exercise regularly. For several months, even my short runs became less and less frequent. By the summer of that year, I was feeling guilty about not being more active physically. In addition, I was feeling increasingly lethargic, and I knew I was gradually getting out of shape. Over the years, my weight had gradually crept up from around 160 pounds at the time of the 1985 marathon to somewhere in excess of 180 pounds, the heaviest I had ever been. I knew that I needed to make some changes and get back to being more active again, and I felt I needed a new challenge, but I didn't really know what I wanted to do.

It is strange how a seemingly minor event can sometimes set in motion a series of additional events that ultimately result in a radical, unforeseen change in the course of one's life. Maybe it can be considered an example of chaos theory in action in everyday life. One day in late summer 2002, I had come home from work and was looking through my mail. My eyes happened to dwell on a flyer from AARP, an organization that I had somewhat unenthusiastically decided that I might as well join after reaching the milestone of turning 50 years old in 1995. The flyer contained information about what they called the TriUmph, a short distance triathlon series that AARP was sponsoring in various locations around the country at that time. (I did not know very much about triathlons at the time, and it was not until months later that I eventually learned that these relatively short distance triathlons were usually referred to as "sprint distance" races.) I could easily have thrown out that flyer along with all of the junk mail that always seems to fill my mailbox, but something about it caught my attention. I pulled it out to take a closer look. As I read through it, a light went on. I was intrigued by the fact that the triathlon was geared primarily toward people over 50 years of age, and particularly toward those who had never done a triathlon before. I learned that the Honolulu race was scheduled for December 15, and that a training program was being offered for people who wanted some help in preparing for the event. When I considered the distances involved—a 400-meter swim, a 12-mile bike, and a 5K run, for a total of a little over 15 miles—I thought, "Even I might be able to get through that."

The AARP flyer piqued my interest because I had actually given some very vague thought to the idea of doing a triathlon way back in the mid 1980s. I had worked for a while with a colleague who was an avid athlete and who had talked about wanting to do "the Ironman" over in Kona, which, of course, was then still very much in its infancy. When I initially heard her talking about it, I couldn't help but ask myself if I too might possibly be capable of doing it. When I learned exactly what it involved, however, it didn't take me long to come to the conclusion that it was completely out of the question. I recalled that just a couple of years earlier I had barely been able to finish that first 5-mile run after deluding myself that it was going to be a breeze for me. After such a humbling experience, how could I possibly even think about trying to swim 2.4 miles, bike 112 miles, and then run a full 26.2-mile marathon? All in one day? I didn't give it another thought—at least not for a very long time.

Although I had absolutely no intention of ever attempting to do an iron-distance triathlon, I did briefly entertain the idea of attempting to do a much shorter triathlon. By that time, I had been running consistently for a couple of years, and also swimming with some regularity for over a year, so I was definitely in somewhat better shape physically than I had been when I attempted that first 5-mile run a couple of years earlier. I was still grudgingly resigned to the fact that I wasn't anywhere near as fast as I would have liked to be, but I was gradually beginning to feel a little more confident about my athletic ability. Consequently, I began to vaguely consider the possibility of doing other types of athletic events. I had heard through the local media about the Tinman Triathlon, an event that had recently started up in Honolulu. I learned that "the Tinman" was much shorter than "the Ironman," and I wondered about the possibility of trying to do it some day. I must admit that I was still quite intimidated by the idea of swimming, then biking, then running all in a single event, but it certainly seemed much more feasible than something as outrageous as that extreme event over in Kona.

One major problem, however, was that I did not own a bike. Furthermore, I was financially challenged at that time because I was still in the process of going through both graduate school and a divorce, and I just couldn't see any way that I could justify the expense of buying even an old used bike, let alone find the time to ride it, when I could barely afford the basic essentials of life. Consequently, the whole idea of doing the Tinman, or any other triathlon, was put on the back burner. Nevertheless, a little seed had been planted somewhere in the back of my mind, although it was destined to remain dormant for approximately the next 17 years.

Chapter 9

My First Triathlon

That little seed finally started to come to life in late 2002 when I picked up that flyer for the TriUmph triathlon. I wanted to learn more about the TriUmph event, so I attended the informational meeting where I was happy to learn that the training program was going to be headed by Brian Clarke, a well known figure in the Honolulu running community, whom I had met some years earlier. The fact that I knew the head coach made me feel a little more comfortable about joining the training group, but I must admit that I initially felt more than a little nervous. I think the nervousness stemmed from the fact that there remained a mystique about the word "triathlon" that played havoc with whatever confidence I had developed in my mediocre athletic abilities over the previous 20 years. At the age of 57, I couldn't help but wonder if I still had the ability to do a triathlon at all. It had been so many years since I had fleetingly given those vague thoughts to doing the Tinman.

Inevitably, I also wondered how I would stack up against the other people in the group. I dreaded the thought that I wouldn't be able to keep up with everyone else, particularly on the bike. I actually felt relatively comfortable with my running ability, although I knew I wasn't in particularly good shape at the time. I was at least confident that, if I did some training, I could get through the 5K run portion of the triathlon without collapsing from exhaustion. I also had no doubt that I could swim 400 meters, albeit rather slowly. The bike was the part that really worried me—it had been so long since I had ridden a bike that 12 miles sounded like a pretty long distance. As I was soon to learn, I had good reason to be worried. I really didn't have a clue.

After hearing the presentation about the TriUmph, I made the decision to give it a try, primarily just so that I could say that I had done at least one triathlon in my life. At that point, I really had no intention of continuing to do even short distance triathlons on an ongoing basis, let alone going on to do an iron-distance event. "Check that one off the list, and move on to something else," I told myself. At that time, I could never have foreseen the direction that my life was about to take.

Training for the TriUmph started during the first week of October 2002 and was scheduled to meet three times per week—two evenings and either Saturday or Sunday mornings. It turned out to be what I subsequently learned was a fairly typical triathlon training program in many respects. For the evening workouts, we met at Kalani High School swimming pool at 5:15, and usually did either a combination swim/run or bike/swim workout. For the weekend workout, we would usually meet at 7:00 a.m. at a location like Kaimana Beach in Waikīkī for a combination swim/run or a "brick" (bike/run) workout. Occasionally, Brian would throw in a mini triathlon for us. I remember well the day when we completed our first mini triathlon in late October. We swam all of 150 meters, biked 5 or 6 miles, and then ran a little less than 2 miles. The distances were virtually nothing in comparison to iron-distances. Nevertheless, I can still recall the tremendous sense of accomplishment I felt simply as a result of having done all three sports, one after the other, for the very first time. It was one of those experiences that, I was to find, could really become addictive.

One of the notable changes that occurred in my lifestyle as a result of the Saturday morning training sessions was that there would be no more sleeping in. Not that I had ever been a really late sleeper, at least not since the days of my late teens and early twenties after a night at the pubs and clubs. But I was certainly accustomed to allowing myself the luxury of staying in bed a little longer on weekends than I did when I had to get up for work on weekdays. Instead, I suddenly found myself getting up an hour earlier on Saturdays than I did on workdays, just so I could prepare for my workout. I must admit that I sometimes wondered why I was behaving in such a seemingly strange manner. At the same time, I really liked the way that I felt after I had made the effort to get up so early and get down to the beach or park where we would meet. The early morning is a great time to be outdoors in Hawai'i—a beautiful setting, nice warm weather, but not too hot, not too many people or too much traffic around. It can certainly be one of those times when you feel good just to be alive.

When the training started, I still did not own a bike. I reasoned that, if I were only going to do this one triathlon, there was really no point in going to the expense of buying a bike for myself. "Maybe I can just get by using that old mountain bike that I bought for Nes," I told myself. After all, at almost 5 feet 9 inches, my younger daughter was by then less than 4 inches shorter than me. So I figured her bike would probably be just about big enough for me. That was my first big mistake.

At the first group meeting, I was spared the embarrassment of having to deal with the bike issue. After we had all introduced ourselves, we did a relatively easy swim/run workout, which was fine, except that I noticed not too many of the other guys were swimming in old board shorts like me. It was my first introduction to the world of triathlon gear, and I clearly flunked the fashion test. That, however, turned out to be a relatively minor issue compared with what was to come.

The problems really started when the group met for the first bike ride. When I try to visualize it now, I realize that I must have looked like a complete idiot. My daughter's mountain bike was, inevitably, several sizes too small for me. It finally dawned on me that I had bought it for her a few years earlier when she was probably not much more than 5 feet tall. Not to mention the fact that the rusty old clunker looked completely out of place alongside the sleek, new road bikes or triathlon bikes that most of the people in the group were riding. In addition, my old sneakers, t-shirt, and board shorts just didn't compare to the bike shoes, racing jerseys, and tri-shorts that everyone else was wearing. If the triathlon fashion police had been there, they would no doubt have locked me up and thrown away the key. On top of that, I didn't even own a helmet. I mean, when I was a kid, none of us would have been seen dead wearing a helmet when we rode our bikes. In fact, when I think about it, I'm not sure that bike helmets had even been invented in those days. I soon found out, however, that the rule about wearing a helmet when riding with the group would be strictly enforced. Consequently, I had to borrow one from group members Tom and Donna Mark, who fortunately happened to have a spare one in their car. I would eventually be very glad that our coaches insisted we always wear helmets.

Even on the short ride that we did that day, which was probably no more than 6 miles, I struggled to keep up with the group. Actually, I say "short" now, but in those early days of training anything over 2 miles of riding seemed like an endurance event to me. By the end of that first ride, even if I were only going to do this one triathlon, I knew I had to get another bike. I went home and immediately searched the classified ads in one of the local newspapers. Bingo! I was able to find a used Trek 2500 in pretty good condition for only $300. I went to look at it and took it for a test ride. It turned out to be just about a perfect fit for me, and, of course, it felt so much better than my daughter's old mountain bike. I then went straight to see Frank Smith, one of our coaches, who also happened to be the owner of Island Triathlon and Bike, and bought a helmet, a pair of real biking shoes and some new pedals to match, a bike jersey, some tri-shorts, and a few other bike accessories. The items I purchased were probably all pretty much the cheapest of their kind. I told myself I didn't want to spend too much because I was only planning to do that one triathlon. Or so I still thought.

Once I got going on my new bike, I actually didn't do too badly. I certainly wasn't the fastest rider in the training group, but, to my great relief, I wasn't the slowest either. I didn't fall too far behind the leaders, even when we progressed to doing those seemingly interminable 12-mile rides. I did inevitably fall over a few times because I wasn't able to unclip my new bike shoes from the pedals quickly enough when we came to a stop, but fortunately no major damage was done. The main problem was, when I got off the bike and tried to run, my legs didn't seem to want to move in the way that they are normally supposed to do when I run. Obviously that bike was forcing me to use some muscles that hadn't done much work for many years.

This was the first time I had trained regularly with a group. I had previously done some of my running with friends, but, because of the limitations of my busy schedule with work and family responsibilities, I frequently had to run alone. Actually, I had often enjoyed the solitude of running alone and had never seriously thought about joining an organized training group in the past. Once the training got going, however, I found that there were many things about the group format that I really liked. It provided a structured schedule that I probably would have had considerable difficulty sticking to if I had been training alone. In addition, all of the coaches were helpful and supportive and provided us with all the instruction we needed on the many different aspects of triathlon racing, from technique, to pacing, to bike maintenance, to transitions, to nutrition, and more. After a few weeks, I actually began to feel that I had at least a vague idea of what I was supposed to be doing.

Even more importantly, the group format provided me with an opportunity to meet some great new people. There were around 40 people who had originally signed up for the group, but the typical turnout for any particular workout tended to be somewhere between 20 and 30 people. I tried to make a point of being one of those who consistently came to the workouts, in large part because I was afraid I might not be able to develop the endurance to finish the race if I didn't. Over the 11 weeks of the program, I missed only one of the 32 scheduled workouts. I can now say with some degree of certainty that most people who join athletic training programs bring with them a positive attitude toward life and a level of enthusiasm and determination that can help to create a certain synergy within the group. Consequently, the group can provide an environment that is highly motivating and inspiring as one tackles the various challenges that triathlons present. At times, there was a little friendly competition among members of our group, which added to the motivation, but the competitive aspect was never really serious. Like me, most of the people in that first training group had not previously done any triathlons, and they were looking at it primarily as an opportunity for a new experience of accomplishment in the context of keeping fit and healthy.

Over the years, many of the members of that original group seem to have drifted away from triathlons, but a significant number of them have continued to participate regularly. In the process, several of them have become lasting friends of mine. Without their camaraderie and support I would certainly not have gotten to the point of writing this book. Glenn Perry, Marsha Kitagawa, Bill Darrah, Tom and Donna Mark, Steve Davidson, Bev Csordas, Jeff Smith, Larry Yatsushiro, and Russ Seeney are some of the individuals I know who are still going strong as of 2011. Their friendship and support over the years have meant a great deal to me. Tom and Steve, in particular, warrant a special mention as they have both also gone on to finish iron-distance events. I hope that some of the others will also get to that point one of these days because I am sure they are all capable of it.

That first training program also helped me to get back on the road to a higher level of physical fitness. Although relatively short in comparison to the types of workouts I would later become accustomed to, our training sessions were challenging enough that completing them always gave me a sense of accomplishment, and almost invariably left me in a much better mood than when I started the workout. As our training progressed toward its peak, I was probably putting in a total of around 5 or 6 hours of training per week, more than I had done for many years. As a result, I could feel myself getting fitter and stronger week by week, and I gradually became more and more confident that this triathlon thing was something I could do.

By the time race day came around, I had lost a few pounds, and my endurance had increased to the point where I knew, in my head, that I was capable of finishing the race. Nevertheless, as I drove out to Schofield Barracks on the morning of the race, I still felt nervous and began to wonder if I could really do it. The swim took place in the Richardson Pool at Schofield, which is located up on a plateau in Central Oʻahu where temperatures tend to be a little cooler than in Honolulu. We had done a couple of training sessions at Schofield, so I had an idea of what to expect. But, by mid-December, the water felt bitterly cold compared with the Kalani High School pool where we had done most of our swim training. Together with the tension generated by the race atmosphere, it made swimming seem like hard work, and I found myself almost gasping for breath at times as I went up and down the lanes. I now think of a 400-meter swim as being short indeed, just about long enough to get warmed up. On that day, however, it seemed almost interminable, although it actually took less than 10 minutes. I was greatly relieved when I finally climbed out of the water and made my way into T1, the first transition area, where my bike was patiently waiting for me. It was a pleasant surprise to find that the bike ride was actually quite enjoyable, on roads free of traffic, with expansive views of both the Waianae and Koʻolau mountain ranges, early in the day on a fine December morning. After getting into T2, the second transition area, and putting my bike back on the rack, I found that I was still able to maintain a steady, moderate pace throughout the run, which allowed me to finish the 2002 Honolulu TriUmph Triathlon in a time of about a minute under an hour and a half—an outstandingly mediocre performance, to be sure. Nevertheless, I felt a tremendous sense of accomplishment when I crossed the finish line, with my two daughters, and granddaughter, Hina, all there to cheer me on. All that training had paid off. I had done it. I had finished my first triathlon!

One of the nice things about the TriUmph was that there was a Beginners' Division in each age group. Although I was some distance behind most of the more experienced athletes in my age group, I did manage to finish in third place in the Beginners' Division in the age group, not too far behind a couple of other guys from our training group, Gary Jennings and Glenn Perry. I was thrilled to be able to get that award, as it showed me that, even in a triathlon, mediocre athletes can win things sometimes. I also think that the sense of accomplishment that I derived from finishing the race and winning that modest award was one of the things that helped to motivate me to keep going beyond that first triathlon. In particular, it helped me to start believing in myself as a triathlete. It was another small step toward acceptance of my mediocrity. On the one hand, I have to admit that I still had some underlying resentment about the fact that I was not very fast in comparison to a lot of the athletes in the race. On the other hand, however, I felt extremely good about what I had accomplished. It had given my confidence a huge shot in the arm, and I had at least developed a sense of being minimally competent as a triathlete. It was, in fact, a real revelation to learn that I could do this.

An even more important motivator was the great sense of camaraderie that had developed within the gang that I had trained with for the TriUmph. This was a bonus to the sense of accomplishment that I think we all felt after finishing the triathlon. We had trained together three times a week for 11 weeks, raced together, and enjoyed several potluck dinners and brunches together after our training sessions. By the time we finished that first triathlon, some of us, at least half of the group in fact, very much wanted to continue training together and keep up the fitness momentum that we had begun to develop. Even before that first race was completed, we had begun talking about what we might do next.

Chapter 10

On to the Tinman

After the celebrations following the TriUmph were over, the consensus among the group seemed to be that we should plan to do Brian Clarke's training program for the Tinman triathlon, which was scheduled to start in April 2003. I was excited that I was finally going to have an opportunity to take on the challenge of the Tinman so many years after I had first given it those vague thoughts back in the mid 1980s. However, the start of that training program was still a few months away, and I didn't want to lose the gains in fitness that I had begun to develop during the training for the TriUmph. So, together with Glenn Perry, I decided to continue training with Brian Clarke's next running clinic, which started shortly after the New Year. Again, I found that I really enjoyed the camaraderie and friendly competition of the group-training format, which provided that added incentive to be consistent and disciplined in my training. Not unexpectedly, I didn't even come close to placing in my age group in any of the races that we entered. Let's face it. If you're as mediocre as I am, you really can't expect to win awards very often. Nevertheless, I was pleased with my performances in the shorter distance races, which ranged from 5K to 10K. I was definitely running much better than I had been when we started training for the TriUmph, and, to my surprise, my race times were actually not too far behind the times that I had been able to put in for those distances back in the mid 1980s when I was almost 20 years younger.

The running clinic culminated with the Norman Tamanaha 15K run in March 2003. (This event is now held in August as the first race in the Honolulu Marathon Readiness Series of events.) I had not run 15K continuously since some time in the late 1980s, so it was definitely a challenge for me to build up to that distance. Unfortunately, although I thought that I was fairly well prepared by the training, for some reason I just didn't have much energy on race day and struggled to get through the course in about 1 hour 45 minutes. I had been hoping to finish in less than 90 minutes, so I was quite disappointed with my time, and somewhat frustrated with myself for not being able to do better. I knew in my head that I had done the best I could on that particular day, but deep down it was still difficult for me to accept that my performance was not as good as I had hoped for, and far below the level that I wished it could have been. I was, however, eventually able to console myself with the thought that at least I had managed to finish a distance that I had not attempted for many years. I think I knew at some level that it was at least another small step forward on a journey of some kind, although I had no idea at that time exactly where that journey would lead me.

The next step in the journey was training for the Tinman, which was scheduled to take place in July 2003. This proved to be an interesting experience because, unlike the TriUmph training group that had consisted mainly of people more than 50 years old, the Tinman group included a fairly wide range of ages. Although at least half of the "senior citizens" from our TriUmph group were signed up, many of the athletes were considerably younger, with some even in their 20s. It was also a much larger group, with as many as 80 people signed up, although again some tended to be more consistent in their attendance than others. Some of the group members were solid, young athletes, maybe not outstanding but certainly fast enough to make us older folks look slow. On the other hand, I was relieved to find that we oldies could keep up with at least a few of the younger folks. Frankly, it was comforting to learn that some of those youngsters were just as mediocre as we were.

I was again determined to be one of the consistent ones in this training group because the Tinman training represented what seemed at the time to be a significant step up in terms of the volume of training. Our group workouts, particularly the bike rides, tended to be somewhat longer than they had been in the TriUmph training, as they obviously needed to be for a race that was about twice as long. Initially, the idea of riding my bike continuously for up to an hour and a half seemed like a rather daunting prospect. In addition, I sometimes felt frustrated that, no matter how hard I trained, I was never able to get up to the level of some of the faster guys. But, at the same time, I did feel a growing sense of accomplishment as I gradually found my endurance increasing to the point where a ride of 25 miles began to seem like a distance that I could handle without having to worry about the possibility of passing out from exhaustion.

Another factor that helped to build my endurance was doing some additional workouts outside of the group-training schedule. During the previous two clinics, I had done a few additional workouts on my own on a somewhat sporadic basis, as Brian Clarke had encouraged us to do if we had time. However, it was not until the Tinman training that I started doing some of these additional workouts on a regular basis. A few of us, including Glenn Perry, Peter Biggs, Kieran Yap, and myself, started to meet on Sunday mornings with Greg Austin, one of our coaches, either at Kapi'olani Park or at Glenn's house. From there, we would go for a 20 to 25 mile bike ride, sometimes followed by a run of anywhere between 2 and 4 miles, depending on how we felt. I also started to make a point of going down to Kapi'olani Park after work once a week for a 10K training run on the Tinman course, and to Ala Moana Beach for an extra swim workout. As a result of all that consistent training, by the end of the clinic I was quite familiar with all three parts of the course in the upcoming race, and I was beginning to feel fairly comfortable about my ability to complete the required distances in all three sports.

Despite my increasing confidence, as a novice triathlete I was still prone to many of the foibles that often befall newcomers to the sport. For example, I had once gone on a short bike ride on my own and had parked my truck on Kaimanahila Street near Triangle Park, which is located in the Kāhala area just to the east of Diamond Head. The truck was parked on a slight downhill slope, about 20 or 30 meters away from a stop sign. I finished my ride feeling very pleased with myself for having done an extra workout. After dismounting from my bike, I removed the front wheel before lifting the bike onto the rack that I had purchased for the bed of the truck. I then leaned the front wheel of the bike against the left rear wheel of the truck. After setting the bike securely on the rack, I proceeded to change out of my bike shoes and jersey, and into my slippers and t-shirt. Then, after guzzling some water to quench my thirst, I got in the truck and started to drive away. As I came to a halt at the stop sign just ahead, I was surprised to suddenly see a bicycle wheel roll past the driver's side of the truck. It went straight through the stop line and across the road, where it came to a stop after bumping into the side of a parked car. For a few seconds, I was wondering what kind of idiot could have rolled a bicycle wheel down the street. Then it dawned on me that it was my wheel. As I jumped out of the truck and ran across the road to retrieve the wheel, the driver of the parked car got out and began examining the side of her car for damage. Feeling rather embarrassed, I apologized profusely. Although there was no visible damage to her car, she just glared at me and did not even bother to acknowledge my apology. Because there was no damage done, there was not a lot she could say. But, if looks could kill!

When Tinman race day arrived, I was feeling nervous and more than a little bit intimidated. It was only my second triathlon, and the scale of the event seemed so much larger than that of the TriUmph. Around 1,000 people had entered the race, and a lot of them appeared to be experienced athletes. There we were, all standing on Ala Moana Beach just after sunrise waiting for the start. I found myself wondering for a while whether I was really supposed to be there. Finally, I told myself to just get in the water, warm up while waiting for my starting wave, and then do the best I could. Somewhat to my surprise, it actually turned out quite well. The swim, the bike, and the run all went smoothly with no significant mishaps, and I was elated to find that I was still feeling relatively strong when I crossed the finish line in a time of about 2 hours 45 minutes. Although I placed only 551st overall, and 24th out of 44 finishers in my age group, a performance that would certainly have to be considered mediocre by any objective standards, I felt extremely satisfied with what I had been able to do. I had finally been able to fulfill an ambition that had been lurking deep in the back of my mind for many years. I had finished the Tinman! In addition, I was pleasantly surprised to find that my aging body still had the ability to keep going continuously at what felt to me like a fairly high level of intensity for the better part of 3 hours.

Along with a number of my comrades in training, I was finding that the desire to keep up the momentum seemed to grow with each successive event. After each race was completed, the question that we asked each other was, "What's next?" I found that I was becoming hooked on the athletic lifestyle and that being an athlete was gradually becoming a more integral part of my identity. By the time the Tinman was over, I was putting in at least 8 to 10 hours of training every week, and I was loving it. More and more, I was thinking of myself as an athlete, rather than just some guy who exercised in his spare time and occasionally entered a fun run or a swim. In many respects, I had begun to reorganize my life around my participation in athletics rather than just fitting exercise into my busy schedule whenever I could. I recall going to a celebration party after one of the events. We had planned it so that each of us would get up to say some words of appreciation for the coaches. When my turn came, the first thing that came out of my mouth was, "Hi. My name is Brian, and I'm a triaholic!"

In addition to the sense of accomplishment that my first two triathlons had given me, I really liked the way that I was feeling as a result of the regular training. Overall, I was feeling fitter and stronger than I had in many years, and my attitude toward life seemed to become proportionally more positive. That is not to say, however, that I felt great all of the time. There were times when I felt tired as a result of my busy work schedule combined with the increased volume of training. But, for the most part, it was a good kind of tiredness that allowed me to sleep soundly every night. I did notice, however, that, on some days, particularly the longer weekend workouts, I would not exactly be feeling on top of the world when I started out. Maybe it had been a particularly busy week at work, or I had not gotten as much sleep as I should have, or maybe there had been some other stressors in my life that took up some of my time and energy. On such days, it would seem like a real effort to keep up with other athletes, and I would find myself slipping into a negative mindset. I am usually a pretty easygoing and even tempered person, but there is certainly a side of me that can sometimes manifest itself as moodiness and frustration. In the context of a workout, my negativity was usually directed at myself for not being able to perform the way I would have liked to. Occasionally, however, it would manifest outwardly with comments about other road users such as, "What the hell does that jackass think he's doing?!" Once in a while, those feelings were even expressed more directly, such as yelling at and flipping off an inconsiderate motorist during one of our bike rides. I found, however, that, if I just kept going with the workout at my own pace, the negativity that was initially present would gradually dissipate, and I would almost invariably end the workout in a much more positive frame of mind. Often, after completing a workout that I initially thought I was never going to make it through, I would feel a sense of exhilaration that seemed to carry over into other areas of my life long after the workout was over.

After the Tinman, a few of us older guys, including Glenn Perry, Jeff Smith, Steve Davidson, and Peter Biggs, decided to take on the challenge of doing the Waikiki Roughwater Swim, training with Dave Washburn in a program that he called Swim Safari. Those workouts were a lot of fun. Two mornings during the week, right after sunrise, we would swim at Kaimana Beach in Waikīkī, and, on Saturday mornings, the training took us out of town to various beautiful beaches around the island of Oʻahu. Most swim coaches will tell you that you have to do intervals in a pool regularly if you want to get faster. I know they are absolutely right. But I'm sorry; I don't really want to hear it. This is one of the areas in which it is very clear to me that getting faster and maximizing my performance are not my top priorities. I love swimming in the ocean, but I can take it or leave it in a pool. Give me a choice between a swimming pool and the clear blue waters of somewhere like Waimea Bay, watching green sea turtles and tropical fish as we swim, and I'll take Waimea any day, especially when followed by a big, tasty brunch at a place like Café Haleiwa, which became one of our rewards for a good workout. Swim Safari was also comprised of another group of positive people, and I made a number of new friends in the group, including, in particular, Stella Cabana, an ambitious and determined athlete, who later became a great training buddy when we started training for longer distance triathlons.

Unfortunately, Swim Safari culminated in the near disaster that was the 2003 Waikiki Roughwater Swim. Along with Jeff Smith, I was one of the fortunate ones who decided to pull out of the event after going out for a warm up swim. I swam out about 300 to 400 meters from the shore, at which point I could already tell that there was a pretty strong current that day. I had done WRS only once before, and that had been 8 years earlier on a day when the current was favorable. I was not at all confident that I was a strong enough swimmer to handle an unfavorable current for 2.4 miles. I felt like a bit of a wimp at the time, but as the morning progressed I began to realize that I had made the right decision. The waves were actually not that big, 2- to 3-foot faces with an occasional 4 footer, so it wasn't too difficult to get through the break. But the longshore current out behind the break was really mean that day. By the time they reached the first turn buoy, which is officially listed as being 677 meters from shore, all but the strongest of swimmers were simply not moving forward at all. In some cases, they were literally moving backward, despite stroking as hard as they could. Out of over 900 people who started the race, less than 400 were able to finish. Another couple of hundred swimmers managed to make it back to shore under their own power, but the rest had to be rescued one way or another. From the shore, it was a wild scene with several helicopters hovering over the course and dozens of rescue boats bringing in people that they had pulled out of the water. Even Dave and our other coaches ended up being pulled out somewhere around the halfway mark because it seemed unlikely that they would be able to finish within the allotted time limit. The whole experience very much reinforced what I had learned from the days soon after I first arrived in Hawai'i when my friends and I would go bodysurfing at places like Makapu'u, Sandy Beach, or Pounders—the ocean can be a lot of fun, but you have to treat it with a great deal of respect.

Swim Safari was followed by another round of training with Brian Clarke for the 2003 edition of the TriUmph triathlon, which was scheduled to take place on November 23rd. The course for the race was moved from Schofield Barracks to a new location at the old Barber's Point military base at Kalaeloa, near the southwest corner of the island of O'ahu. The format for the training was basically the same as the previous year. The composition of the group was also similar to that of 2002, although some members of the original group did not return, and a few new members came in. Among the new members was Jodie Hagerman, who over the years has become one of my best friends in the triathlon community. Not long after Jodie joined the group, we were running together and talking, and I learned to my surprise that she happened to be the sister of another good friend whom I had known since our time in graduate school at the University of Hawai'i. As one of my old friends used to say, Honolulu is a big city now, but it's still a small town. It's one of the things that I love about living here.

The 2003 TriUmph also went smoothly for me and it became another step in my evolution as a triathlete. I didn't manage to place this time, even in the Beginners' Division, for which I was still eligible having raced in only two previous triathlons, but I was able to improve my time by a few minutes over the previous year, finishing in just over 1 hour and 25 minutes. It was actually a little hard to make a direct comparison of the two performances because the conditions on the two courses were slightly different. Nevertheless, I was pleased with my effort, and I chose to regard it as a significant improvement.

Unfortunately, the 2003 TriUmph proved to be the last event in that series because AARP decided not to continue it in 2004. In my opinion, the cancellation of the series was a great pity, because it provided an excellent opportunity for older people to stay physically active, to take on a new challenge, and to "get their feet wet" in the sport of triathlon. I think I can speak for many of my friends who began with me when I say that we might never have gotten started as triathletes if it had not been for this event.

My performance at the 2003 TriUmph meant that the year had ended on another positive note. It was something of a revelation to me that, even in my late 50s, there was still room for progressive improvement in my performance if I kept training consistently. With each new event, I felt that I was making progress and my confidence in my capacity for endurance was gradually growing. As a consequence, I was slowly becoming more comfortable in the role of athlete. In addition, I had moved at least a few steps closer to rising above that old feeling of resignation and coming to a deeper acceptance of my athletic mediocrity. However, I was not completely there yet.

Chapter 11

Upping the Intensity

A particularly important development in my own progress, and I think in the progress of several of my training buddies, took place soon after the 2003 TriUmph. We had learned that the inaugural Honolulu Triathlon was going to take place in April 2004, and a lot of us wanted to give it a try. It was going to be a big day that included the trials for the U.S. Olympic triathlon squad, as well as the age group event on a slightly different course. After having successfully completed the Tinman in 2003, an Olympic distance triathlon definitely seemed feasible because it essentially involved only a longer swim—1500 meters as opposed to 800 meters. After Swim Safari, I knew I could swim that distance quite comfortably (as long as the current wasn't too strong). The Honolulu Triathlon therefore seemed like the logical choice for our next challenge.

The problem was that Brian Clarke was not able to offer a training group for the Honolulu Triathlon. Consequently, those of us who were interested in doing it had to look for other options. One of the gang, Jeff Smith, made contact with another training group, Boca Hawaii, run by a transplanted Brazilian triathlete named Raul Torres de Sa, who used to go by the nickname "Boca," hence the name of the group. Fortunately, Raul was enthusiastic about putting together a group primarily for us older folks, and so, in January 2004, the Boca Masters group was born. Once again, I certainly did not see it at the time, but my participation with the Boca Masters group turned out to be a critical turning point in my progress as a triathlete.

Up to that point, I had enjoyed Brian Clarke's training groups a great deal. In terms of the details of the training, the groups were systematic and well organized, and particularly suited for beginners, as pretty much all of us had been when we started in 2002. The coaches who worked with Brian were always helpful and encouraging, and their guidance and support had helped me to gain the confidence to accomplish the goals that I had set for myself up to that point. Some of them, like Brian himself, had been top class athletes in their respective fields and had gladly shared their experience and knowledge with us. When I had started training with Brian in late 2002, I wasn't entirely sure that I would be able to swim 400 meters, get out of the water and immediately bike 12 miles, and then run 5 kilometers. A little over a year later, I felt very confident that I would be able to swim 1500 meters, bike 40K, and then run 10K, in order to finish my first Olympic distance triathlon.

By the time we started the Boca Masters group, I felt that I was ready for a somewhat different approach to training. In general, the Boca Hawaii training program had a reputation for being geared toward "hard core" athletes who were more focused on speed and competition than any of us had been. Raul himself had a reputation as an experienced veteran of multiple endurance athletic events, including numerous iron-distance triathlons. Consequently, I must admit that I felt a little intimidated when I showed up for our first training session. I soon found, however, that I really had no reason to feel that way. It certainly helped that the majority of the athletes in the Masters group were people that I already knew from Brian

Clarke's training program, most of them just about as mediocre as I was. There were also a few new people, like Lori McCarney, Steve Edwards, and Barry Kurren, all of whom proved to be great additions to the group. In addition, Raul had an infectious enthusiasm for the sport of triathlon that he readily communicated to us. One of his mottos is "Train with passion." Indeed, training was steadily becoming a true passion for a lot of us in the group.

Our first coaches for the Boca Masters' group were Jay Paul and John Sarich. Jay, whom I mentioned before, was in his late 30s at the time. I was surprised to find out that he was actually a relative newcomer to the sport because he had already made a name for himself as one of the top triathletes in his age group in Hawai'i. John was of the same generation as most of us in the group, and actually a little older than me. Superbly fit for his age and strong as an ox, in many ways John epitomized the ideals of maintaining lifelong physical fitness and taking on new challenges in life.

The training with Jay and John involved a somewhat greater volume, and certainly more of a focus on intensity, than we had been accustomed to in the past. But I found myself enjoying the challenges that we encountered in many of our workouts. I wanted to keep getting better, so I worked very hard in training, and, in retrospect, I probably over-trained a bit. The volume was nowhere near as great as I would later become accustomed to. At that point in time, however, my body probably was not quite ready for the workload that I was putting it through. Consequently, I think my immune system was a little weaker than usual because I ended up getting sick three times during that year.

The first race of the year was the Lanikai Triathlon, a sprint distance event that has since become a popular fixture as one of the first events on the O'ahu triathlon calendar each year. At that time, it was held in late March, which is still around the tail end of the rainy season in Hawai'i. I recall traveling along the Pali Highway from my home in Honolulu to Kailua, on the windward side of the island, on the day of the race. It was about 5:00 a.m., so it was still very dark on the highway once we got out of town. The wind was howling, and it was absolutely pouring with rain as I drove, accompanied by my long-suffering girlfriend, Joni, over the Ko'olau Mountains. By the time we got to the start of the race at Kailua Beach, I knew that Joni was thinking that I had to be crazy to be out there so early in the morning in that kind of weather doing a triathlon when I could have been at home sleeping. I must admit that I did have a few similar thoughts myself. Nevertheless, once I got there, I couldn't wait to get started. I got out of my truck, checked in and racked my bike in the transition area. As the start of the race approached, I put on my swim cap and goggles, and eagerly headed out into the rather chilly and choppy waters of Kailua Bay. By the time I finished the entire triathlon, the rain had just about stopped, but the roads were still wet and slippery, and the wind was still blowing pretty hard. Despite all of that, I was again feeling that now familiar sense of accomplishment and elation that comes at the end of a race when you know that you have given it your best shot. I think it was at that point that I really knew I was addicted.

That initial success at Lanikai was followed by my first major disappointment as a triathlete. In April 2004, during the week before the Honolulu Triathlon, I came down with one of the worst upper respiratory tract infections that I had had for years. It dragged on throughout the week without much improvement, even though I took a few days off from training. On the day before the event, I was still hoping that I might recover enough to be able to race, so I decided to go ahead and check my bike in at the transition area. When I got up the next morning, however, I still had a hacking cough and felt unusually weak. At that point, I knew there was no way that I would be able to do the race. Reluctantly, I went down to the bike corral, took my bike out, and informed one of the course marshals that I would be pulling out. I stayed for a while to watch and cheer on my friends with as much enthusiasm as I could muster. But, long before any of them finished, I was feeling so lousy I had to go home and go back to bed disappointed and demoralized. I had trained extremely hard and was very much looking forward to achieving another goal that had seemed to be well within my reach, so it came as a bitter blow to be forced to pull out.

I've learned several times during my career, if one can call it that, as a recreational athlete that setbacks and disappointments can sometimes eventually lead to positive things in the longer run if you can find a way to put them behind you and move on. In retrospect, I can now say that pulling out of that race may not have been such a bad thing at all because it left me with the nagging feeling that I still had something to prove to myself, which served as an added incentive to keep pushing ahead. By that time, I had become firmly committed to the goal of completing an Olympic distance triathlon, and it bothered me no end that I had not yet been able to accomplish that goal. The situation was complicated by the fact that there were no other Olympic distance triathlons on the Oʻahu race calendar until the following year's Honolulu Triathlon. At that time, I had never really given much thought to going off the island of Oʻahu, much less outside of the state of Hawaiʻi, to do a triathlon. Incidentally, there are really only two drawbacks to living in Honolulu. The first is that the cost of living is considerably higher than most other parts of the country. The second is that it is a long way to anywhere else. In any event, spurred on by lingering feelings of frustration about not being able to participate in the Honolulu Triathlon, as the summer of 2004 went by, I became increasingly focused on trying to find a way to compensate for that failure to accomplish my goal.

Chapter 12

Endurance Starts to Call

Training for the 2004 Tinman with the Boca Masters group began almost immediately after the Honolulu Triathlon. It was during that time that I first began to have some vague thoughts about possibly attempting to do a longer distance event. By that time, I had been around people like Raul, Jay, and John for a few months, and I had listened to some of their talk about their experiences in iron-distance events, as well as in half-iron-distance events. The latter, consisting of a 1.2 mile swim, a 56 mile bike, and a 13.1 mile run, for a total of 70.3 miles, seemed to be regarded as being the next logical step up after an Olympic-distance triathlon for those who wanted to take that next step. Through Boca Hawaii, I had also met a number of other athletes who had either completed or had firm plans to do some of these longer distance races. We were fortunate enough to come into contact with some excellent athletes through the Masters group. Wil Yamamoto and Rachel Ross actually trained with our group for a while, although they were really in a class of their own, and Tim Marr helped out with some of our coaching. All of them subsequently went on to great accomplishments in the sport of triathlon, not only in Hawai'i, but also nationally and internationally, Wil and Rachel as top age groupers, and Tim as an accomplished professional triathlete. We Mediocristanis may never be able to compete with athletes of the caliber of Tim, Wil, and Rachel, but we can certainly still learn from them and be inspired by them. The contact I had with these fine athletes, who seemed to have so much confidence in their own ability, was one of the things that began to allow me to think about the possibility of expanding my own horizons.

Through our association with all the people who were training or had trained with Boca Hawaii, I also met some seemingly pretty mediocre athletes like myself who had been able to successfully complete either a half or full iron-distance event. One person in particular was Gerald Lee. Gerald was not part of our Boca Masters' group, but he had trained with Boca in the past. I'm not sure exactly when I first met him, but I remember being impressed by his determination when I heard him talking about his experiences, including one at Ironman Canada, in which he had managed to finish just about 10 minutes short of the 17-hour deadline. I am sure Gerald will not object when I say that he was obviously not an outstanding athlete in terms of his ability level, but equally obviously, finishing an iron-distance event had been a truly outstanding accomplishment for him. I certainly found his experience to be truly inspirational.

People like Gerald not only provided a source of inspiration but also helped me to develop a more healthy perspective on my own less than outstanding athletic abilities. At that point in my life, I had been reminded many times, in no uncertain terms, of my mediocrity as an athlete. Although I had, by that time, been able to accept that reality to some degree, I had still not completely come to terms with it. On the surface, I could acknowledge and even joke about my mediocrity, but at a deeper level, I still resented it. As I look back now, I think the essential problem was that I was still a little ashamed of my mediocrity. Deep down, I wanted to be worthy of respect as an athlete, and I think I wanted that respect from myself at least as much if not more than from others. The problem was that there was still at least a small part of me that held on to the idea that, if I were not able to perform at an outstanding level, then I didn't really deserve that respect. Consequently, even as a supposedly mature adult in my late fifties, it was still hard to fully accept the simple fact that I was never going to be an outstanding athlete. After listening to people like Gerald, however, and witnessing the amazing determination and perseverance of numerous other obviously mediocre athletes, it gradually became clearer to me that my ability level was really not the thing that mattered. Over time, I came to recognize that, if I simply choose to take on the challenge and then give it my absolute best shot, I can justifiably be proud of my accomplishment no matter how mediocre my performance is in comparison to others. As a psychologist, I'm sure that I already knew that as a general principle because I have often attempted to convey similar ideas to some of my clients. In retrospect, it seems so glaringly obvious that I can't believe it had never really occurred to me in exactly those terms in relation to my own athletic activities. To put it in simple terms: you don't have to *be* outstanding in order to *do* something outstanding.

Let me now get back to my question for Jay, to which I made reference at the beginning of this part of the book. Inspired by the example of some of the athletes I was meeting, around the middle of the year 2004, somewhere in my mind something began to stir. Maybe it had to do with the idea of wanting to accomplish something that I could truly view, at least by my own standards, as outstanding, although I can't say I was specifically thinking in those terms back then. Maybe it had something to do with needing to compensate for not being able to fulfill my goal of doing the Honolulu Triathlon a little earlier that year. Maybe it simply had to do with wanting to see if I might be able to emulate the experiences of the inspiring athletes that I had been meeting. I can't pinpoint the exact moment in my memory, but it was some time during the spring or early summer of 2004 that I first vaguely began to wonder, "Could I too possibly be capable of doing an Ironman? If not a full thing, maybe a half?"

These were the thoughts that led to the question that I posed to Jay as we were running around Ala Moana Beach Park one summer evening that year.

It was always a pleasure to train with the coaches and athletes I met through the Boca Hawaii program because of the positive and encouraging attitude they almost invariably exuded. I particularly appreciated the belief that the coaches always seemed to have had in me, even when I didn't necessarily have that belief in myself. Jay responded to my question by saying that he knew I'd been thinking about it and that he had no doubt that I was capable of doing it if I put my mind to it. I was flattered by the belief that Jay had in me, but I still wasn't ready to take that leap of faith in myself. By that time, I had done the math in my head—numerous times, in fact. I had figured that, even if things went well, finishing an iron-distance event might easily take me as much as 16 hours to complete, maybe more depending on all the unpredictable factors like ocean currents, weather conditions, and flat tires, not to mention other potential catastrophes that could easily become the stuff of nightmares. Because of all of those concerns, I was not at all confident that I would be able to make it within the 17-hour time limit, even if I managed to keep going all the way to the finish, and I certainly wasn't sure that I could do that. Despite the confidence that I had built up over the past year or so, I just wasn't yet convinced that I had the endurance to keep going for that long a period of time. Sometimes, when I thought about what might be involved in attempting to do an iron-distance event, I even had visions of becoming exhausted and either collapsing or having to pull out of the race long before I got to the finish line.

Despite those reservations, I remember talking with one of the other members of the Masters group, Larry Yatsushiro, about the possibility of attempting a longer distance event. At that time, I essentially concluded that 140.6 miles in single day was way too much for me to take on, but I wondered if half of that distance, 70.3 miles, might just about be feasible, particularly if I had a training buddy of similar ability. Larry and I had some discussions about possibly entering the Keauhou Triathlon, a half-iron-distance event on the Big Island, in May of the following year, 2005. We had, by then, met a number of athletes who had done that race in the past, so we had at least a vague idea of what to expect. Based on what we had heard from them, it sounded like a challenging event, but we figured we just might be able to get through it if we kept training hard...and if everything went well on race day.

By the middle of the summer, despite numerous lingering doubts about my ability to finish, I had made up my mind that I wanted to take on the challenge of a half-iron-distance event the following year. I figured that, if I could gradually keep increasing the volume and maintain the consistency of my training, maybe I would have at least an outside chance of finishing that distance. I had heard through the grapevine that some athletes whom I had met through Boca were planning to do the new Honu Half Ironman in 2005. (The Honu event had actually made its debut on the Big Island a little earlier in 2004 as an Olympic distance event. In 2005, it became the Honu Half Ironman, and then a year or two later it was renamed as Ironman 70.3 Hawai'i, although many local athletes still refer to it simply as "Honu.") I was, however, somewhat intimidated by what I had heard about Honu. It sounded like it was going to be a race geared toward serious athletes—you know, the outstanding kind, not the mediocre kind like me—on a course that would be even more challenging than the Keauhou Triathlon. In addition, the unofficial word was that Keauhou was more of a "people's event," along the lines of the Tinman, albeit well over twice as long. Not wanting to be too ambitious, I decided that I wasn't ready to take on Honu, which seemed a little bit too extreme, and signed up for the 2005 Keauhou Triathlon. It was around that time that some of my friends in the Masters group began questioning my sanity, and I must admit I sometimes wondered about that myself. I was going to be the first one of our gang to attempt a half-iron-distance event. Was I getting into something over my head?

Incidentally, Larry Yatsushiro unfortunately was not able to attempt any of the longer distance events at that time due to some pretty serious health problems. Fortunately, he was able to make a successful recovery, and I do know that he was able to complete Ironman 70.3 Hawai'i eventually. I remember him as a tough, determined athlete, and I hope he will be able to move up to the full iron-distance some day because he is certainly very capable of it. I did try hard to persuade some of my other training buddies, like Glenn Perry and Peter Biggs, to consider signing up for Keauhou also but to no avail. One other friend, Tom Mark, who had loaned me a bike helmet that first TriUmph training session a couple of years earlier, also deferred at that time. Tom subsequently did decide to take on the challenge of the half-iron-distance and ended up having an excellent performance at Ironman 70.3 Hawai'i in 2007. He is an extremely disciplined and determined athlete who subsequently went on to become the second person from our original 2002 TriUmph group to finish an iron-distance event. He was able to accomplish that goal on the challenging course at Penticton, Canada, in 2008. Then, two years later, in August 2010, despite dealing with nagging injuries that would probably have sidelined a lot of people, he was able to successfully finish Ironman Canada for the second time—a truly great accomplishment!

Much of the process of making the decision to enter the Keauhou Triathlon took place during the time leading up to Tinman 2004. At that time, I was becoming more and more hooked on the athletic lifestyle, and I approached every event with the expectation that I was going to improve my performance in some way. Despite the fact that I got sick again not long before the Tinman, I was able to recover well enough to have what I felt was a fairly decent race. On the one hand, I was satisfied with my performance because I was able to improve my time by several minutes over the previous year. On the other hand, however, I didn't feel quite the same sense of accomplishment that I had experienced the year before. Perhaps I was already looking beyond that event. Next year's Keauhou Triathlon was already very much on my mind, and I figured I was going to have to put in the performance of my life if I was going to finish that event. Finishing the Tinman, even with an improvement over the previous year's performance, seemed to be a relatively small accomplishment in comparison with what I would have to do at Keauhou.

In addition, I was also aware that I still had some unfinished business to complete. I desperately wanted to make up for the debacle of Labor Day 2003, so my immediate goal for the summer of 2004 was the Waikiki Roughwater Swim. Despite my lack of enthusiasm for swimming pools, I forced myself to do some pool training under the coaching of Joe Lileikis at the Oʻahu Club. Joe is another great coach who brings a tremendous amount of enthusiasm to his work. Many of my friends have trained with him at some point in time, and I think I can safely say that all of us have been inspired by his approach to coaching, by his example as a top class swimmer, and, in recent years, by the courage he has brought to dealing with some potentially life-threatening health problems. Not even Joe could get my swimming ability above the mediocre level, but training with him certainly helped to build my confidence in my ability to rise to the challenge the WRS would pose.

Raul also helped some of us from the Masters gang who were planning to do the WRS by taking us out for some training on the race course, which was extremely helpful in building our confidence. In July, during the course of our swim training, some of us entered the Cholo's 2000 at Waimea Bay, one of the four events in the annual North Shore Swim Series. I had previously done that event a couple of times in the 1990s, and I had always enjoyed it greatly because of the spectacularly beautiful setting and the incredibly clear water in Waimea Bay. By the time the WRS came around, I was feeling much more confident in my ability to do a long distance open ocean swim. Conditions for the event were not ideal by any means, but certainly not as bad as the year before. After swimming out from the start at Kaimana Beach and making the first turn 677 meters from the start, I found myself battling a fairly strong current for much of the 2305 meter leg that runs roughly parallel to Waikīkī Beach, and also down the 842 meter channel back to the shoreline in front of the Hilton Hawaiian Village Hotel. As a result, I eventually finished the 2.4-mile swim in 2 hours 23 minutes, approximately 40 minutes longer than when I had first done it in 1995, even though both my technique and my speed had improved considerably during that time. I was reminded again what a huge difference the current can make in an open ocean swim.

Even though my time was quite slow, I was thrilled that I had finished the Waikiki Roughwater Swim after the disappointment of the previous year. It was one more step toward wherever my journey as an athlete was taking me. About ten of us from the Boca Masters group celebrated our success by indulging ourselves in a huge buffet lunch at the Hale Koa Hotel after the race, and I vividly remember one of my friends, Marsha Kitagawa, splurging on the array of delicious desserts that were presented to us. An occasional episode of guilt free indulgence is one of the rewards for all of that training that we do. Incidentally, Marsha is another person who has shown a great deal of perseverance in her training over the years. Despite her tendency to minimize her ability as a runner, she has gone on to finish several marathons over the past few years. In addition, in 2010, she was able to finish her first Ironman 70.3 Hawai'i and then greatly improved her performance in her second appearance at the event in 2011. Like many of the other recreational athletes that I have come to know over the years, she provides a great example of the way that commitment and consistency in training can pay off in the long run.

As part of my preparation for Keauhou the following year, I decided that it would be a good idea to further build my endurance by training for the Honolulu Marathon in December 2004. I had not done another marathon since that first one in 1985, and for a long time I had assumed that I probably never would. By the fall of 2004, however, I finally felt that I was ready to take on the challenge again.

Along the way, I decided to do the Ko Olina Triathlon in early October. At that time, Ko Olina was set up in between the sprint and Olympic distances, but with a unique format, featuring a swim across four small man-made lagoons with a short run between each lagoon. Unfortunately, I got sick again, for the third time that year, about a week before the race. Joni and I went on a cruise in September, and, by the time our ship got back to Honolulu, both of us had come down with a really bad case of the flu. I was completely incapacitated for a couple of days, but managed to recover just about enough to be able to compete in the race. It was, however, an ordeal that I would never want to repeat. The run, in particular, although only about 4.5 miles, was absolute torture. Joni, my loyal supporter, was even less well recovered and could barely walk back to the car by the time we left. I couldn't help but feel a bit guilty that I had dragged her all the way down there, and I also found myself wondering what the heck had motivated me to go ahead with the race in the condition that I was in. After having had to pull out of the Honolulu Triathlon due to sickness earlier in the year, I just wasn't willing to even consider pulling out again. All of this seemed to be more evidence of my growing addiction to the sport.

After Ko Olina, I threw myself with full force into training for the 2004 Honolulu Marathon with the Boca Hawaii clinic. This was my first Boca training group that was not set up primarily for the Masters folks, so most of the people in the group were considerably younger. It proved to be another opportunity to meet some seasoned athletes who already had a lot of experience in longer distance events. The group also included some other athletes who were relative newcomers to long distance triathlons but who already had their sights clearly set on big goals like Ironman Canada in 2005. Many of those athletes were really strong runners, and I can recall feeling more than a little intimidated by them at the time. As I got to know them, however, I found that they were a great group of people who were supportive of those of us whose mediocrity was somewhat more obvious.

My main training buddy for the marathon that year was Jodie Hagerman, who ran at approximately the same pace as I did. As I mentioned above, I first met Jodie in Brian Clarke's group when we were training for the 2003 TriUmph. In the process of training for the marathon, I got to know her better, and she has remained, to this day, one of my best friends. She, too, is a strong and determined athlete whose uncompromising efforts in training and resilience in rising above numerous challenges in her life inevitably provide inspiration to everyone with whom she trains. Running all those miles with her helped immensely in building up the endurance and confidence that I needed to finish the second marathon of my life, almost 20 years after my first one.

On race day in December 2004, Jodie and I ran together for most of the course, but I "hit the wall" and started to feel my energy fading at about mile 24, and eventually finished a couple of minutes behind her in a time of about 4 hours and 33 minutes. Despite the fact that the last couple of miles were rather painful, I was thrilled, and actually quite amazed, that the reward for all of that hard work in training was that I had been able to run a marathon well over an hour faster than I had done 19 years earlier. That success helped me go into 2005 with a much more optimistic and confident attitude. I still couldn't even imagine myself actually doing a full iron-distance event, but I was at least beginning to believe that I really was capable of finishing the half-iron-distance event at Keauhou. I couldn't wait to get going with the training for it.

Chapter 13

Half Way There

In early 2005, I was in for quite a shock when I was informed that the Keauhou Triathlon was being cancelled and my entry fee would be refunded. Competition from the new Honu Half Ironman, which was to be held in early June just a couple of weeks after the Keauhou race had been scheduled, had apparently caused such a drop in the enrollment for Keauhou that it was not feasible to go ahead with the race. Initially, my reaction was one of great disappointment, and I worried that I would have to give up my primary triathlon goal for the second year in a row. Fortunately, however, disappointment was once again to turn into opportunity for me. I soon found out from friends that there were still slots available for Honu, and a lot of them encouraged me to go ahead and send in my entry as soon as possible. Although I had by then been told by a number of people that the course at Honu was actually not that much more difficult than the Keauhou course would have been, I still felt quite intimidated by the prospect of entering this race. Putting aside my previous doubts, however, I told myself that I couldn't let this opportunity pass. I had to at least give it a shot. I decided to sign up right away before it was too late.

The year 2005 turned out to be an excellent one for me in many respects. I initially continued my training with the other "senior citizens" in the Boca Masters group leading up to the Honolulu Triathlon. As with the previous year, the first event of the triathlon season on O'ahu was the Lanikai Triathlon, which happened to take place a few weeks before my 60th birthday, thankfully in much better weather than the previous year. The timing of this event proved to be fortunate for me. To my amazement, I placed third in the 55–59 age group. In the past, I had occasionally placed in my age group in sparsely attended fun runs, as well as in a few biathlons when I had done them as part of a team. Plus, of course, I had managed to take third place in the Beginners' division in the 2002 TriUmph. I had, however, always tended to regard those as relatively minor achievements, attributable to being in the right place at the right time in a small enough pond, or to having the right biathlon partner, rather to any real ability on my own part. To actually place as an individual age-grouper in a triathlon seemed like a huge accomplishment for me. It seemed to be more evidence that, despite my age, I was gradually getting better and better. When I looked at all the race results, however, I was immediately humbled and brought back to the reality of my mediocrity by the realization that if had been in the 60–64 age group, I actually would not have placed. Damn, I thought, some of those old timers sure are fast!

It was during the early part of 2005 that I began to consider treating myself to a new bike. When I had first started biking in 2002, I had found it to be hard work, probably because I had just not been accustomed to using the necessary muscles for many years. As time went by, however, and my body became more accustomed to pushing those pedals around for extended periods of time, the more I found that I really enjoyed biking. Although many of the roads on the island of O'ahu are not as bike friendly as they might be ideally, it is still a beautiful setting for being out on the road. Plus, we are fortunate that the weather is favorable for biking throughout virtually the entire year. I found that I particularly liked the experience of being able to cover fairly long distances under my own power with relative ease as compared to running or walking. Over a 2-hour period of time, for example, I might have been able to cover about 12 miles if I were running. In contrast, on my bike, I could cover a distance of about 30 to 35 miles, which allowed me to go for workouts in parts of the island that I would rarely, if ever, have been able to include in a run. As a bonus, that 2-hour bike ride didn't seem to take as much out of me physically as a 2-hour run would have done. Because I was enjoying the biking so much, I reasoned that if I were going to be doing this triathlon stuff for the long haul, maybe it might be worth considering at least a modest upgrade. Up to that point, my old Trek 2500 had served me well, but it was definitely beginning to show signs of its age in a number of ways. I therefore began to consider possible options.

As I have noted, one of the themes of this book is simplicity. I selected this as a theme because I think it essentially captures the approach that I bring to my participation in athletics. I prefer to keep things simple as much as possible, and not make them more complicated than they need to be. I try to maintain that approach not only in the process of training and racing, but also in relation to the gear and equipment that is needed. Triathlon is a sport that requires a good deal of equipment, in comparison, for example, to just running or swimming. Consequently, it can become quite an expensive sport in many ways, even if you don't do a lot of traveling in order to participate in races, which can significantly add to the expense. Bikes are always the single most expensive item on the list of equipment. By early 2005, I had been around the sport long enough to be well aware of all the many possible choices that were available if I decided to get a new bike. I knew a number of athletes who had spent many thousands of dollars on high-end triathlon bikes or road bikes, and, in some cases, both. I have to admit that, when I saw some of my training buddies riding those expensive machines, I would sometimes get a little envious and start thinking that maybe I needed to get something like that for myself. At that time, however,

I knew that a near top of the line triathlon bike could easily have set me back upwards of $5,000. Did I really want to spend that much?

Over the years, I have inevitably spent quite a lot of money on my athletic activities. Without a doubt, it has been worth every penny of it because of the rewards and benefits that I have gotten from those activities. At the same time, because so many products are marketed to the triathlon community, I have come to the conclusion that it is very easy to spend a great deal more than is really necessary to enjoy the sport and to achieve most of one's goals. Consequently, I have tried to make a point of avoiding unnecessary spending. When I considered all the other priorities in my life, I found it difficult to justify spending $5,000 or more on a bike that would, at best, offer an athlete of my ability nothing more than a marginal improvement in performance. Ever since I first became involved in the sport of triathlon, I have never been primarily focused on competitive race performance. I certainly always try to perform at the best of my ability, and I am always thrilled when I do manage to get a podium place in my age group as I had done at Lanikai. However, my main reasons for becoming involved in triathlons were for the sense of personal accomplishment and to maintain my physical health and fitness. Ultimately, therefore, I just couldn't see the point of spending a great deal of money on a bike that wasn't really going to contribute any more than a less expensive model to the fulfillment of those priorities.

When I went to see Frank Smith at Island Triathlon and Bike, I had decided that my upper limit was $2,000, and I must admit that I still felt a little guilty about even going up to that relatively modest level. I looked at a number of different triathlon and road bikes and eventually decided on a Felt F-35 road bike, which I equipped with easily removable aerobars for triathlon use. I also decided to have the Felt fitted with a 30-speed Ultegra gearing system, which was technically a downgrade from the 20-speed DuraAce system that originally came with the bike. The older I get, the more I am glad that I chose to go with the triple crank, especially on steep hill climbs. My bike is certainly never going to impress any of the elite triathletes, but it has proved to be a trusty steed and more than adequate for my needs over all the years since I bought it. At this point in my life, I still feel quite content to ride it for as long as it lasts, and as I long as I am able to last as an athlete, which I hope will be into my 80s or 90s.

By late spring of 2005, equipped with my new bike, I felt ready to take on some new challenges. Boca Hawaii runs many training clinics throughout each year, and Raul happened to have one starting in April that was specifically geared toward the Honu Half Ironman, for which I had, by then, signed up a couple of months earlier. When the Honu clinic started, I decided to transfer from the Masters group to the Honu group, even though the Honolulu Triathlon, for which the Masters group had been training, had not yet taken place. Making that transfer was something of a bittersweet experience for me. On the one hand it meant leaving the comfort zone that I had developed with a great gang of comrades. I had been training continuously with many of them for the last 2 ½ years. On the other hand, it was an opportunity to meet and learn from a new group of friends, some of whom had a considerable amount of experience in longer distance endurance events.

We had already been through what were for me some pretty grueling workouts with the Masters group, often at what I perceived as a fairly high level of intensity. Our Saturday morning workouts, for example, had included various combinations of swims of up to 2,000 meters, bike rides of 30 miles or more, and runs of up to 7 miles. So, in some ways, I felt reasonably well prepared to make the transition. Nevertheless, the move to the Honu group definitely represented a step up to another level in terms of training volume. On one of our first sessions, we did a pretty hard ocean swim workout at Kaimana Beach, followed by a run of "just" 9 miles at what was for me a pretty decent pace. At that point, I sure was glad that I had had the foresight to train for that marathon back in December.

A few weeks into the Honu training I vividly recall having one of those "breakthrough" days that give your confidence such a qualitative boost. First, we biked from the Boca Hawaii store in Kaka'ako over to Tantalus, a popular location for hill workouts on the slopes of the Ko'olau mountains just a couple of miles behind the city of Honolulu. It is a great workout—nearly 5 miles of almost continuous climbing, with about 1,500 feet of elevation gain. On that day, we did the equivalent of almost 2 ½ full loops of the hill—roughly 12 miles of hard climbing altogether. After returning to the Boca store, we were supposed to run at least 40 minutes and up to one hour if we felt like it. Although it was hard work all around, particularly toward the end of the workout in the heat of the day, I was able to push myself to keep running for the full hour after the ride. I felt a particular sense of satisfaction because a lot of athletes who were considerably younger had chosen to do only the minimum 40-minute run. I knew I was pretty slow in comparison to many of the people in the group, but it was on days like this when I really began to feel that my inherent mediocrity did not matter that much. By pushing myself as hard as I could, I was able to somehow rise above that mediocrity by accomplishing something that I initially was not at all sure that I would be able to do.

Raul's coaching prepared me well for the events of 2005. The Honolulu Triathlon turned out to be a great event for me. I went into it with the attitude that it was just another long training session in the run up to the Honu Half Ironman. As usual, my performance was unquestionably mediocre by any objective standards, but I worked hard and felt strong throughout the event, finishing in around 3 hours and 10 minutes on a fairly challenging course. I didn't come close to placing in my age group, but I certainly hadn't expected to. I was just pleased that I was able to maintain what I felt was a good steady pace throughout each of the three stages of the race. At the finish, I was still feeling like I had the ability to keep going without too much difficulty if I had to, so I was very happy with my performance overall. Not only had I achieved that elusive goal of completing my first Olympic distance triathlon, but I was beginning to feel that I was well on track toward my new goal of finishing a half-iron-distance event.

The highlight of the training for Honu was a weekend of workouts on the Big Island that would give us a chance to get a feel for the Honu course. When I saw the training schedule that Raul had planned for us, my initial reaction was, "How the hell am I going to be able to do all of that in one weekend?" After arriving late Friday afternoon, we were scheduled to meet for a 40 minute warm up run, just to get the blood flowing again after a day in the office and the flight from O'ahu. On Saturday morning, we would first bike

56 miles or more over virtually the whole course of the race from Mauna Lani to Hawi and back. Then we would run for 40 minutes again before taking a break for lunch. I hoped that I would then somehow be able to find time for a quick nap, if time permitted, because we were scheduled to meet again for a 1-hour swim workout at Hāpuna Beach at 4 o'clock in the afternoon. Sunday morning had us scheduled to run 15 miles on a fairly flat but very hot course starting from Hāpuna, along the old road to Puakō, down to the end of Puakō Beach Road. Then, we would continue running along the coastal trail toward the Mauna Lani Resort, out to the highway above Mauna Lani, and then all the way back along the same route to Hāpuna. This would be followed immediately by a 1-hour bike ride.

One of the great things about my triathlon experience has been developing the willingness to challenge myself to go beyond my perceived limits. When I went into that training weekend on the Big Island, I know at the back of mind the idea still lingered that a mediocre athlete like me would never be able to do all that we were expected to do. To my great surprise, however, I was able to successfully finish all of the workouts that weekend, without quitting, passing out, or otherwise failing to complete what I had somewhat apprehensively set out to do. Ultimately, I felt a tremendous sense of exhilaration at having done so, although I must admit there were some difficult moments along the way. On Saturday, in particular, I was really starting to struggle in the blistering heat as we tackled the second half of the run. Immediately prior to the run, we had completed a pretty tough bike ride, which had presented us with some fairly strong trade winds as we climbed that seemingly never-ending hill going up to Hawi. I remember one of my new training buddies, Asako Shimazu, encouraging me to keep going when I was almost ready to throw in the towel as we toiled up and down the last few hills before the finish in the blazing sun on the old road between Puakō and Hāpuna Beach. I had to slow down to a walking pace part of the way up the final short but steep hill, but I managed to keep moving forward without stopping and finally made it to the finish. After the morning workout had been completed, I found myself wondering how I could possibly be ready to swim for a full hour less than four hours later.

When I returned to the bed and breakfast place where Joni and I were staying in order to grab some lunch, I even had thoughts of just going back to sleep and skipping the swim workout altogether. I have to admit that I did manage to find time for a short nap after lunch, but I'm glad I didn't skip the swim. Hāpuna is a beautiful, long sandy beach with spectacular views of Mauna Kea and the Kohala Mountains in the background. During the summer months, the ocean on the west side of the Big Island is usually quite calm, and the water is crystal clear. It is hard to imagine a better place to swim. I definitely still felt tired as I dove into the water, but the coolness of the water was refreshing, and I was immediately thrilled by the sight of a sting ray, which was cruising slowly over the sandy bottom just a few yards from shore. It lifted my spirits, and I began to feel more and more energized as we swam back and forth across the bay. By the time we got out, I could hardly believe it, but I felt great. After a day like that, our dinner in Waikoloa was more than just a get together for the group—it was a real celebration! The long run the next day was certainly not easy in the usual west Hawai'i summer heat, but I had more than enough energy to complete it and the short bike ride that followed. By the time the weekend was over, I felt like Superman, or at least a mediocre version of Superman. Mediocreman perhaps? I had managed to complete everything that the weekend schedule called for, and, at the end of it all, I felt invigorated rather than exhausted. What a revelation! Most importantly, it was at that point that, for the first time, I felt confident that I was ready for the challenge that Honu was going to present.

When I had signed up for Honu, I still had no plan to attempt a full iron-distance event. I greatly admired my coaches and new training partners who had done all of those events, but I still couldn't really envision myself as one of them. I told myself that I would see if I was capable of enduring the half-iron-distance at Honu, and that if I could achieve that goal, that would be enough for me—at least I thought it would. There was, however, within the 2005 Honu group, a sub-group of 15 or 20 people who were training not only for Honu but also for Ironman Canada in August of that year. Some of them had done one or more iron-distance races in the past, and others were planning to do one for the first time. A few of them obviously had a lot of natural athletic talent ("real athletes" I would have called them at one time). But I was surprised to find that many of the others seemed to be pretty ordinary people like myself in terms of their athletic ability. Although most of the people in the group were considerably younger than me, I was both surprised and impressed to find that a couple of the guys, Chuck Miller and Terry O'Toole, were almost my same age. That certainly made me think. Regardless of age, the thing that everyone in that Canada group seemed to have in common was that they were obviously determined and committed to the process of training for the race. I found it hard to believe how hard and grueling some of their workouts were. But, as I observed their progress in training, along with my own, and listened to their stories, I think some of their determination and commitment must have gradually rubbed off on me.

In addition to the people who were planning to go to Canada in 2005, there were a number of other people in the group who were in the process of developing plans to do an iron-distance event the following year. For a lot of them, it would be their first attempt at that distance. Some had thought of doing Ironman Canada, others were considering Ironman New Zealand or Ironman Brazil. I had really enjoyed the camaraderie, inspiration, and support that came from training with a group of people who were all committed to achieving a common goal, and I began to think that it would really be a lot of fun to train with a group of friends for one of these events. However, I still had deep-seated doubts about whether I had what it would take to be able to finish a full iron-distance event, so I was not yet ready to make a commitment to take on that challenge. Consequently, I decided to wait and see how I did at Honu before making any decision about trying to go up to the next level.

The Honu Triathlon turned out to be a wonderful experience—another natural high in many ways. There is something very special about doing a triathlon in Hawai'i, particularly on the Big Island with its open roads and expansive scenery. Hawai'i is, in many ways, the birthplace of the long distance triathlon, so it is easy to feel a sense of connection with the roots of the sport. In addition, Hawai'i is just a great setting for both training and racing. The natural environment provides an abundance of spectacular scenery, and the tropical climate allows for outdoor training, including swimming in the ocean without a wetsuit, 365 days a year. I feel extremely fortunate to be able to live and train in such a beautiful place, and I know that I'm more than a little spoiled when I start complaining that the water can get a little chilly during the winter months.

Another thing that made Honu special was that so many friends were there to support us. Joni, who had previously had a career in nursing, came along with me, and volunteered in the medical tent on race day. Bill Darrah and Marsha Kitagawa from the Masters group took us out to dinner a couple of days before the race and came out to cheer us on. After I finished, my marathon running buddy Jodie was there to greet me with a lei, and there were congratulations from all my Boca training buddies who had also finished the race. I felt a great sense of elation as we ate, drank, and talked together during the awards ceremony. I had finished the Honu Half Ironman! It was an accomplishment that I could not even have dreamed of when I first started training for the TriUmph in 2002, only 2 ½ years earlier.

I was very pleased with my race at Honu, to say the least. The 1.2-mile swim took me a little over 46 minutes, which was about as good as I had ever been able to do for that distance. I was fortunate that the ocean conditions had been excellent—almost flat with very little current. The bike ride from Mauna Lani up to Hawi is always a challenge with the hills and the winds, but I paced myself fairly well and still felt pretty strong when I headed out of T2. The run was the toughest part. Although there had been some wind and a little cloud cover on the bike course up in the hills toward Hawi, by the time I started out on the run course down by the ocean at Mauna Lani, the sun was almost directly overhead in a virtually cloudless sky, and there seemed to be virtually no wind on many parts of the course. To put it bluntly, it was brutally hot! At times I felt like walking, but with the help of some Hammer Gel, and what must have amounted to gallons of water and Gatorade, I was able to keep running, or at least shuffling, all the way. A couple of miles before the finish, with the adrenaline that comes with the anticipation of the finish, I began to get my second wind. I was able to pick up the pace for the rest of the way, crossing the finish line with the clock showing 7:08:59. I was ecstatic! When the results were posted, I was profoundly humbled when I saw that the winner of my age group, Ed LeTourneau, a truly outstanding triathlete, had finished in the amazing time of 5:22. Consequently, I was again reminded in no uncertain terms of my inherent mediocrity. By that time, however, it didn't matter at all. I had accomplished something that was, for me, truly extraordinary. Although I was tired at some level, the sense of accomplishment was so great that I felt like I was walking on air for the rest of the day. I was also amazed that, after a good night's sleep, I again felt a sense of invigoration rather than fatigue. It was another revelation to me. So the half-iron-distance really wasn't too bad. Although I didn't do a great deal in the way of physical activity on the day after the race besides an easy swim, I couldn't wait to get back to serious training again. Just two days after the race, I was back out on the road happily running again and still feeling like I had just won a gold medal at the Mediocre Olympics.

Chapter 14

Let's Go for the Iron!

During the celebrations that took place after Honu, I remember talking with an athlete from somewhere on the mainland who commented that it had been a really tough race, taking into account the challenging bike ride and the heat during the run. He went on to say that in some respects it was probably more difficult than some full iron-distance races that he had done. I don't remember the man's name or where he was from, but his words had a big impact on me. This was another example of those seemingly minor events that can end up having an impact that seems far out of proportion to the nature of the original event. This brief encounter did, in fact, become part of another significant turning point for me. After hearing what he had said, in the context of feeling so good after finishing the race, all of a sudden it became easy, almost natural in fact, to psychologically take that next step. I immediately found myself thinking, "If I can complete a race like Honu under these conditions, maybe, if I choose a race where the course is not too difficult, there's at least a possibility that I could finish an iron-distance event after all."

This is not to say that I had complete confidence in my ability to do so at that time. Although, as I have mentioned, some vague thoughts of attempting that distance had been circulating in the back of my mind for a year or so, there had always seemed to be an element of fantasy in those thoughts. In addition to the same old doubts, the task of preparing for such an event still seemed overwhelming in many ways. Nevertheless, in the weeks that followed, I began to research some of the events in more detail. The first step was just looking through the special issue of *Triathlon* magazine, called *The Road to Kona*, which had been included in our race packets at Honu. I paid particular attention to the races in Brazil and New Zealand because I knew that some of the people in our training group had been thinking about participating in those events for the following year. I scrutinized the websites for all the different events and then talked with some athletes who had some familiarity with the courses. I knew well that no iron-distance course could ever be described as easy, but I got the impression that either Brazil or New Zealand would be a relatively good choice for a beginner (as opposed to somewhere like Lanzarote). At first, I was leaning toward the race in Brazil, which, I learned, was held on a relatively flat course in and around the resort city of Florianopolis in the southern part of the country. It seemed like a fairly good course for a first-timer, and I liked the added bonus of going to a somewhat exotic part of the world that I had never visited before. However, New Zealand looked very enticing also, and it was definitely a lot easier to get to from Hawai'i with a simple non-stop flight across the Pacific from Honolulu to Auckland. It was a difficult decision to make.

One of the other considerations that went into the decision was being able to train with at least a few people who were at about the same level as me, or at least not too much faster. During the summer of 2005, several of my training partners made the decision to do Ironman New Zealand. Although I knew some of them would be a lot faster than I could ever hope to be, I figured that there were at least a few who would probably finish the race at around the same time as me, give or take an hour or so. More importantly, I liked them all a lot, and I thought it would be a great group of people to train and travel with. "Okay," I thought, "New Zealand it is." The decision was made.

The process of making that decision gave me ample motivation to keep up a serious program of training during the summer of 2005. For some time, I had been planning on joining Brian Clarke's trail running group, which visited various scenic locations around the island of Oʻahu. I had done a certain amount of hiking on several of the islands in years past, and I had always enjoyed getting out of the hustle and bustle of the city into such quiet, beautiful natural settings. I had always found it to be a great way of relieving stress and developing a greater appreciation of all that life has to offer. Spending time up in the mountains, looking down on the rest of the world, always seemed to make me feel more relaxed and helped to give me a more positive perspective on whatever was on my mind. I thought that running in that type of natural environment would be a nice change from the routine of road running that I had become accustomed to over the years. I was not disappointed. During our weekday evening sessions we would run in the popular and well-maintained Tantalus-Makiki Valley trail system in the Koʻolau Mountains above the city of Honolulu. The start of this trail system is only about 2 or 3 miles from the downtown area, although, when you are out there on the richly forested mountain slopes with no concrete in sight and no traffic noise, it often seems that the city could easily be thousands of miles away. Running on those trails also forced me to do some serious hill work on a regular basis, so I felt that the training really helped to build both my endurance and my sustainable speed on the run.

The trail training culminated with a visit to the Big Island for the Volcano Wilderness runs in late July. Athletes had a choice between a marathon, a 10-mile run, and a 5-mile run, with most of each course being off road. I hadn't done any runs longer than the 13- to 15-mile range since the previous December, so I didn't feel that I was quite ready to run another marathon, particularly on such a challenging course. The 10-miler, therefore, seemed like the best option.

There is such an amazing variety of natural beauty in Hawai'i that it would be difficult to choose one particular place as being the best of the best. Nevertheless, there is something special about the area around Kīlauea volcano, with its contrasting landscapes of barren lava and lush tropical forest replete with magnificent 'ōhi'a trees and hāpu'u ferns. On top of that, the marathon course had a reputation for being one of the most difficult in the country, if not the world. The Wilderness runs were definitely a "must do" type of event while they lasted. Unfortunately, they have been discontinued in recent years because of the ongoing output of volcanic fumes from Kīlauea crater, which tend to be blown across parts of the course by the prevailing trade winds. Hopefully, there will come a time when these races can start up again.

About two weeks prior to the Volcano runs, I again did the Tinman Triathlon. I felt that I was in much better shape than I had been in the two previous years, and I was looking forward to having a solid race. One of the things that I have learned over the years, however, is not to get too carried away with my expectations because I will never know for sure what may happen on race day. The 2005 Tinman was a case in point. My swim had gone quite well, and I was making good time on the bike, when all of a sudden, about 7 miles into the race, my rear tire went flat. It was the first time I had ever had to deal with a flat tire during a race. By that time, I had become fairly competent, although not particularly fast, at changing flats, so I was able to put the new tube in without too much difficulty, but I inevitably lost a few minutes in the process. My reaction was initially one of frustration and anger. I wasn't going to be able to hit the finish time that I had set as my goal. It sounds completely irrational now, but at the time, the frustration was high enough to make a part of me feel like just calling it quits. However, another part told me to suck it up, get going, and focus on making up as much time as I could. Fortunately, the latter part won.

The rest of the bike ride went well. I felt strong as I came out of T2, and I was able to maintain a good steady pace as I set out on the run. However, in this particular race something happened that really triggered the competitive drive in me. About 4 miles into the run, heading up toward the Diamond Head lookout, I passed a runner who was in my age group, as I could see from the number that was marked on his calf. After I had gone past him, I could hear him pick up his pace, and I was aware that he continued to run close behind me all the way to the final straight. Less than 100 meters from the finish, he sprinted past me. The frustration that had still been smoldering in me since the flat tire returned in full force. I was damned if I was going to let that son-of-a-bitch beat me after I had paced him for the last 2 miles. Digging as deep as I could, I sprinted all out for the finish and overtook him just a few meters from the finish line. I couldn't completely shake the disappointment that the flat tire had prevented me from performing as well as I thought I would be able to, but getting past that guy was at least a small consolation. After the race, he graciously came up, introduced himself, and congratulated me on an exciting finish. His name was Doug Akagi, from California, and he apparently came to Hawai'i to race on a fairly regular basis. I couldn't help but feel a bit guilty about getting so mad at such a nice guy.

During the summer of 2005, I also planned to keep up the swimming as much as possible. I was becoming more confident in my ability to handle open ocean swims, and was able to successfully complete all four races in the North Shore Swim Series as part of my preparation for the Waikiki Roughwater Swim, which was scheduled to take place as usual on the Sunday before Labor Day. I even managed to take third place in my age group for the series as a whole. Yes, you probably guessed it. There were only three of us that participated in all four swims. As further conclusive proof of my mediocrity, I learned that I was 78th out of 79 men who finished all four swims in the series. It just happened that only two of the 77 who beat me were in my age group.

In order to complete my preparation for the WRS, I swam 5K at Ala Moana a week or so before the race, the longest distance that I had ever swum in my life. Now I was really ready to go--or so I thought. When we got to Kaimana Beach for the start of swim, conditions didn't look too bad. It was actually a very pleasant sunny day with some light trade winds. There were some small swells rolling in over the reef, but nothing more than 2- to 3-foot faces as far as I could tell from the shore. However, as we waited, the report came in that there was, like two years earlier, a very strong current that would be against us most of the way. When I heard that news, I could immediately feel my anxiety level go up several notches. Did I really want to attempt to swim that course if it was going to be a repeat of the 2003 fiasco? Eventually, the decision was made for us. Race organizers did not want to risk any such repeat and made what I believe was probably the right decision to cancel the event. It was the first time in its over 30-year history that the Waikiki Roughwater Swim had been cancelled.

Some people had come from the mainland United States or from other countries, such as Australia and New Zealand, to do the WRS, so naturally they were very disappointed. We Hawai'i residents were also disappointed, but at least we would be fortunate enough to have the opportunity to swim the course again when the conditions were more favorable. Three weeks later, a group of around 50 of us set off from Kaimana Beach, this time under almost perfect conditions, and successfully completed the course. Swimming that entire 2.4-mile course outside of the formal structure of a race was another important psychological milestone that helped to boost my confidence as I faced the challenge ahead.

Throughout the latter part of that summer, our preparations began in earnest for Ironman New Zealand. I purchased the book *Going Long: Training for Ironman-Distance Triathlons* by Joe Friel and Gordo Byrn and read it from cover to cover within a couple of days. Joe Friel is a highly respected coach who has written a number of popular books about triathlon training. Gordo Byrn is an extremely accomplished endurance athlete. Their book *Going Long* is the ideal handbook for Iron-distance training. In the coming months, I would often return to certain sections of the book to remind myself about how to maintain my focus. Much of the information wasn't completely new to me, but it helped to reinforce a lot of what I had already learned in training with Boca Hawaii, and also gave me some additional insights into what it would take to make that move up to the full iron-distance. I also made the investment of purchasing my first wetsuit—a piece of equipment that I had never needed in Hawai'i but something I knew I would have to get used to if we were going to be swimming in the chilly waters of Lake Taupo.

The New Zealand gang also started meeting as a group with Raul, who took us under his wing, planned our training schedule each week, and often joined us on some of our longer bike rides. Some of us had already begun to train together on a pretty regular basis during the summer swims. As time went by, I felt that a strong bond began to form amongst the members of the group, and, although I became closer to some than to others, I feel that there will always be a special connection with those comrades who helped me train for what I hoped would be my first iron-distance race. I remember getting together with everyone one Sunday night for a potluck dinner at Kris Chatterjee's house in Waimānalo, where we watched the video of the previous year's event and talked for hours about our plans for the next few months. There was so much excitement and anticipation in the air; it was almost intoxicating!

One of the things that I knew I really needed to do if I was going to be able to succeed in New Zealand was to increase my endurance on the bike. I was now very confident that I could comfortably get through the 2.4-mile swim, even though I knew I would inevitably be toward the back of the pack. I also knew I was capable of running 26.2 miles if I remained consistent with my training, so I figured I could walk or even crawl through the marathon if I had to—as long as I could make it through the bike leg of the race. In the summer of 2005, biking continuously for 112 miles still seemed like an extremely daunting challenge. I had never in my life biked for much more than the 56 miles that I needed to do for the race at Honu, and, apart from the race itself, I had done that distance only a few times during our training earlier that year. Moreover, when I had ridden 56 miles, it was hard for me to imagine how I could have done that distance all over again without needing to stop and lie down for a few hours. I told myself that I just had to start getting used to the idea of three figure distances. The next goal, therefore, became the Honolulu Century Ride, which was scheduled to take place toward the end of September.

To help build up my endurance and strength on the bike, I had signed up for the Boca summer cycling clinic, which started in late July, not long after the Volcano Wilderness runs. This had included some fairly challenging workouts, including a couple of long rides of up to 60 miles, as well as a fair amount of hill work, which provided some solid initial momentum for the New Zealand training. It was at this clinic that I first had the fortune to meet Andrea Huston, a strong cyclist who subsequently went on to successfully finish Ironman Arizona in 2007. I didn't get to know her well at the time, but she was later to become one of my best training buddies.

After the Boca clinic ended, my training continued on a regular basis with the IMNZ gang, and, by the time the Century Ride came around, we had done several longer rides, gradually increasing the distance up to around 80 miles. By that time, the almost 60-mile round trip from Waikīkī to Kailua via Makapuʻu, which had initially seemed so dauntingly long only a few months earlier, had become relatively routine. As our training progressed, I became increasingly confident that I could make it through 100 miles in the Century Ride without my legs seizing up or just falling off.

As we started out from Kapiʻolani Park, together with the thousands of other cyclists who were participating in the Century Ride, some of us initially rode as a group. It wasn't long, however, before we became separated in the crowd of riders, and I ended up riding most of the way with Crystal Kapua. Crystal is a great training buddy who would, I know, readily admit to her mediocre ability as a cyclist. Nevertheless she always brought a lot of heart and soul to her training, so it was always a pleasure to train with her. It was the first Century Ride for both of us, and it happened to come on another brutally hot day. Unfortunately, Crystal did not take in enough fluid along the way and was seriously overheating by the time we got to about 75 miles. As we pulled into the aid station in Kailua, I was starting to get worried about her. She looked completely drained and was saying she wasn't sure she could go on. Fortunately, our coach, Raul, just happened to be at the aid station at that time and knew just what to do. He got one of the big containers of iced water, came up behind her and poured the whole thing over her. Crystal screamed bloody murder, but it definitely succeeded in cooling her down. Following some rehydration with plenty of water and Gatorade, she started to feel a lot better. After about a 15-minute break, we got back on our bikes and headed for the finish. We certainly didn't break any speed records over the last 25 miles, but we made it all the way. We even had enough gas left in the tank to run a couple of miles around Kapiʻolani Park after finishing the ride. I have to thank Crystal for teaching me another important lesson—don't give up no matter how bad you feel!

Our training started to become pretty intense during the fall of 2005. I had decided that I wanted to do the Honolulu Marathon again as part of the build up for New Zealand, so I was doing a lot of the workouts with the Boca marathon group, as well as keeping up the long distance swimming and progressively increasing the distance of our bike rides under the guidance we were getting from Raul. Our training also included what came to be known by some of us as our weekly "torture" session at Boca Hawaii's headquarters in Honolulu. These sessions consisted of 25 minutes of pretty intense work on the turbo trainer followed by 25 minutes of challenging core strength work. Then we would repeat the whole process all over again. I must admit that I always felt some sense of relief when we finally got to the 10-minute cool down period at the end, but at the same time I was thrilled to find out that my old body was not only still capable of working that hard, but seemed to be thriving on it.

Over the course of 2005, I had entered a phase of my life in which training involved a serious time commitment, and, in many ways, it became a major priority for me. At the peak of my training for Honu earlier in the year, I had probably been averaging at least 15 hours of training per week. That amount began to increase even more as we got deeper and deeper into the training for New Zealand. My main focus at that time was the personal accomplishment of finishing that 140.6-mile distance for the first time, and it became the driving force not only behind my approach to training but to the organization of my life in general. Much as I enjoyed my work, for example, there were often days when I just couldn't wait to get out of the office to go swim, bike, or run in the evening. At the beginning of every week, when we saw our training schedule for the coming week, we would express amazement about what the schedule called for us to do, particularly on those long weekend brick workouts. Nevertheless, every week we would find a way to go out and get it done, and by the close of the weekend it would feel so good to know that we had successfully completed everything that we had set out to do. In retrospect,

I can see that I had really internalized Raul's motto—"Train with passion." Training truly had become my passion, and, in many ways, it has remained so, even though I don't always want to keep up the volume of training that is called for when preparing for an iron-distance event.

Despite the high volume of training that we were doing, I was sometimes amazed to find that it actually wasn't as hard to fit it all in as I had originally thought it would be. I think I had assumed that training for the full iron-distance would inevitably involve, in almost every respect, twice as much time as the training we had done for Honu. I mean, twice the distance would seem to require twice the amount of training, right? Consequently, I had often wondered where the heck I was going to find the time to do all of that training while still working full time and taking care of my responsibilities at home. The long rides in particular and, to a somewhat lesser extent, the long runs certainly did take up a lot of time, but I was relieved to learn every workout did not have to be twice as long. I did realize that I had to find a way to manage my time really efficiently, and I was able to become pretty successful in minimizing the amount of unproductive time in my schedule. In the process, I found that I continued to like the way I was feeling. With all the training I was doing, I could feel my strength and endurance steadily growing and my energy level also seemed to grow accordingly. Thus, not only was I able to fit in all of that training, I was also able to remain productive at work and, for the most part, managed to take care of all the essential responsibilities on the home front.

Toward the end of 2005, I took some time to focus particularly on my running, and it really began to pay off. In November, I ran my best half marathon in over 20 years, with a time of about 2 hours and 2 minutes. I was pushing pretty hard in all the training sessions and trying to do a bit extra here and there whenever I could. As a result, I think I overdid it a bit during the week before the Honolulu Marathon. On the Wednesday before the race, I took a day off work and rode on my own for 90 miles, with a short run after, and then followed it up the next day with a solid swim workout, as well as a short but fairly intense final pre-race run with the Boca marathon group. By the evening before the race, I could feel a little soreness in my throat and could tell I was starting to come down with a cold. As I reflected on the year, I was actually pleasantly surprised to realize that, despite all the demands of the busy schedule that had come with all the hard training, it was the first time I had gotten sick that year. In the past, I could usually figure on at least a couple of colds throughout a year. Despite a slightly scratchy sore throat, I was able to finish the marathon in a personal best time of 4 hours 28 minutes, and, although the cold subsequently slowed me down for about a week after the marathon, it was a very minor setback. As the New Year approached, I was feeling fitter than I had ever been in my life, and I was becoming more and more confident that I would be able to finish the race in New Zealand. In addition, and on the surface perhaps somewhat paradoxically, the more my confidence grew, the more acceptant I seemed to become of my mediocre athletic ability. I now realize that can be explained by the fact that I was becoming more and more aware that, whatever I did, I was truly giving it my best shot and making the most of whatever ability I did have. I really couldn't ask myself to do any more than that.

Chapter 15

Disappointment...Big Time!

As we went into 2006, all of a sudden, things literally came to a crashing halt. The New Zealand gang had decided to go for a long bike ride the day after New Year. The rainy season in Hawai'i is roughly from November to April. In the Honolulu city area, it actually doesn't rain very often during that time, but storms in the North Pacific can sometimes bring torrential downpours that can, at their worst, cause serious flooding. By those standards, January 2nd, 2006 was not a particularly bad day. It was cloudy, with intermittent rain as about eight of us headed out on our bikes from Kapi'olani Park in Waikīkī on one of our usual routes that took us round the south east corner of O'ahu, through Hawai'i Kai, Makapu'u, Waimānalo, Kailua, Kāne'ohe, and beyond. I think we had originally planned to go as far as Kualoa and back, which would have amounted to about

90 miles for the day. The weather was not too bad for about the first couple of hours, but, by the time we were about 35 miles into ride, the rain had become much heavier, the roads were wet and slick, and we were all pretty well soaked. I had just taken the lead as we headed into Kāneʻohe town on Kamehameha Highway. At that point, the highway goes down a little hill before crossing a bridge and then going slightly uphill to the traffic light at the intersection of Waikalua Road, so we were going at a pretty good speed, probably somewhere between 20 to 25 miles per hour.

We were planning to make a right turn onto Waikalua Road at the intersection in order to add a couple more miles to the ride and get off the highway for a while. As we approached the intersection, I started to ease over into the right turn lane that begins right after the bridge. Suddenly, I felt my bike begin to slide uncontrollably, and, then, the next thing I knew I was flying over the handlebars. I subsequently learned that there was a lip in the road along the line that separated the concrete of the right turn lane from the asphalt of the through lanes, but I had not been able to see it because of all the water on the road. As I started to move over into the right turn lane, I hit the lip at narrow angle. It threw my front wheel back toward the center of the highway, and down I went. I later learned that several other people I knew had also had crashes at that exact same place.

I can vividly recall feeling my left shoulder and my helmet slamming into the pavement. I can also clearly recall a couple of thoughts that went through my mind, although I'm not sure in which order they occurred. One was, "Thank goodness for that helmet!" In my professional career as a psychologist, some of my work includes neuropsychological assessment, so I am familiar with the potential effects of a traumatic brain injury. I think I was initially in a slight state of shock, but, as I lay on the ground, I knew from the clarity of my thoughts that I was lucky to have avoided what could easily have been a serious concussion and quite possibly permanent brain damage. The other thought was, "There goes New Zealand." I could tell that there was something seriously out of whack somewhere around my shoulder, and I immediately felt a wave of depression come over me at the prospect of not being able to do the race in New Zealand after all of that training that I had done. I had been so close, I could almost taste it, but now, suddenly, it seemed so far away.

By that time, my friends had all stopped and gathered around me to check on how I was doing. I was thinking about trying to get to my feet, but I recall their telling me not to move. I knew they were right, so I just lay back on the wet concrete, with rain water running down the road around me, and resigned myself to the fact that all I could do was to wait for the ambulance. I was relieved that it arrived quickly and transported me away to Castle Medical Center.

Waiting in the emergency room for several hours was probably the most difficult part of the whole experience. Fortunately for me, Joni had been doing some work in the Kailua area not too far from the medical center, so she was able to come to the ER fairly quickly to keep me company. Despite her supportive presence, however, I felt pretty despondent. I was in quite a bit of pain, and I was depressed by the thought of not being able to do the race. In addition, it seemed miserably cold in the hospital, despite covering myself with several blankets. At one point, one of the nurses came in and said she thought I might have dislocated my shoulder. This actually helped lift my spirits a little, because I suddenly had visions of someone popping my shoulder joint back into place and sending me on my way home. However, it was not to be. Eventually the doctor came in with the x-ray results and gave me the bad news—a broken left clavicle, ribs broken in 5 places, and a punctured left lung. He told me that they would have to admit me to the hospital and would probably need to put a tube into my chest to reinflate the lung.

As we go through life, it is virtually inevitable that we all will sometimes be faced with some form of adversity. It is one of those unavoidable facts of life that things don't always go the way we would like them to go. One of the great challenges in life is to find constructive ways of dealing with that adversity. Fortunately, there are relatively few experiences in life that are singularly negative. I certainly can't say that I have always handled adversity well, but one of the things that I have learned is that, if we can find at least one positive thing in the midst of adversity, it can help to sustain us and ultimately allow us to overcome the challenge. For me, one of the most positive aspects of this experience was the tremendous amount of support that I received from friends and family. It was during that time that I realized the full value of all the friendships that I had made through my involvement in athletics. During my waking hours over the five days that I had to stay in the hospital, I rarely went for much more than an hour without someone coming in to visit and "talk story" with me or calling me on the phone. Family and friends brought food, flowers, reading materials, and most of all, their love and caring. Even on that first day, by the time I was settled in my room, several of my friends had come to the hospital to check on how I was doing, which helped me to start developing a more positive outlook. Their continuing presence helped to keep my spirits up during most of my hospital stay. I have to admit there were still times I felt depressed and sorry for myself, particularly during the nights when the pain made it hard to sleep or even get comfortable. But, at other times, I felt positively ecstatic and truly overwhelmed by the outpouring of support that I received.

When I came out of Castle Medical Center on January 7th, my left arm was in a sling and I was still in pain, particularly from the ribs, so I knew that I was a long way from being ready to race. After all that training, however, it was really hard for me to accept that I was not going to be able to race in New Zealand. I knew I wouldn't be in top shape, but I still held on to a sliver of hope that I might be able to recover sufficiently so I could at least start the race, and hopefully finish as well, even if it took me 16 hours, 59 minutes, and 59 seconds. I had had plenty of time to do the calculations while I was in the hospital. The race was scheduled to take place on March 3, which was still about eight weeks away. I was well aware it was a long shot, but I knew that fractures typically take six to eight weeks to heal, so I figured maybe there was just enough time.

On the day of my discharge, I was not feeling that great. I had not slept well the previous night because it was difficult to find a comfortable and pain-free position, so I was tired, lethargic, and a bit grouchy. Nevertheless, I felt restless after I got home, and was anxious to get back to some type of physical activity as soon as possible. I got up early the next morning and drove down to Kapi'olani Park to meet up with the New Zealand gang before they left on their bike ride. They were all happy to see me out of the hospital, and I told them I had not completely given up on doing the race. It gave me a bit of a lift to see my friends keeping up the good work, but at the same time it was difficult to watch them as they rode away from the park without me.

With my arm still in a sling, all I could do was to set off for a walk. I forget exactly how far I walked that morning. I think it was probably about 6 miles. I knew that if I wanted to have any chance of racing in New Zealand, I had to keep as physically active as possible, and walking was the only realistic option for a while. Over the next few weeks, I must have put almost as many hours into walking as I would have done into all of the three sports combined if I had not been injured. Just about every day I walked for a couple of hours. On one occasion, I walked for 4 hours and covered over 14 miles. It allowed me to feel that I wasn't giving up completely on my goal. One of the other good things about my walks was that I would almost invariably meet a few people that I knew who were out running or biking. So, as well as helping me to maintain some degree of fitness, the walking also helped keep me in everyday contact with friends in the athletic community.

A few days after being discharged from the hospital, I followed up with my primary care physician at Kaiser. I knew he had some triathlon experience, having done the Tinman in the past, and I suppose I hoped that he might be able to do something to speed up my recovery in some way. Most of all, I wanted to know more about my prognosis. Was there any chance that I would be able to recover in time to race in New Zealand? He didn't seem to think so, and he really wasn't able to tell me very much, except that collarbone and rib fractures are usually just left to heal on their own, as one of the consultants at Castle had already suggested. I was disappointed to say the least. I knew that already. He did say that he would refer me for a consult with orthopedics, but that was on a routine basis and would probably be scheduled in a couple of weeks. "A couple of weeks? That's way too long," I thought. I needed to know as soon as possible. I tried to convey to him my sense of urgency and pleaded with him to try to arrange an expedited consult. I thought for a while that I had got through to him, but, later that day, I received a phone call informing me that the appointment with orthopedics would indeed be about two weeks away. I was really irritated at that point, and my initial reaction was to voice a few choice words for my doctor. Then it occurred to me that maybe there was something else that I could try. One of my training buddies in the New Zealand gang, Kelly Tam Sing, just happened to be an emergency room physician with Kaiser. I called him immediately and left a message asking if he could help speed things up. A couple of phone calls later, I had an appointment for a consult in orthopedics for the following day. Sometimes it's good to have the right connections. Kelly had really come through. "Maybe there's still some hope," I thought.

When I went in for the orthopedic consult, all I really wanted was to be told that I could get clearance to race by March 3rd. Unfortunately, it was not to be. When the physician's assistant looked at the x-rays, he was concerned that the fracture of the clavicle was badly displaced. I might be a candidate for surgery, he felt. The surgeon agreed that the fracture might not heal well if left alone and that it would probably be smart to do a fixation of the bone. I liked my surgeon immediately. He had a casual and friendly manner, but, at the same time, he was knowledgeable and professional. After talking with him for a while, I felt confident in his opinion. He showed me the x-rays, and I knew he was right. I agreed to go ahead with the surgery. The bad news was that, although they would schedule it as soon as possible, there was no way I would be ready to race by March 3rd. I finally had to resign myself to the fact that I was just not going to be able to do the race in New Zealand in 2006. It was a bitter pill to swallow.

On January 27th, I went in to Kaiser Medical Center for the surgery. Going in, I was a little nervous but also eager to get the surgery done and get started on my rehabilitation program as soon as possible. Coincidentally, one of the nurse anesthetists, Harlyne Caruso, was another training buddy who was also going to be racing in New Zealand—another example of Honolulu still being a small town. It helped put me at ease to see a familiar, friendly face as I was going through the preparations for the surgery. I can clearly remember being wheeled into the operating room and then, the next thing, I was waking up in the recovery room. In the process, I had become the proud owner of a bionic clavicle, the fracture being joined by a titanium plate that was held in place by seven small screws. I must say that, since then, that little plate has done its job extremely well.

After coming out of the hospital on January 28, my main focus was preparing for the trip to New Zealand. During the time following my injury, everyone in our training group had encouraged me to make the trip even though I was not sure that I was going to be able to race. At first, I was not sure that I wanted to go if I couldn't race. After having the surgery, I knew that I was supposed to keep my arm in a sling until well after the date of the race, and I worried that I was just going to be dead weight for the group if I went along with them. In addition, I was secretly concerned that watching them participate in the race might make me feel even more depressed. As it turned out, however, there was absolutely no basis for either of those concerns. Making that trip would, in fact, turn out to be one of the best things I could have done for myself in terms of the psychological aspects of my recovery.

Although I knew by the end of January that I would not be able to race in New Zealand, I was determined to maintain as much of my fitness as I could. I had worked far too hard to just let it slip away. However, having the surgery meant that there would be an extended period of time when my training options would be quite limited. I was under doctor's orders to keep the shoulder immobilized for several weeks, so there was no way I could realistically consider riding a bicycle on the road. I tried getting on my turbo trainer a few times, but it initially felt awkward and uncomfortable with my arm in the sling, so I decided that it was better to put that on hold for a couple of weeks, at least until I felt more accustomed to doing things with the sling on. The immobilization of the shoulder also made it pretty much impossible to do any type of swimming. In any case, I had orders to stay out of the water for several weeks while the surgical incision healed. In addition, my surgeon advised me not to run for at least the first month or more, as he was concerned that the pounding might interfere with the healing of the bone. The only thing I could do was to keep walking. I became increasingly grateful that I could at least do that. It was frustrating, to say the least, not to be able to train with my friends, but I have always enjoyed walking and hiking, and it was definitely one of the things that helped keep my spirits up as I prepared for the trip to New Zealand.

On February 24th, we boarded the plane at Honolulu International Airport bound for Auckland, New Zealand. The adventure of visiting new places has always held a strong attraction for me, and New Zealand certainly did not disappoint. The scenery around Lake Taupo was beautiful, the weather, although a little cooler than Hawai'i, was still warm and sunny, and the people that we met in the stores and restaurants were friendly and welcoming. In addition, I found that sharing a house with a group of friends who were all focused on a common goal was uplifting for me in a lot of ways. I very much enjoyed the camaraderie and all the fun that we had together. I also found that I was able to help out with transportation, cooking, and other logistical issues, so it turned out that I didn't have to worry too much about feeling useless after all. Most importantly, I was able to draw a great deal of inspiration from the commitment and determination of my friends. When I returned to Honolulu, I was more determined than ever that I was going to do the iron-distance as soon as I possibly could.

Although the trip to New Zealand was a great experience for me personally, March 4 unfortunately turned out to be another day of disappointment in many respects. The weather in Taupo had been almost ideal up to that point, and everyone was looking forward to having relatively good conditions for the race. However, during the night before the race was due to begin, a storm system began to move into the area from the south, and the wind began to pick up. At one point, I was awakened by the force of the wind against the window of my room, and I recall thinking how ominous it sounded. By the time we all got up in the morning and headed down toward the start of the race, the wind had reached gale force level. When we got to the start area, we were informed that the start of the race would probably have to be delayed, and the whole race might possibly have to be cancelled. I couldn't believe our misfortune, and I can only imagine how frustrated and disappointed my friends must have felt after putting all of that time and energy into preparing for the race.

While my comrades were waiting for some type of decision from the race organizers, I walked down to the shore of the lake to see what the conditions looked like. The wind was so strong that I had to lean into it at almost a 45-degree angle as I walked toward the lake in order to avoid being blown backwards. I later heard that there were sustained winds in the area of at least 30 to 40 miles per hour, with gusts as high as 50 miles per hour in places. Through the gradually emerging daylight I could see that the surface of the lake, which had been almost completely flat on previous days, was full of whitecaps, with swells of maybe 2 to 3 feet rolling in toward the shore. Knowing how chilly the water was likely to be, it certainly didn't appear very inviting, but I saw no reason why our gang from Hawai'i would not be able to handle it. There were, in fact, some guys in our group, like Kris Chatterjee, Kelly Tam Sing, and Greg Kugle, who were experienced surfers as well as excellent swimmers, and probably would have been quite comfortable in 8- to 10-foot waves. In fact, everyone in our group had some degree of experience dealing with ocean swells and currents, and wind chop on the surface of the water. I wondered, however, what the bike ride would be like under such windy conditions.

As we waited, it soon became evident that there would not be enough time to complete the entire race. At that point, we just began to hope that the whole race would not be called off completely. We were told that it would be a while before a final decision would be made, so some of us walked into the town to get some breakfast and kill time. Even though I wasn't racing, the seemingly endless waiting was stressful for me, and I was impressed by the way that everyone in our group seemed to take it in their stride. I wondered how I would have handled it if I had been in their shoes. I was not at all sure that I would have been as calm and collected as they all seemed to be. When we made our way back to the large tent that had been erected near the transition and finish areas, they all waited patiently, even when the wind was so strong that it began lifting the roof of the tent so high that some of the huge supporting poles came off the ground and began to swing dangerously to and fro amongst the crowd. Under the circumstances, I was amazed to see that Crystal was even able to lie down and go back to sleep for a while. Eventually, after a wait of several hours, we learned that a decision had been made to eliminate the swim completely, and to run the race as a duathlon, with a 56-mile bike ride followed by a half marathon.

By the time the race finally got started it was already around midday. By that time, the wind had dropped a little, but it was still strong, so conditions were very challenging, particularly on the return leg of the bike, which was directly into the teeth of the wind. As a spectator, I began hearing reports to the effect that it was taking athletes only about one hour do the 28 miles on the outward leg of the ride but as much as two hours or more to do the other 28 miles on the return. In light of the severe conditions, I was greatly relieved that everyone in our group was able to finish safely, and I felt proud of them all for having been able to deal with the uncertainty and the long wait before the race and still go out and have a good race despite the adverse weather conditions.

An important milestone in my recovery took place while we were in New Zealand—my first run. Crystal, Stella, and Amy Wieland had planned to do a short training run a couple of days before the race. After having done some type of errand in town, I was walking over toward the area where they were planning to start, thinking that maybe I could meet up with them and go for a walk while they were running. As I got closer, I saw them a little way ahead of me just starting out on their run. I had been under orders not to do any running before my next appointment with my surgeon, which was scheduled for the day after my return from New Zealand. However, I had been feeling good, and my intuition told me that the healing process was going well. In a split second, I made the decision to run after my friends and try to catch them up. Although it was a little awkward with my arm still in the sling, it felt so good to be able to run again. They had started slowly, so I was able to catch them up within a few hundred meters. Despite their concerns, I ended up running for about 4 miles with them. After that, I continued to run a few miles each day, and, by the time we left New Zealand, I had completely ditched the sling. A couple of days after the race, some of our group decided to go to the bungee jump over the river near Taupo. When I saw them jump, I was sorely tempted to have a go, but wiser heads among my friends prevailed, and I eventually allowed them to talk me out of it.

I returned from New Zealand more determined than ever that I was going to do an iron-distance event some day. At first, my thought was to return to New Zealand the following year. Some of my friends had, in fact, got me a poster signed by Cameron Brown, the great Kiwi triathlete who has won Ironman New Zealand multiple times, with words of encouragement to "kick butt" at Taupo in 2007. That poster, incidentally, still hangs on the wall of my office, and I try to take inspiration from it whenever my motivation starts to flag.

As it subsequently turned out, however, a totally unexpected series of events eventually resulted in my going in a very different direction. We initially learned that, because of the problems in New Zealand, Ironman North America had opened up a limited number of slots in some of their 2006 events for U.S. citizens who had been entered in the race in New Zealand. As soon as I heard about that, I told myself that I was going to see if I could get into one of those events.

Everyone in our group was well trained and ready to go, and some of the gang wanted to enter one of the events as soon as possible. Stella and Kris signed up for Ironman Arizona, which was only just over a month away. Kelly couldn't go to Arizona at that time, so he decided to go for Ironman Coeur D'Alene in June. Because of other commitments, Crystal and Amy couldn't make either of those races, and they were initially thinking of Ironman Florida in November. For a while, I was still debating which one I wanted to try to do. After my follow up visit with my surgeon on March 7th, I was officially allowed to stop using the sling. However, he wanted me to hold off on swimming and biking on the road for a few more weeks, which meant that all I could do apart from running were some turbo trainer workouts, which I had already been doing for a couple of weeks before departing for New Zealand. Consequently, I didn't think I could possibly be ready for Arizona in April, and I knew there was no way I could keep up with Kelly if I tried to train with him for Coeur D'Alene. At that point, the decision was pretty clear to me. I knew that Crystal and Amy would be great training buddies, and they were probably going to maintain about the same race pace as me overall. Florida it would be! That would also give me plenty of time to get back in shape.

The problem was that I didn't know if I would be able to get one of the slots in Florida because I had actually withdrawn from the race in New Zealand after I realized that I wasn't going to be able to participate. Nevertheless, it seemed like an opportunity that was too good to pass up, so I was determined to try. In retrospect, the series of events over the months that followed turned out to be rather comical. My initial request for a slot in Florida was, in fact, turned down because I had eventually withdrawn from the race in New Zealand following my injury. I basically pleaded by phone with the Ironman North America office to let me have a slot. After some communication back and forth over several days, I eventually learned that my wish had indeed been granted. I immediately sent in my application. A few days later, I checked the website and saw that my name was actually on the official list of entrants. I was ecstatic—back on track again! Now I knew where I was going, or so I thought.

Now that I had a specific new goal in mind, I immediately started back into serious training again. I signed up for the Honolulu Triathlon in May and for Honu in June, and then joined the Boca training group leading up to those two races. Before long, I was running 12 to 15 miles again, and doing workouts of up to two hours on the turbo trainer. I had to go through a few sessions of physical therapy to get full strength and range of motion back in my shoulder, and then I was ready to start swimming again. Eventually, on April 12th, my surgeon cleared me to start swimming and get back on the road again with the bike. My first bike ride the following Saturday morning was a real breakthrough psychologically. It felt great to back on the road again on such a beautiful day. I remember that Karen Oshiro, an excellent all round athlete who has been a Boston Marathon qualifier and who had been a member of the group that had done Ironman Canada the previous year, kept me company much of the way on that first ride. We rode at a consistent pace with the Boca group out to Waimanalo and back, a total of about 45 miles. "Not bad for my first ride back on the road," I thought. In addition, we stopped along the way back for a short but steep run from the highway up to the lookout at Makapu'u. The run was very tough, in close to 90-degree heat by that time of day, but I felt good all through what was my first really hard workout after the injury. It got me off to a good start in the process of regaining the confidence that I could soon get back to a level of fitness that would allow me to finish Ironman Florida in November.

Shortly after that, Stella and Kris successfully completed Ironman Arizona, and both of them had great races. It was the first full iron-distance event for both of them, and I was so happy for them. After the disappointment of New Zealand, all of their hard work had finally paid off. In addition, their success provided additional inspiration and motivation for me. I knew that, if I had done the race in Arizona, I would probably have been a little slower than Stella, and considerably slower than Kris, but after having trained alongside them for so many months, their success made me feel more confident than ever that I, too, would eventually be able to emulate their accomplishment.

The first real challenge during my recovery was the Honolulu Triathlon, which had been moved to May 14th after being held some time in April the previous year. The new date was good because it allowed me to have at least a few weeks back on the road with the bike before the race. In addition, the course had been greatly changed, with the swim at Ala Moana instead of Waikīkī and the bike leg going out toward Pearl Harbor instead of toward Hawai'i Kai, so it was like a new event on a faster course in many respects. It would be a good test of how well my recovery was progressing. It proved to be a bit tougher than I expected. I had no problem finishing the race, but I was rather disappointed with my time—a little over 3 hours. I felt I should have been capable of much better that. "Maybe it was just one of those days," I told myself. I didn't want to believe that maybe I had actually not recovered quite as much of my fitness as I would have liked.

The next big challenge was at Honu on June 3rd. This was going to be only my second time racing the 70.3 mile distance, but by the time race day arrived I felt my recovery was going well, and I had high hopes for a good performance—maybe too high in light of my performance at the Honolulu Triathlon. In early May, we had gone back to the Big Island for the same tough training weekend that we had done the previous year, and although it had definitely been hard work, I had felt pretty strong throughout the weekend. By the time race day came around, I even had visions of improving my time over the previous year, and maybe getting down under 7 hours.

It was not to be. To start with, because of a relatively strong morning breeze, conditions for the swim were not as good as they had been in 2005. There was a little more surface chop, and there seemed to be considerably more of a current against us as we swam across the bay at Hāpuna. As I came out of the water, I glanced at the time on the clock—over 52 minutes—about 6 minutes slower than the previous year. Not a good start. The bike ride also seemed to be a lot tougher than the previous year. I just didn't feel like I had much power in my legs, and it seemed like I was constantly struggling against the wind, no matter which way I was going. By the time I went into T2, I knew I was way behind schedule if wanted to go under 7 hours. To make things worse, I was only about a mile or so into the run when my legs started cramping. That had never happened to me before, so it really took me by surprise. For a while, it was bad enough that I even found myself wondering if I was going to have to pull out. I had to stop running and just hobble along quite slowly for a while. I massaged my legs, and downed as much fluid as I could at the next aid station. Eventually the cramps began to ease up, and I was able to keep going, although the cramping returned intermittently throughout the first two thirds of the run. At the aid station around mile 9, I drank some cola, and it seemed to give me a lift, so that I was eventually able to finish fairly strong, without any further cramping. However, I was not at all happy with my performance. My finish time was over 7 hours 24 minutes, not only way over the 7 hours that I had hoped for, but about 16 minutes slower than the previous year.

Although at some level I knew that it was unrealistic, I had come to expect that if I simply kept on training more and more, my performances were just going to keep getting better and better with every event. Consequently, I came away from the finish line at Honu feeling frustrated and disappointed with myself. Despite all I had learned about myself as an athlete, there were still times like this when it was difficult to fully accept my mediocre performance as being the best I could do under the circumstances. In reality, I had given it my best shot, but in my mind my performance somehow didn't seem to be good enough. As I waited for the awards ceremony and the food a little later that afternoon, I just couldn't shake the thought that I should have been able to do better.

Chapter 16

Opportunity Knocks

I tried to console myself with the thoughts that at least I had been able to finish the race and that I was still on track to reach my goal of finishing Ironman Florida in November. However, I was still feeling a little dejected as we sat in the pavilion eating our belated lunch during the awards ceremony after the race. I hadn't even bothered to check the printout of the race results, not wanting to have to push my way through the crowd to see the board where the results were posted and also not wanting to see in black and white how poorly I had done. The following sequence of events seems almost surreal as I think back.

Before I continue with the story, I must explain that, although Honu is only a half-iron-distance event, it is one of the qualifying races for the Ironman World Championship in Kona in October.

Consequently, although the location may be a little remote for many athletes who do not live in Hawai'i, it is still a big event drawing entrants not only from the islands but also from various parts of the United States mainland and from a number of foreign countries. One of the benefits for those of us who are fortunate enough to live in Hawai'i is that there are a limited number of Kona slots available specifically for Hawai'i residents. I am very grateful for this arrangement because it basically gives us an extra bite at the apple, as it were, when it comes to having the opportunity to qualify for Kona. The previous year, I had not even bothered to submit my name for the Kona qualification process. All I had wanted to do was finish on my first attempt at the half-iron-distance. In addition, I had assumed that I would be so far back in the pack that I wouldn't have a chance of qualifying for Kona. Moreover, at that time, I was still not sure that I ever wanted to attempt a full iron-distance event, so I didn't think there was any point in submitting the necessary paperwork. However, after the Kona qualifiers were announced in 2005, I had been surprised to learn that I was actually next in line for the State of Hawai'i resident slot in my age group, despite the fact that I was a considerable distance behind the qualifier, Dave Kerr, an experienced triathlete whom I had previously met in Honolulu but did not know well. Consequently, when I submitted my entry for Honu in 2006, I decided to go ahead and send in the paperwork necessary to prove my State of Hawai'i residency, just in case I got lucky.

Returning now to the story, the awards ceremony had reached the point at which the master of ceremonies, Guy Hagi, was getting ready to announce the names of the Kona qualifiers. Some of us were talking about which of our friends might have qualified. One of my friends, Arlene Kim, asked me whether or not I would take the Kona slot for my age group in the event that I qualified for it. Arlene's question took me aback, because, after seeing my very disappointing finishing time, I had not even considered the possibility that I might qualify for the Kona slot. I had not been too far away from getting a Hawai'i resident slot in 2005, but my time in 2006 was so much slower that I had completely given up any thought of being a qualifier. I didn't even answer her question directly. I basically just said something to the effect that, after such a poor race, there was no way I could possibly have qualified.

Soon they reached the point of announcing the qualifiers for my age group, the male 60 to 64 year olds. I remember hearing them call out the name of Chuck Miller, a good training buddy who had put in very good performance at Ironman Canada the previous year. I had gotten to know Chuck quite well over the course of the previous year or so, and I knew that he was always considerably faster than me, particularly on the bike and the run. During our training, I had commented to Chuck that I thought he might have a good chance of qualifying, but he had told me before the race that he was not going to take the Kona slot if it came down to him because of other commitments. As they called his name several times, we waited to see who would be next in line. In the back of my mind, I found myself wondering if there was any possibility it could be me, but immediately banished the thought. I knew that Chuck had finished way ahead of me, and I assumed that there had to be several other eligible athletes that had also finished ahead of me.

I took a sip of my beer and sat back, waiting and wondering if the next name called would be someone that I knew. All of a sudden, I heard Guy Hagi calling out my name. I was surprised by the immediacy of my own reaction. I had not consciously thought about a direct answer to Arlene's question, but perhaps her question had triggered some sort of decision-making process in my mind at an unconscious level. As soon as I heard my name, without stopping for a moment to think, I jumped up, pumped my arm in the air, and called out, "Yes!" as loudly as I could. I then marched straight to the front of the pavilion to collect my ticket to the big race. Opportunity had knocked, and I had grabbed it without hesitation. In little more than a second, my dejection had turned to elation. I could barely believe my good fortune. I was going to Kona!

It would be an understatement to say that I was exhilarated, but at the same time I immediately knew that there was going to be a great deal of hard work ahead. After I collected my entry ticket, I happened to see Fish Arabia, another excellent all-round endurance athlete whom I had known for several years, whose accomplishments have included a number of ultra-distance runs. I called out to him, "Now I really have to do some serious training!" By the time I got back to my table, I was surrounded by friends who showered me with hugs and congratulations on getting the Kona slot. I was touched because everyone was so genuinely happy for me. The value of that kind of support and camaraderie is immeasurable, and it is definitely one of the things that has made training and racing such a rewarding activity for me. It was reassuring to know that I would have plenty of friends on my side as I prepared for the race in October. Nevertheless, I was also very much aware that I had many hours of arduous training ahead of me if I were going to have any chance of finishing that race.

Several of my friends from the Boca training program had also qualified in their respective age groups, including Wil Yamamoto, Rachel Ross, and Uʻilani Pauole. They were all excellent age group athletes who were way out of my league, so I knew I wouldn't be doing much training with them. Nevertheless, we kept in touch throughout the training process, and they were all very supportive of my efforts. In addition, Laurie Sloan, another Honolulu athlete, had also qualified in the female 55 to 59 age group. I had seen her at a few athletic events around Oʻahu in the past but had never gotten to know her. As it turned out, Laurie and I were able to do quite a bit of training together during our preparation for Kona. She was a bit faster as a swimmer and runner than me, but we kept a similar pace on the bike, so we were able to do several of our long rides together.

As soon as I returned to Honolulu, I immediately began to focus on what I would need to do over the next 20 weeks in order to finish the race in Kona. Previously, I had never really had the time or inclination to keep detailed training logs, but I suddenly became obsessed with setting up a detailed training schedule all the way through to the race, which was scheduled for October 21st. One of the first things I did was meet with Raul, who generously gave me his advice about how to prepare for Kona, and subsequently sent me a training schedule every week. At the beginning of each week, I would take what I had tentatively outlined in my own plan and integrate it with the input that I got from Raul. That way I ended up with a training schedule that gave me all the workouts that I needed and that I could also fit into my personal schedule. (See Appendix 1 and 2.)

As I went through my training, I was truly relentless in my pursuit of a goal that not very long ago would have seemed like an absolutely impossible dream. I was well aware that I was relentlessly pursuing a performance that was going to be distinctly mediocre in comparison to most of the other athletes that would be participating, but that was just fine. I was very clear about my personal goal. One way or another, I was going to find a way to make it to the finish line within the time limit. During over 4 months of hard training, I rarely missed a workout that I had planned. I also never perceived the large volume of training that I was doing as a burden or a chore. On workdays, I couldn't wait to get out of the office to go train. On weekends, I was up long before the crack of dawn, and ready to get going. In short, I was a man on a mission.

In many ways, training for Kona became the number one priority in my life over the next 4 months. Training, along with related activities such as preparation for and cleaning up after workouts, probably averaged 20 to 25 hours a week and even more during some of the peak weeks. On most weekdays, it was usually anywhere between 2 to 4 hours per day, usually after work in the late afternoon and early evening. On Saturdays and Sundays, I found that I was often devoting virtually the whole day to training or associated activities such as bike maintenance, not to mention taking much needed naps after the long, arduous training sessions. In the process, I became more efficient in my time management than I had ever been before, or have ever been since for that matter. Despite this singular focus on training, I managed to maintain a fairly full schedule at work and to keep the house clean and tidy enough to prevent it from descending into chaos. I was also able to maintain all of the important relationships in my life without completely alienating anybody that I am aware of, although I know I was not always able to give to my relationship with Joni the attention that it deserved.

In addition to religiously following my training schedule, I thought it was important to enter a number of athletic events along the way in order to maintain something of a race mentality during the time leading up to Kona. During the summer, I was again able to successfully finish all four swims in the North Shore Swim Series. At the same time, I wanted to get used to putting in some high mileage on the bike as soon as possible, so I also started doing some longer bike rides almost immediately after Honu. In June and July, these rides included several lengthy jaunts with Tony Pace and Emy Ching, who were putting in a lot of miles in preparation for the approximately 200 mile Seattle to Portland ride that they were going to be doing toward the end of July. One day, I thought we were planning to do about 75 to 80 miles, but we kept adding on a mile here and a couple of miles there. We eventually hit 100 miles—only my second century ever after the Century Ride in 2005. By that point, I had had enough, but amazingly they just kept on going. They later told me that they ended up doing over 130 miles that day.

The long bike rides every weekend, often done in the company of Laurie Sloan, were never easy, particularly when they were followed by a run of up to 10 miles on some occasions. However, they definitely started to pay off. By the end of August, I felt pretty comfortable doing rides of between 70 to 90 miles, so I decided to enter the Dick Evans Memorial Road Race for the very first time. This is the 112-mile race around the island of Oʻahu on which the bike leg of the original Ironman race was based. It tends to be viewed as an event for hard-core cyclists (as opposed to mediocre triathletes like me), so once again I felt intimidated. I had been hoping to talk Laurie into doing it with me, but she couldn't fit it into her schedule, so I knew I was going to be on my own. While waiting for the start of the race in Hawaiʻi Kai, there were times when I wondered if maybe this wasn't such a good idea after all. I had visions of being stuck out there on the other side of the island in last place and unable to make it back to the finish. Nevertheless, I was determined to give it my best shot.

I was greatly relieved that I was just about able to keep up with the pack for the first 30 miles, simply because the whole pack of about 200 cyclists always rides together, at what they consider a moderate pace, with a police escort up to that point. However, the pace quickened significantly as we got into Waipahu, and then the pack rapidly broke up after we started to climb the hill up Kunia Road into the center of the island. I suddenly had visions of my worst pre-race fears becoming a reality. I soon found myself almost at the very back. For most of the rest of the race, I was riding on my own, with only a handful of other stragglers behind me. It was definitely a challenging ride. After the long climb up Kunia Road, there was at least a little relief as the course went up and down for a few miles before the long descent to Haleiwa. After that, however, I found myself riding into a pretty strong headwind all the way along the North Shore and down the windward side of the island. I must admit that I did feel a little discouraged at some points along the way. At such times, it occurred to me that it would feel really good to just stop pedaling and go have a beer somewhere. Nevertheless, by constantly reminding myself about my ultimate goal, I managed to keep on moving forward with only a very brief stop at the aid station in Kāne'ohe. Then, as my energy was starting to fade, the support and encouragement that I received from the Boca athletes who were manning the final aid station in Kailua helped keep me going over the last few miles. I finally finished in about 7 hours 15 minutes. I was thrilled just to have made it to the finish line, and, on top of that, I wasn't last. I even forced myself to run for about 40 minutes after the race and then followed it up by doing the Waikiki Roughwater Swim the next day. It was another breakthrough weekend. I can't honestly say that 100-mile bike rides ever really became routine for me, but by the time I completed the Honolulu Century Ride in late September, I had done a total of five rides of 100 miles or more since June. With each one, I was feeling more and more confident that I could at least make it through the bike leg in Kona.

For the first time in several years, I was not formally training with a group. On the one hand, I thought it would be good psychological preparation for the race to get more experience doing some of my workouts on my own. On the other hand, I didn't want to be doing all of my training alone. I had come to greatly appreciate the camaraderie and support that came from training with groups of other athletes, so I decided to email my training schedule to my friends and invite them to join me for my workouts whenever they could make it. I was always happy when some friends would come out to join me, particularly on the long bike rides. I also started going out to Hawai'i Kai every Sunday morning to meet informally with a group of friends for a long run. The composition of the group varied from week to week, but there were usually at least half a dozen people and sometimes more than twice that number. After the run, we would all hang out for a while and get something to drink from Starbucks or Jamba Juice, so it was a good opportunity to socialize with other athletes and talk about our plans for upcoming races. Over the years since then, I have continued to do that Sunday morning Hawai'i Kai run on a regular basis, and it has become one of the staples of my training regimen. In the process, I have made or solidified friendships with a lot of other athletes. Some of the friends who have consistently been present over the years include Karen and Eric Sanders, Emy Ching, and Jodie Hagerman, all of whom are not only excellent athletes but also great people whose inspiration and friendship I very much value. Although we have sometimes thrown in some variations, our basic route has usually been from Hawai'i Kai to Makapu'u and back, a distance of just over 10 miles, to which some of us would add more distance depending on our individual training needs. It is a beautiful route, with excellent views of the O'ahu coastline and mountains, and three good hill climbs along the way, so it makes for not only an enjoyable but also a challenging run. That basic course, with the addition of however many extra miles I felt I needed to do, served me well in my preparation for Kona.

Although I was always happy and grateful when friends would join me for workouts, because of the volume of training that I was doing as well as the idiosyncrasies of my schedule, a lot of my workouts inevitably had to be done alone. I began to appreciate more and more that doing some training alone is particularly important in psychologically preparing for an individual endurance event like an iron-distance race. I knew that during the race, no matter how many of my friends were there as fellow competitors or supporters, it was ultimately going to be me against the course. Consequently, I knew I had to get some of that experience in training. In addition, I found that training alone gave me some valuable time to reflect on what I was doing as an athlete and on various aspects of my life more generally.

During the build up for Kona 2006, one of the things that I sometimes reflected on was how far I had come in my athletic endeavors and also how much my perspective had changed over the time since

I started training for my first triathlon less than 4 years earlier. Over that 4-year period, I had frequently been amazed by my ability to get through long, demanding training sessions that I could not have imagined being able to do just a short time earlier. As I looked back, I recalled the days when I thought that swimming 500 meters and then going for a 30-minute run, all at a relatively moderate pace, was a pretty tough workout. Or the days when I considered riding from Kāhala to Hawaiʻi Kai and back, a round trip of about 12 miles, to be a long ride. Or those early days when running any distance at all after getting off my bike seemed like awfully hard work. Now, a workout like a 60-mile ride from Waikīkī to Kailua and back, followed by a 4-mile run around Diamond Head would be considered relatively short and quite routine. I recalled the very first day that I rode the Tantalus loop back in 2003 and felt that it was really a big deal. Now, one of my favorite late afternoon workouts during the middle of the week was to ride two loops of Tantalus, which meant almost 10 miles of climbing, and then do a tempo run of about 6 miles back into Mānoa Valley with a few hills along the way. It was never an easy workout, but it was something that I came to know I could do comfortably. Plus, on those days when I still felt strong enough to pick up the pace as I came back down the valley over the last couple of miles of the run, there was a real sense of exhilaration and wonder that my old body was still capable of doing that. On other weekday afternoons, I would make sure that I was ready to leave the office by about 3:30 p.m. so I could head over to Ala Moana Beach, where I would typically swim somewhere between 2000 and 4000 meters, followed by a relatively flat 6- to 8-mile tempo run through Waikīkī or Kakaʻako. I now considered that to be one of my easier workouts for the week.

Although I derived a great deal of confidence from all of the training I was doing on Oʻahu, I still had some nagging doubts about my ability to tackle that infamous course in Kona. At times, some of those potentially self-defeating, catastrophic thoughts would begin to creep into my mind. What if there were an unexpectedly big, late-season southerly swell rolling into the bay on race day? Could I handle the kind of currents I might encounter? Although I had developed some confidence in my open ocean swimming ability and

I knew I could make it comfortably through 2.4 miles under reasonable conditions, I wasn't accustomed to heading directly out to sea continuously for 1.2 miles before turning back toward the shore. What if there were gale-force tradewinds blowing across the highway on the way up to Hawi? Could I make it all the way up that hill, and could I make it back down without being blown off the road? And even if I made it up to Hawi, would I have enough energy left to ride all the way back to Kailua-Kona? What if I just ran out of gas? Would I be able to push myself to keep going, or would I just fall by the wayside?

I decided it would be a good idea to confront my fears directly by heading over to the Big Island for a couple of weekend training sessions on the actual Kona course. Fortunately, Laurie Sloan had a similar idea, so I again had the benefit of her company on the long bike rides. I would fly over from Honolulu on Friday evening and try to get in a short run or swim before the end of the day. Laurie and her husband, Bruce, would come over on Saturday morning, and then Laurie and I would ride the course with Bruce acting as our traveling aid station. On the first trip, toward the end of August, we were able to ride over 100 miles on the Saturday, which was an extremely hot day as usual for that time of the year in Kona. I will be forever grateful to Bruce because I don't think we would have made it without his assistance. As we biked in the blazing heat through the lava fields of west Hawai'i, it was very comforting to know that Bruce was going to be waiting for us a little way ahead with a refill of ice cold drinks.

Laurie and Bruce would return to Honolulu after dinner on the Saturday, but I would stay on until Sunday so I could become familiar with the run course. On the Sunday during that first trip, my stomach was acting up, but I managed to run from Kailua-Kona down Ali'i Drive to the turnaround point at Keauhou and back, plus a few extra miles in the opposite direction, for a total of about 16 miles. Throw in a couple of short swims and it was a pretty solid weekend. However, because I wasn't feeling my best during that Sunday run, the weekend didn't do as much for my confidence as I had hoped it would.

The second Big Island training trip about a month later was even more valuable. On the Saturday, I put in a total of about 115 miles on the bike, followed by a short run. It was a certainly tough day, but I was pleased that I felt that I could easily have done more if necessary. The next day, I ran for a total of 18 miles, including the whole of the second part of the course out to the Natural Energy Lab and back. It was another brutally hot day out on Queen Ka'ahumanu Highway, but I felt strong all the way. At any time other than race day, there are no water stops at all on that part of the course. However, the night before I had driven out toward the Energy Lab and left bottles of Gatorade by the side of the road every couple of miles. In that heat, I certainly needed every drop. After the run, it felt wonderful to go for a swim in Kailua Bay just to cool off. With only three weeks to go before the big day, that weekend represented the peak of my training. By the time I got on the plane to go back to Honolulu that Sunday afternoon, I could relax with the thought that all I had to do was taper down over the next few weeks. After wondering for four months whether I was going to be able to get this point, I was finally just about confident enough to say that I was ready to take on the challenge of Kona.

Chapter 17

The BIG Day

I arrived on the Big Island on the Wednesday before the race. Throughout the next three days, the town of Kailua-Kona was absolutely crawling with super fit athletes and expensive bikes, and it was sometimes a bit difficult to fully comprehend that I was also going to be participating in whatever event it was that all these people were going to be doing. At times, it seemed like I was in a fantasy world.

Surprisingly, I was able to sleep well the night before the race, perhaps because it all did seem so unreal. It was only when I got up at about 3 o'clock on race morning that it finally sunk in that this was the real thing. It was time to get ready for action. Joni and I were staying at King Kamehameha's Kona Beach Hotel, which must be the most conveniently located hotel for any triathlon. The swim start, T1, T2, and the finish line are all right next to the hotel. Being so close to everything meant that I had lots of time to get ready for the start without any rush or logistical hassles. After my usual breakfast of banana, with cereal and skimmed milk, plus some extra sweet bread, I walked down to the start area for body marking and a final check to make sure my bike was ready for the road. I then had plenty of time to go back up to the hotel room to relax for a little while and put on some sunscreen before taking my bottles of Gatorade and Spiz down to my bike and then heading over toward the swim start area.

Waiting on the pier to get into the water before the start of the swim, I did start to feel a little nervous. For a while, all of those old questions and doubts were coming up again. Had I really done enough training? Would I be able to endure and overcome everything that infamous course might throw at me? I tried to breathe deeply and tell myself that I knew I was capable of doing whatever was needed to finish the race. I also remember talking with an athlete from the Big Island who, I learned, had done much less training than I had and still seemed confident enough. That eased my mind a bit. As the time got closer to the start, I was feeling a little more calm and composed. Nevertheless, the nervousness, probably fueled also by an element of impatience, wouldn't completely abate.

After what seemed like a very long wait, it was finally time to get in the water. As I did, my nervousness quickly seemed to dissipate. The warm, leeward waters of west Hawai'i felt soothing as I swam slowly out toward the starting line. I stopped to look around and saw a mass of spectators lining the shore and huge signs announcing that this was indeed the Ford Ironman World Championship. A big smile came over my face. I thought, "I really am doing this! Me, participating in a World Championship!" In some ways, it had all seemed way too good to be true, like it was part of a fantasy. But, right then, I was fully aware that it was real. At the same time, I was completely ready to get started with the challenge. At that point, I really didn't care where I placed or how mediocre I was in comparison to anyone else. I knew that I had been extremely fortunate to have the opportunity to qualify. But, at the same time, I had earned the right to be there. In addition, I had trained my ass off, and I was determined to give it everything that I had. There was no doubt in my mind that, one way or another, I was going to finish that race.

The swim start at Kona has a reputation for being chaotic, with about 1800 swimmers starting en masse as soon as the starting gun goes off. However, I found out, as the start area filled up, that, if I hung out 15 to 20 meters behind the start line, it really wasn't as crowded as I thought it was going to be. It seemed like an excellent starting point for a relatively slow swimmer like me—out of the crowd but not too far back, with less than half a minute of swimming to get over the start line. When I had arrived on the Wednesday, there had been some fairly good-sized waves sweeping into the bay, which had worried me a little, but by race morning they had largely dissipated. As I looked out into Kailua Bay, I could see some small swells rolling in and breaking against the wall a few hundred meters along the coast from the pier, but there was certainly nothing to worry about, and the water was as clear and beautiful as it almost always is in Kona. What a great way to start the day!

The professionals were off as scheduled at 6:45, and, then, 15 minutes later, the other 1700 or more of us age-groupers were all on our way. Inevitably, there were a few bumps with other swimmers during the first few hundred meters, but it wasn't long before I was swimming in relatively clear water, and I told myself to just take my time and enjoy the journey. I knew it was going to be a long day, so I was in no hurry at all. The first half of the swim went very well. As usual, there were lots of fish and beautiful coral heads to keep my attention along the way, and the time went steadily by. At one point close to the turn around, I saw down in the deep water far below me a small hammerhead shark. I glanced at my watch after going around the Body Glove boat at the halfway mark and saw that my time was about 49 minutes. I wasn't thinking about it at the time, but it occurred to me later that the leader of my age group was probably finishing the swim at around that same time or shortly after. I was just happy that it was close to my average time when I did 2000 meters in training at Ala Moana. "Good enough," I thought. "If I can do the same on the way back, that will be under 1:40. I'll be in good shape."

The second half of the swim proved to be a little tougher. I felt that I was swimming comfortably at my usual slow, steady pace, but there must have been a fairly strong current against us as we swam back toward the pier. As we got closer to shore, I had a feeling that it was taking longer than I thought it should. I hauled myself out of the water and looked at the clock. With my relatively poor eyesight, I initially saw my time as 1:46—just a little slower than I had hoped for. However, once I got closer, I realized it was actually 1:56. For a moment, I felt a surge of disappointment. "Damn, I should have been able to do better than that," I thought. Then I reminded myself that I was well under the swim time limit and there was a long day ahead of me. There was no rush and no need to get down on myself. I headed toward the transition area, changed into my bike gear, powered up with Gatorade and gel, and got myself mentally ready for the second act.

By the time I came out of T1, I was happy to be getting out on the road on my trusty Felt F35. Although it wasn't fancy, it was a machine that had served me well so far, and I had come to feel that I could rely on it to get me through the challenging course that lay ahead. I had made it through the swim, and I focused on the simple thought that it looked like a really nice day for a long bike ride. I caught a glimpse of my family and friends cheering me on as I rode up Palani Road. That gave me a good psychological lift. All I had to do next was keep my bike moving forward for another 7 or 8 hours.

There was a rather unusual weather system moving quickly through the islands that day, so conditions were apparently variable depending on where you happened to be on the course at any particular time. By the time I had completed the first few miles around Kailua town and started heading north on Queen Ka'ahumanu Highway, I found myself heading into a wind that seemed to be coming from approximately a northwesterly direction. It wasn't a particularly strong wind, but the direction was unusual. The prevailing winds throughout the Hawaiian Islands are the trade winds, which blow 75 to 80 percent of the year and typically come in from an easterly to north-easterly direction. The area around Kailua-Kona, however, tends to be protected from the trade winds by the combined mass of three huge mountains—Mauna Kea and Mauna Loa, both of which are well in excess of 13,000 feet, and Hualālai, which rises to over 8,000 feet almost directly behind the town of Kailua. Typically, the prevailing wind in the Kailua area in the early morning is a sea breeze coming in from approximately a south-westerly direction, so there tends to be something of a tailwind when you are heading north on the highway for maybe about the first 20 miles until you start to feel the trade winds in the Waikoloa area, as Laurie and I had found on our training rides. When I hit that headwind instead, I knew right away it was going to be a long ride. Instead of cruising steadily along the slightly undulating sections of the highway going out of town at 18 to 20 miles an hour as I had done in training, I was often down to only about 15, and, of course, considerably slower on the uphill sections.

By the time I was approaching Waikoloa, about 20 miles out of town, the wind had shifted, and I actually had a tailwind for a little while, but it didn't last for long. The climb from Kawaihae to Hawi along Akoni Pule Highway was a long grind, as it always is, and parts of it were especially difficult against a wind that once again had changed direction. Songs such as Bob Seger's "Against the Wind" would start to run through my mind, but then I would try to shift my focus back to the song that I had used as a theme song and inspiration during training—"Running Down a Dream" by Tom Petty. The title captured the essence of what I was doing, and it helped keep me going on some of the more challenging parts of the ride. Another song that would run through my mind was "Keep Right On to the End of the Road." In case you are not familiar with it, the song was originally written around the time of the First World War by the great Scottish entertainer, Sir Harry Lauder. Some years later, it was adopted by my hometown soccer team, Birmingham City Football Club, as the club song. I recalled big games in the days of my youth when a full house of almost 50,000 fans at the old St. Andrew's stadium would be singing their hearts out. I hoped the song would spur me on in the same way that we had hoped it would motivate the players back then.

When I got to the turnaround in Hawi, I decided that it was time to take a short break. By that point, I had covered about 60 miles, and although I had purposely tried to make a point of not pushing too hard, it had definitely been a solid morning's work. It felt so good to get off the bike, sit down, take off my shoes, drink my fill of Gatorade, and eat part of a Clif Bar. It briefly occurred to me how very easy it would be to just lie down, relax, and forget about the race. But after about a 2-minute break, I quickly put that thought out of my mind, and told myself to get back on my bike and get moving again. There was still a lot of work to do.

On the return from Hawi, the first few miles to Māhukona are all downhill, so it was an opportunity to make up some time. After that, the road goes up and down for a while before another fairly long downhill stretch into Kawaihae. The climb out of Kawaihae is not long, less than a mile, but it is one of those hills that always feels like it is much steeper than it looks. In the heat of the day, it seemed like a killer to me, as it usually does. But at least by the time I got to the top and turned back onto the Queen Kaʻahumanu Highway, I could tell myself I was on the last leg of the bike course. At that point, however, there were still over 30 miles to go, and they were not particularly easy miles. In addition to dealing with the rolling hills, I still seemed to be riding into at least a mild headwind much of the way, and I found myself counting down the mile markers one by one to mark my progress. Many of them seemed to go by all too slowly. Toward the end, my feet were hurting, my rear end was sore, the muscles in my legs were aching, and there were times when I just wanted it to be over. At such times, I reminded myself that were thousands of athletes who would kill for the opportunity to be right where I was. I told myself to just suck it up and keep going. By the time I got to the airport at Keāhole, the wind seemed to become more favorable, and the going finally got a little easier. Only 7 more miles to go. So far so good. I just hope I don't get a flat tire!

I rolled into T2 with a bike split of about 7 hours 40 minutes—without question, about as mediocre as it gets at Kona. But the main thing was that I had made it through that critical second stage of the race. I had consciously tried not to push too hard on the bike, and I had made a point of trying to keep my cadence up around 90 revs per minute as much as possible. At times, I told myself pointedly to hold back and take it easy because I knew I could easily burn myself out on the bike if I did not pace myself carefully. As I dismounted, I found that my restraint had paid off. My running legs felt good as I moved through the transition area. I was ready to tackle the marathon.

I told myself that I was going to take my time in transition, spending over 12 minutes to do a complete change of clothing, relax a little, and drink plenty of fluids. I also used some of that time to read all of the messages of encouragement in the cards that some of my friends had given me before the race. Taking a break also gave my heart and lungs a much-needed rest from all of the work they had been doing. By the time I got up to leave T2, I was feeling refreshed and rejuvenated.

One of the benefits of being relatively slow on both the swim and the bike was that, by the time I got out of T2, the sun was starting to drop into the western sky. Thus, I didn't have to deal with as much heat as those athletes who were out on the run course in the middle of the day. That's not to say it was cool by any means. I imagine the temperature must have remained in the low 80s until well after dark. Plus, it was humid, as it tends to be in Kona, so I found myself sweating profusely even after the sun had gone down. I made a point of drinking enough to ensure I didn't get dehydrated along the way. Initially, I was taking in either Gatorade or a combination of water and gel in order to maintain a good intake of calories along with the fluid. There eventually came a point, however, about 15 miles into the run, when my body just couldn't take any more sugar. At that point, I switched to a combination of water and chicken soup, the saltiness of which was just what my body needed, with a few sips of cola thrown in whenever I needed an extra bit of a lift. At one of the aid stations, I even felt chipper enough to joke with one of the volunteers who handed me a cup of chicken soup and asked him if they had any Portuguese bean soup, a popular local favorite, on the menu.

In retrospect, I probably went out just a little bit too fast for the first few miles of the run. I had been feeling surprisingly fresh and strong when I left T2, and I was able to comfortably maintain about an 11-minute-mile pace on the way out to the first turn around point at Keauhou, which is about 5 miles into the run. On the way back, however, I began to feel myself slowing down. By that time, it was starting to get dark, so I grabbed one of the glow sticks that were being handed out. I also turned on the headlight that my good training buddy Crystal had given me for the race. Later in the race, the headlight turned out to be very helpful in those pitch-black areas out on the highway and down the road to the Natural Energy Lab where street lamps are conspicuous only by their absence. I would highly recommend a headlight as an accessory if you happen to be a slow poke like me.

By the time I got back into Kailua town approaching the 10-mile mark, I could feel my energy level starting to decline. I had been able to keep running pretty much all the way up to that point, although I did briefly slow down at the aid stations, mainly because I always seem to have a hard time running and drinking at the same time without spilling liquid down the front of my shirt. In the middle of Kailua town, there is a short but fairly steep hill on Palani Road between Kuakini Highway and Queen Kaʻahumanu Highway. Under ordinary circumstances, it would not be too bad to run up. At 12 hours into the race, however, it was just too steep for me to keep running, so I reluctantly slowed to a walk as I started to climb the hill. Fortunately, a number of my friends from Boca Hawaii were right there on the medial strip in the middle of Palani Road just above what is known as "hot corner." Jay Paul and Asako Shimazu jumped up when they saw me and showered me with words of encouragement as they walked with me up to the top of the hill. Never underestimate the value of the support of friends. Their show of support and encouragement gave me the psychological lift that I needed, just at a point where my determination was beginning to get a little frayed around the edges. As I turned left onto Queen Kaʻahumanu Highway, I felt renewed and ready to start running again.

As I headed out of town along the highway, I was surprised at how well I was able to keep running. I had always thought of the run as being, in relative terms, the strongest of the three triathlon sports for me. But, after such a tough bike ride, I had expected this run to be a really difficult one, and it would not have surprised me if I had been forced to walk much of the way. As I have said, I had initially been disappointed with my swim time, and my bike time was also a bit slower than I would have liked ideally. However, the longer the run went on, the happier I was that I had paced myself conservatively on the swim and the bike. It was certainly no great surprise that I found myself toward the back of the pack throughout the race, but I had easily made the time cutoffs for the swim and the bike, and I found that I was far from being in last place, as I had sometimes feared that I might be. Not, I should now add, that there is anything at all wrong with being in last place. My admiration and respect go out to all who are willing to take on the challenge and give it their all, no matter where they place and even if they are not able to finish. If you know that you have indeed given it your best shot, then you have, without a doubt, done something extraordinary.

As we got further into the run, I found myself not only going strong and steady but also passing quite a few people. Overall, I was, in fact, able to move up 80 places during the course of the run. About a mile or so out of town along the highway, to my great surprise, I suddenly came up on my training buddy, Laurie Sloan. I knew she would have been out of the water well ahead of me, and I anticipated she would maintain her lead over me on the bike as we were probably going to be riding at about the same pace. In addition, she was usually a faster runner than me, so I was expecting her to finish way ahead of me. Unfortunately, she had been forced to slow down to a walking pace, and I could tell she wasn't feeling well. I tried to say something encouraging to her as I went past her, but I knew she was in for an ordeal the rest of the way. I'm glad to say that she was able to finish the race, which is certainly a testament to her determination. But, at the same time, I felt bad for her because she had trained so hard, and I know she felt that she was capable of doing better.

The second turnaround, at the end of the road by the Natural Energy Lab at about the 18-mile point, was a critical point in the race psychologically for me. Although I had been running fairly well up to that point, there was still an element of doubt that had crept back into my mind somewhere along the way. As I was approaching the turnaround, I knew there were still over 8 miles to go, certainly a long enough distance to crash and burn somewhere out there on that dark highway. As I headed back toward town, however, any lingering doubts gradually began to fade, and, with each successive aid station, I felt more and more confident. I was on my way home!

Along with the chicken soup and water that I had started taking in at the aid stations after mile 15, I was also drinking the occasional cup of cola. I then also downed part of a can of Red Bull that I had stashed in my special needs bag, which I was able to pick up near the Natural Energy Lab. I'm sensitive to the effects of caffeine because I don't usually consume caffeinated drinks in my everyday life, so I found that the cola and Red Bull gave me another good lift. After that, although my legs were starting to feel tired and heavy, I found it was relatively easy to keep up a slow, steady jog between aid stations. About a mile after the Energy Lab, I was surprised again as I came up behind Dave Kerr, another of the athletes from Honolulu, who was also in my age group. It was Dave's second year in a row at Kona, having qualified at Honu the previous year and then winning a lottery slot in 2006. I had not trained with Dave, but I had met him several times, and I knew he had much more experience in long distance triathlons than I did. Thus, I had expected him to finish far ahead of me. As it turned out, however, I gathered that he had not been able to train as much as he might have wanted to ideally. In any event, as I went past him, he graciously congratulated me on running a good race, a nice gesture, which gave me permission to figuratively pat myself on the back and tell myself that I really was doing a pretty good job.

Incidentally, I was fortunate to miss some of the worst effects of that strange weather system while I was on the road near the Natural Energy Lab. I later learned that it had poured with rain for a while in Kailua town, and some athletes, as well as a lot of spectators, had gotten soaked in the process. I saw a few drops of rain at one point when I was going out of town, but otherwise it was completely dry. It occurred to me afterwards that my timing had been perfect. Sometimes it's good to be slow.

The last few miles of the run were, in many ways, the highlight of the whole event. By the time I got to mile 22, there was no longer any doubt in my mind that I was going to finish. As I got closer and closer to Kailua town, I could hear the music and celebrations at the finish line gradually getting louder and louder. The adrenaline really started to kick in, and an almost euphoric feeling started to come over me. I was even able to pick up the pace a bit as I headed up the little rise in the highway before making the right turn down Palani Road into the center of the town. Almost there! Down Palani

Road, left onto Kuakini Highway, right onto Hualālai Street, and then the final right turn onto Aliʻi Drive. To be approaching the finish line in Kona was an absolutely incredible experience. I really felt like a world champion as I passed hundreds of cheering spectators along the last few hundred yards before the finish. My daughter, Jen, and my then 6-year-old granddaughter, Hina, who had been so supportive of my athletic endeavors, spotted me as I approached. I was thrilled when Hina was able to jump into the road and run with me across the finish line. Actually, I now feel fortunate that she was able to share that experience with me because, for some reason not entirely clear to me, family members are no longer allowed to run across the finish line with athletes.

As we ran past the crowds of cheering spectators over the last few yards, I heard the announcer, Mike Reilly, calling out my name. Then, we were going up the ramp, crossing the finish line, and it was over. I had done it. I was an Ironman! I had crossed the finish line in a time of 15 hours, 13 minutes and 59 seconds, in 1560th place overall. I had comfortably accomplished my primary goal of finishing the race with plenty of time to spare, and had even achieved my secondary goal of going under 16 hours. I was 32nd in my age group, out of 41 people who were registered for the race and 35 who actually finished the race. A profoundly mediocre performance, no doubt, but that was completely inconsequential at that point. All that mattered to me at that moment was that I had done what I set out to do—I had conquered that infamous course in Kona! I felt a tremendous sense of accomplishment surge through me. I had done something that, just a few short years earlier, I could never in my wildest dreams have imagined doing. Although I wasn't thinking in exactly those terms at the time, I can now say without a doubt that I was able to transcend my inherent mediocrity, and in the process found my own personal "Black Swan," and, oh, what a positive one!

When I later looked at the full race results, I was impressed to see that the winner of my age group had finished in just seconds over 11 hours flat. Although I reckoned that I might have been able to improve on my own time if I had started doing triathlons when I was younger, I know I couldn't even have gotten close to an 11 hour finish when I was in my 20s and 30s, let alone in my 60s. At that point, however, comparisons with other people were completely irrelevant. I knew that I could look in the mirror and, with complete honesty, tell myself that I had accomplished something that was, for me, truly extraordinary.

Immediately after crossing the finish line, I found myself surrounded by volunteers who were congratulating me and checking to see if I was okay. I was actually surprised at how good I felt after more than 15 hours of physical exertion. Someone gave me a lei, and someone else gave me something to drink, and then someone escorted me through to the back of the finish area, where lots of friends and family were waiting to greet me with hugs, lei, and congratulations. For a while I felt like I was on top of the world. Lots of pictures were taken. I recall feeling energetic enough to lift Hina onto my shoulders at one point. Slowly, the euphoria began to subside, and I began to feel like I needed to take the weight off my feet, but I declined to go to the medical tent. By that time I just wanted to get out of my running gear and take a shower, so I headed back to the hotel, along with Jen, Hina, and Joni. My good training buddies, Crystal and Amy, who had been so supportive all through my training and had even made signs especially for me during the race, also came along to keep us company.

I had fully expected that I would be exhausted to the point of collapse if I made it to the finish line, but, to my great surprise, after a shower and a change of clothes, I felt ready to go out and party. There must have still been some adrenaline in my system after the excitement of the finish, along with caffeine from the cola and the Red Bull. Jen and Hina were both very tired after such a long day and needed to get some sleep, but Joni, Crystal, Amy, and I decided to go back down to the finish line to watch the remaining athletes finish. There was quite a bit of drama as the time approached the midnight deadline. Everyone was waiting to see if Sister Madonna Buder, the then 78-year-old nun who seemed by have made endurance triathlons another calling in life, would be able to finish before the deadline. We were getting updates on her progress over the public address system every few minutes, and it seemed touch and go whether she would make it or not. She finally came through the finish line around one minute before the deadline to the loudest cheers of the whole night. It was a spectacular and uplifting finish to a day that had, for me, truly been an experience of a lifetime.

At midnight, far from wanting to go to sleep, I was still feeling exhilarated. By that time, I was also feeling very hungry, so a big meal seemed like as good a way as any to end what had definitely been one of the most incredible days of my life. To our dismay, we found that all the restaurants in the Ali'i Drive area were already closed, so we had to drive a mile or so out of the town center to Denny's, where we all enjoyed what was either a very late dinner or a very early breakfast.

I was surprised at how good I felt when I got out of bed on the morning after the race. I certainly wouldn't have wanted to go out and do the race all over again, but, despite only sleeping for about 4 or 5 hours, I felt surprisingly alert and energetic. A group of about 12 of us went for a big celebration breakfast at Aloha Café in Kainaliu, a few miles outside Kailua-Kona. For Laurie Sloan and I, as finishers, it was a wonderful opportunity to savor that feeling of accomplishment in the company of family and friends who had been so supportive throughout our training, as well as during the race itself. Moments like that are to be treasured as things that make all the effort of training and racing worthwhile. The official awards banquet later that day was another great opportunity for Laurie and I to celebrate our achievement with friends and other athletes. What an incredible weekend it had been!

Joni and I returned to Honolulu on the Monday evening after the race. During the time before our departure, I had some time to take it easy and unwind in Kona. Some people recommend taking a couple of weeks off completely after an iron-distance race, which is probably good advice. But I had absolutely no desire to slow down. By Tuesday, I was already looking forward to my next goal. I could hardly wait to get back to training again.

After returning to Honolulu, I immediately resumed my training with the Boca Hawaii group that was preparing for the Honolulu Marathon in December. My goal at that point was to complete not only the race in Kona but also all three components of the original Ironman course on the island of O'ahu in the same year. I had already done the Dick Evans Memorial Road Race and the Waikiki

Roughwater Swim in September as part of my training for Kona, so the Honolulu Marathon was all that remained. I initially had vague hopes of setting a personal record for the marathon, maintaining a 10-minute-mile pace and finishing in less than 4 hours 22 minutes. But, in retrospect, I can see that I wasn't strongly committed to that particular time goal. My focus was more on just finishing the race and enjoying the camaraderie of the group while we were training. Consequently, although I kept training consistently, I probably cut myself a bit too much slack in terms of intensity. As a result, I didn't set my PR and ended up falling short of my time goal by about 9 minutes, finishing in 4 hours and 31 minutes—not quite as good as the previous year but a satisfying performance nevertheless.

The marathon finish was a great way to end what had truly been one of the most eventful years of my life. Emotionally, it had been something of a roller coaster ride, having gone from dejection and disappointment after the crash in January, to astonishment in June when I learned that I had qualified for Kona, to exhilaration and elation after finishing my first iron-distance triathlon, at the World Championship in Kona of all places. Finishing the marathon, and thus completing the three Oʻahu events that formed the basis of the original Ironman, was just a little more icing on the cake.

When I looked back over the year, the following scenario occurred to me. If I had not had that crash in January, I would have done the shortened race in New Zealand. I would then almost certainly have chosen to go to Arizona in April with Kris and Stella. If I had been able to finish the race in Arizona, it would obviously have been a huge accomplishment for me. But, then, having achieved that goal, I probably would not have felt a need to enter Honu in June. Of course, if I had not entered Honu, I could not possibly have qualified for Kona. What a revelation! That crash, as devastating as it had initially seemed, had actually given me an opportunity to go to Kona to participate in the World Championship. How incredibly fortunate I had been!

Chapter 18

More Challenges

Just as 2006 had been a year of downs then ups, 2007 turned out to be the other way round. In fact, a number of new challenges lay ahead during the next two years. Initially it seemed like things were continuing to move along just fine. In early 2007, I was at the height of my addiction to training. I was feeling really fit and strong and probably in the best physical shape of my life. I was definitely enjoying all aspects of the training, and I looked forward to each workout with great enthusiasm. I seemed, in fact, to have an almost unending appetite for endurance training. I was also planning ahead for my next goal, which was to break that 10-minute-mile pace for a marathon. I decided to set 4:20 as a specific time goal. I had already made tentative plans for a trip back to England some time later in the year to visit family and friends, and I thought it would be great to do some type of athletic event while I was there. After looking at a number of possible options, I decided that I would take a journey up to the north of Scotland in order to run the Loch Ness Marathon, which was set to take place in early October. That was to be my primary goal race for 2007.

During the first half of the year, a number of my friends were training for Ironman Austria in July. Although I wasn't planning to do that race myself, I was able get in plenty of long workouts with them, including a 112-mile bike ride around the island of Oʻahu one weekend in April. I was also continuing to participate in some of the shorter distance triathlons during the first half of the year, and I had pretty good races in both the Lanikai and Honolulu triathlons. I was able to set a personal record for the Olympic distance in the Honolulu Triathlon, finishing almost 15 minutes faster than I had done the previous year. At that point, everything seemed to be going well, and I felt that my fitness had returned to at least the level it had been prior to the crash in January 2006. Immediately after finishing the Honolulu Triathlon, a few of us, including Asako Shimazu, Lilian Kanai, Terry O'Toole, and Lee Ann Hernandez, even biked for about another 45 miles out to Waimānalo just to make sure we got in all the miles we felt we needed for the day. By that time, Saturdays or Sundays like those, with 6 hours or more of training, had become a routine part of my weekly schedule just like another day at the office.

Next up after the Honolulu Triathlon was Honu in early June. My primary goal for Honu was to set a PR, which I was able to do fairly comfortably. For much of the race, I also seemed to be on track to achieve my secondary goal—to break 7 hours. Then, for the second year in a row, I had some cramping in my legs during the run, which slowed me down quite a bit although fortunately not as much as the previous year. Consequently, I ended up going about a minute over the 7 hours, which, I must admit, was a little disappointing because I had been starting to feel that I could accomplish whatever goal I set my mind to whenever I wanted to.

Despite that minor disappointment, my confidence was still very high, perhaps a little too high. A certain amount of overconfidence was beginning to creep in. When things are going well, it is sometimes hard, even for someone who should have learned from many years of experience, to remember that life can sometimes throw you an unexpected curve ball. At that time, my participation in athletics was still very much focused on personal accomplishment and improving my performance in my goal races. So, after just missing out on my 7-hour time goal at Honu, I threw myself into training hard for the Loch Ness Marathon. I was more determined than ever to achieve my marathon goal, and, as I moved ahead with my training, I rather unrealistically failed to envision the possibility that there would be any obstacles along the way. As part of my preparation, I entered the Hibiscus Half Marathon in Honolulu a little later in June, more as a training exercise than a goal race. I was able to put in what I felt was a solid performance on a hot and humid summer morning. That performance left me feeling that I was well on the way to achieving my marathon goal as long I remained consistent with my training over the next few months. I decided to focus particularly on increasing the intensity of my workouts in order to improve my speed.

Then, one Thursday evening in July, disappointment struck again. I had been running hill intervals of a little under a mile in duration on Kīlauea Avenue, which has, from a runner's point of view, a moderate incline overall. I had been pushing myself pretty hard and had just completed three intervals followed by a fairly fast tempo run for a couple of additional miles when I started to feel a sharp pain in the base of my right foot. It didn't occur to me at the time, but I later realized that I had probably been so focused on trying to improve my performance that I had made the mistake of overtraining. Over the previous month, I had been running almost every day of the week, and this was my second high intensity workout that particular week, having run intervals on the track at Kaiser High School just two days earlier. Initially, I assumed that the pain would just go away after a day or two, but to my dismay it didn't. I decided to lay off running for a few days, after which there was some degree of improvement, but then the pain would return with full force after a few miles whenever I started running again. I began to wonder for the first time if the problem might affect my performance in the upcoming marathon.

After a few weeks with no significant lasting improvement, it was completely messing up my training plans. Every week that I couldn't do all of my planned workouts was a setback, and my plans didn't call for any setbacks. I don't like going to the doctor unless I have to, but eventually I had no choice but to get my injury checked out. I pretty much knew what the problem was, and my physician merely confirmed the diagnosis—plantar fasciitis. I tried just about everything to fix the problem. I bought a splint and a special sock to keep my foot flexed while I was sleeping; I bought over-the-counter and then custom inserts for my shoes; I tried rolling my feet on a special roller that I bought and on a spiked rubber ball that my friend Eric Sanders gave me; I did all kinds of stretching exercises; I went to see a chiropractor who scraped the bottom of my foot with a special tool. Nothing seemed to work. I would sometimes get partial relief for a few days, but the pain would come back, often worse than before. If I tried to run for more than about 6 miles, the pain became almost unbearable. As time went by and the marathon got closer, I became increasingly frustrated and discouraged. Just before my departure for England, I considered getting a cortisone shot in my foot. But I knew that would only be a temporary fix that might actually aggravate the problem by masking the pain, so I eventually decided against it.

Because I could not run anywhere near as much as I wanted to, I tried to maintain my fitness, and work off some of my frustration, by increasing the volume of swimming and biking, particularly the biking, which had not been a focus of my training since Honu in early June. Laurie Sloan had qualified for Kona again, and she liked to have company on her long bike rides, so a number of us started to join her whenever we could. In August, I went over to Kona with Laurie and Bruce for a training weekend like we had done the year before. Unfortunately, I hadn't been doing nearly as much mileage on the bike as Laurie had, so I wasn't quite ready for the 100 miles or more that she had planned. It was another brutally hot, but also windy, west Hawai'i summer day, which made for a challenging ride. I was able to make it through about 75 or 80 miles, before I finally threw in the towel and reluctantly decided to accept a ride back into Kona in Bruce's rental car. I concluded that my lack of running was having a negative effect on my conditioning, and I felt very frustrated by it.

Laurie had thought about doing the Dick Evans bike race as part of her training program, but she had always felt a little intimidated by it, which I could fully understand, having felt that way myself the previous year. Around the middle of August, a few of us, including Asako Shimazu, Tony Pace, and I, encouraged her to give it a try and told her that we would ride with her to keep her company. However, at the time, less than a month before the Dick Evans, none of us had built up the necessary endurance for a 112-mile bike race. In early July, Asako had successfully finished Ironman Austria. It was her third iron-distance event in less than two years, improving her performance each time, which was an accomplishment that I found very inspiring in light of the fact that her ability level overall was probably about the same as mine. She had, however, been taking a well-deserved break from long distance bike rides during the weeks after the race in Austria, so getting quickly back up to the 112-mile distance was going to be a challenge for her. Tony and I were probably good for about 70 or 80 miles but not much more than that. With well under a month to prepare, we increased our mileage as much as we could, although we never got close to the full race distance. We got to the point that we felt we could probably finish the 112 miles, although I think we all knew it would be a stretch to do it within the 7 ½-hour time limit that had been set for that year.

On the day of the Dick Evans race, Asako, Tony, and I were waiting near the start, but Laurie was nowhere to be seen. We later found out that Laurie's apprehension got the better of her, and she wasn't feeling well, so she reluctantly decided that she couldn't do the race. At that point, we figured that we might as well go ahead and give it a try, seeing that we were already there and ready to go. It turned out to be another disappointing, and also quite disturbing, day. For some reason, I was not feeling particularly strong that day, and I found myself falling behind Asako and Tony as we were going up Kunia Road into the center of the island. They had to wait for me to catch up at the top of the hill, and I found myself cursing the plantar fasciitis and beating myself up for not being as fit as I felt that I should be.

About 50 miles into the race, as we cycled along the Haleʻiwa bypass, we were alarmed to see that there had been a crash on the road ahead. As we pulled up behind the group of riders who had stopped, we could see one rider lying on the road with paramedics attending to her. We were shocked to find out that it was our friend, Lee Ann Hernandez. I was relieved to see her finally move her extremities, but it was obvious that she was badly hurt. We later learned that she had fallen hard after clipping the wheel of another rider while riding in a tight group at a pretty good speed. As a result of the fall, she had sustained a severe concussion. Fortunately, Lee Ann, who is now Lee Ann Watanabe, is a real fighter, and she was able to make an amazingly rapid recovery. Despite being hospitalized for several days after the accident as the result of a subdural hematoma, she was back on the road again within a matter of weeks. By May of the following year, she was able to finish Ironman Brazil on her first attempt at that distance—a tremendous accomplishment and a testament to her determination and motivation to recover.

Although we had all been shaken by Lee Ann's injury and we remained very worried about her, we tried to press on. It was another hot and windy day, and we became increasingly aware that our progress was slower than it should have been. By the time we reached the little town of Kaʻaʻawa, about 75 miles into the race, we were all thirsty and running low on fluids. It was still a few miles to the next aid station, so we stopped, probably for longer than we should have done, at a convenience store to refill our bottles. By the time we reached the final aid station in Kailua, at about the 100-mile mark, Tony's legs were cramping badly, and he decided that he had had enough. Asako and I managed to keep going, but we were way behind schedule. After we made another brief stop to check on a rider with a flat tire, a couple of the course marshals came by on a motor bike and told us that we were not going to make it within the time limit. They also told us that we would have to give them our timing chips. We reluctantly complied with their request. By that time, I was so frustrated and annoyed that I actually felt like throwing mine at them, but I managed to restrain myself from actually doing so. Afterwards, we were determined that we were not going to give up, so we continued riding and finally made it to the finish line

20 minutes or so over the time limit. It was at least some consolation that we had been able to hang in there to the end, but I was still disappointed that we had not succeeded in finishing within the official time limit. I knew, on the one hand, that we had given it our best shot under the circumstances, and I should, by that time, have been satisfied with that. However, at the same time, I just couldn't completely silence that part of me that was saying I had failed to perform as well as I should have been able to do.

By the time I left for the United Kingdom, I was feeling increasingly discouraged. The Dick Evans race had not gone so well, and the plantar fasciitis was not getting any better, so the volume of running that I had been doing was far below what I had originally planned. Consequently, my goal of running the marathon in 4:20 was receding further and further into the distance. In fact, I was beginning to wonder if I was going to be able to do the race at all.

I arrived in London in late September and drove immediately up to Birmingham, my hometown, for a few days. Then I went to spend a few more days in Torquay, in the south west of England, before heading up to Scotland. During that time, I tried to keep running as much as I possibly could, but I wasn't able to get anywhere near marathon distance. I think 10 miles was about as much I was ever able to struggle through, and, by the end of that I was limping along at a slow walk. I tried to compensate by doing as much walking and hiking as possible, but then I started to get shin splints, particularly in my left leg, which made running and even walking more of an ordeal. By the time I got to Inverness in early October, I even looked into the possibility of transferring my registration from the marathon to the 10K race, which was held on the same day. I was told, however, that it was too late to do that. I probably should have pulled out at that point, but I guess I have a bit of a stubborn streak when I have set my mind on something. I had been looking forward to this marathon for months, and I just couldn't allow myself to pull out completely, even though I knew there was, by then, absolutely no chance that I was going to set that PR.

I must say that the Loch Ness Marathon was an excellent event. The course was relatively flat for the most part, with just a few short and not too steep hills. The weather on race day was ideal for long distance running—cool but sunny and dry. It occurred to me that the location and conditions would have been perfect for a PR. On top of that, the scenery in the Scottish highlands is absolutely magnificent. I would highly recommend the race as a destination event. Just don't try to do it if you are suffering from plantar fasciitis. On race day, we were taken by bus from the historic city of Inverness to the start line, which is way out in the country, seemingly miles from anywhere. I was fervently hoping that we wouldn't meet any oncoming traffic as the buses barreled along little country lanes that were barely wide enough for one vehicle, let alone two. After we arrived at the start area, I struck up a conversation with Tom Brown, a runner from the Edinburgh area, and a woman from South Africa, whose name I don't recall. The three of us ran together at a pretty good pace for the first few miles, but, after about 6 miles, the woman gradually began to pull away from Tom and me. By that time, the pain from both the plantar fasciitis and the shin splints was getting progressively more intense and difficult to tolerate, and I gradually found my pace getting slower and slower. I think the early pace had also been a bit too much for Tom, who was a few years older than me, so together we ended up trying to maintain a combination of walking and running for the rest of the race. Actually, there was considerably more walking than running as the race went on, but Tom's company certainly made the whole experience much easier to endure. We eventually made it to the finish line in 5 hours and 45 minutes—not only a far cry from the 4:20 that I had originally been hoping for but also a personal worst to boot. It had been a real ordeal, but at least I was able to give myself credit for making it to the finish line under some very challenging circumstances. In addition, despite all the pain and disappointment, I have to say that it was still a great experience to run a marathon in such a beautiful natural setting.

 When the race was over, I found that I had a considerable amount of swelling in both my feet, and it just wouldn't go down. It probably didn't help that I went hiking in the Ben Nevis area the next day because I wanted to make the most of my visit to the Scottish Highlands. A couple of days after the race I flew from Inverness down to London and then returned to Honolulu the following day with my feet and lower legs still quite swollen. It was at that point that I knew I really needed to take a break from running for a while.

After I got back home to Honolulu, the swelling in my feet went down over the first week, but it was a couple of months before the plantar fasciitis finally went away completely. Taking a complete break from running was the only thing that helped to cure it. During that time, I maintained my fitness by swimming and also doing a certain amount of biking, but some of my drive and enthusiasm had been sapped by the disappointment of not achieving my goal in the marathon and by not being able to do any more running. Earlier that year, I had started swimming regularly with Stefan Reinke on Tuesday mornings at Kaimana Beach and Friday mornings at Ala Moana. Stefan is a great coach and an excellent all round athlete who always exudes enthusiasm for training in general and for swimming in particular. In addition to coaching with Boca Hawaii, he led these twice-weekly swim workouts for a number of years, without charge, welcoming all comers regardless of ability level. I always knew that I was going to get a good workout whenever I swam with Stefan. I also did quite a bit of aqua-jogging with another good friend, Shoko Paul, in lieu of running. I had been told that aqua-jogging can help to maintain fitness for running during times when you are not able to run. I'm not sure about that because I felt like I was starting from scratch when I eventually did start running again, but I must say that I thoroughly enjoyed the aqua-jogging as a form of exercise that puts a minimal amount of stress on the body. In addition, if you are able to do it with a few friends, it certainly allows for a lot more conversation than swimming.

Although the latter half of 2007 had been extremely frustrating because of the plantar fasciitis, my motivation to continue athletic activities in the future had actually remained high. I had enjoyed the experience in Kona so much that I was highly motivated to do another iron-distance event in the near future. Although I had been more than satisfied with my performance in Kona, I wanted to see if I might be able to improve my time the next time around. I had been further inspired by the stories of my friends who had done Ironman Austria earlier in the year. Toward the end of the year, a group of athletes with Boca Hawaii, led by Raul himself, had been starting to make plans for a trip to Ironman Brazil in May 2008. After attending the first organizational meeting for the Brazil trip, I immediately decided that I was in. The opportunity to go and race in a place like Florianopolis, with a group of good friends and with a native Brazilian as our coach and guide, seemed way too good too pass up. As a bonus, we planned excursions to the Amazon and then to Rio de Janeiro after the race. Not only was I envisioning having a great race, but I was also looking forward to a fabulous vacation afterwards.

The next few months were essentially a rebuilding phase for me. By January 2008, the plantar fasciitis had completely gone away, so I was able to start running again without any pain. That same month, I joined the Boca cycling clinic, and some of us made a point of going for at least a short run after all of our rides. I was thrilled to be able to resume running on a regular basis. With my enthusiasm renewed, I was soon again immersed in a full schedule of endurance triathlon training. With no small amount of overconfidence, and again seemingly oblivious to the possibility of any further setbacks, I was already looking forward to setting a personal record in Brazil. The course looked challenging enough, but definitely easier than Kona, so I set a primary goal for myself of finishing in 15 hours or under, which definitely seemed feasible, as long as I continued training as consistently as I had done in the past. It was in the bag, or so I thought.

For several years, athletic training had been, to say the least, a major focus in my life. At certain times it had, in fact, been my primary focus. I viewed my life as having five main areas to which I devoted most of my time and energy—my work, my relationships with my two daughters and granddaughter, my relationship with Joni, my household responsibilities, and training. I had managed to maintain a fairly full schedule at work, and, being self-employed, I was fortunate to have the flexibility to always make sure that work activities didn't interfere too much with my training schedule. I had usually been able to take care of enough household responsibilities to prevent the place from getting too chaotic and disorganized. I had also managed to maintain a fairly good relationship with Joni, although I must admit there were times when my devotion to athletics definitely caused some tension in the relationship.

I had also managed to find enough time to maintain great relationships with both my daughters and my granddaughter, and I was happy that things seemed to be going relatively smoothly in all their lives. Jen had been through a divorce around the time when I had first been getting into triathlons. That had been a challenging time for her, but she had dealt with it remarkably well and was moving ahead nicely in her career and in her life more generally. Nes had been through a number of personal struggles during her adolescence and early adulthood, and her struggles had periodically necessitated more of my attention. By 2008, however, she had managed to graduate from college, had a good steady job, and a fairly stable relationship with a young man I really liked named Omar. Her life seemed to be on a positive track for the most part, although I have to say that it was still like pulling teeth to get her to keep her room clean.

Then, in March 2008, some major personal problems took center stage in my younger daughter's life, and I found myself confronted with some difficult choices. Although Nes prided herself in being independent in a lot of ways, I could see that she needed a lot more of my support and guidance at that time, and it was evident to me that the balance in my life had to shift. Inevitably, that meant less time and energy available for training. For the first time since I had started participating in triathlons, my participation in training sessions with the Boca group began to dwindle, and I was forced to reconsider whether I could realistically make the trip to Brazil. Despite the difficult time that she was going through, Nes actually encouraged me to go ahead with the Brazil trip, because I had already bought my ticket, obtained my visa, and had even been to the doctor for all my shots in preparation for the trip. Under the circumstances, however, it was very clear to me that it was not right to leave home for the best part of a month and put my personal goals before the needs of my daughter, so I decided to pull the plug on the trip.

I have never had any regrets about the decision to pull out of the trip to Brazil. There is no doubt in my mind that it was absolutely the right thing to do, and I'm very glad, in fact, that I had not become so absorbed with my drive for personal accomplishment that I lost sight of my daughter's needs. At the same time, I did feel disappointed that I was not able to go to Brazil and set that personal record that I felt was well within my grasp. I had set it firmly in my mind as a goal that I wanted to achieve, and I have always been very committed to accomplishing my goals once they are clearly set, so it was definitely hard to put that goal on hold.

Without a clear focus for the rest of the year, I gradually began to lose some of my motivation to train as consistently as I had previously done. Nevertheless, I did continue to participate in a few events. Before I pulled out of the Brazil trip, I had done the Lanikai Triathlon, at which time I was still in pretty good shape, so I managed to finish second in my age group. I'm sure that by now it won't surprise you to learn, however, that there were only four of us in that age group. My only other triathlon of the year was the Honolulu Triathlon in May, although by then I had already slacked off on the training and didn't have a particularly good race. I decided to skip the Honu 70.3 race in June because I knew I just wasn't ready for it. After that, I didn't have a great desire to enter many races. In September, I did half of the Honolulu Century Ride as one of the escorts for a group of participants from Japan, which was a lot of fun and didn't require too much effort. In order to have something to motivate me to keep up some training, I did decide to enter the Val Nolasco Half Marathon in November. By the time race day arrived, however, I hadn't done as much running as I should have done if I had wanted to perform to the best of my ability, so I ended up just taking my time and not really racing it. Although I didn't feel that I had accomplished much, I enjoyed just participating in the race and had fun running alongside Marsha Kitagawa for the last few miles, during which time I found myself, for the umpteenth time, trying to convince her that she should do an iron-distance event some day.

In terms of athletic accomplishments, the one bright area for the year was my swimming, thanks in no small part to Asako Shimazu, who had endured back surgery in April of that year following a skiing accident, and Wendy Miki, a diehard triathlete who has completed many iron-distance races and has also endured more than her share of injuries and misfortunes over the years. Incidentally, Wendy became Wendy Miki Glaus after she married Eric Glaus, another hardcore triathlete if there ever was one, in November of that year—a match made in triathlon heaven. Over the previous year or two, Asako and Wendy had helped to keep me motivated enough to keep coming out for Stefan's group swims on Tuesday and Friday mornings almost every week. We rarely missed a workout, even on those winter days when the water temperature seemed like it was barely above freezing, although in reality, it probably never gets much below 70 degrees in Hawai'i. How spoiled we are! As a result of all that regular swimming, I was able to perform well enough to feel very satisfied with my effort in the Waikiki Roughwater Swim on Labor Day. Then, a little later in the year, I was able to set a personal record for the 2000-meter distance at the Turkey Swim, a fun event which is sponsored by Nu'uanu YMCA, and which is held at Ala Moana Beach every year just before Thanksgiving. That was my big accomplishment for 2008. It wasn't quite what a personal record in Brazil would have been, but at least it was something.

Chapter 19

Second Time Around

By the end of 2008, I was greatly relieved that Nes seemed to be in a more stable place in her life. She had, in fact, by that time recently completed a move to southern California to join her boyfriend, Omar, who had been stationed there a little earlier in the year. Consequently, I began to feel free to devote more time to training consistently again, although my earlier lack of consistency, combined with the usual excess of eating over the holidays, had left me in considerably less than tip-top shape, particularly when it came to biking and running. Around that time, I was invited to join a small group of athletes who were going to be training with Tim Marr, who had by then firmly established himself as one of Hawai'i's top professional triathletes and who was also in the process of getting started as a head coach in his own right. We had all trained with Boca

Hawaii in the past, and Tim had sometimes been one of our coaches there. Over the course of time, some of us had become interested in joining a smaller group that was a little less intense than many of the Boca training groups seemed to have become. In addition, most of us were a little older (and considerably slower) than the majority of the people training with Boca at that time, so Tim's group seemed to be a more mellow alternative. As it turned out, I liked it so much that I have continued to train with this group of friends ever since then. In retrospect, I can see that the change of groups reflected a subtle change in my orientation to athletics, which has continued to evolve since that time, although I didn't become fully conscious of the change until over a year later.

"Teem Marr," as our team has unofficially come to be called, based on the way Tim's lovely Brazilian wife, Mariane, pronounces his first name, was comprised of a great group of athletes. The composition of the group has changed a little since the beginning of 2009, but many members of the original group have remained pretty much ever-present, including Karen Sanders, Lilian Kanai, Chuck Miller and his wife Stephanie Marshall, Jodie Hagerman, Lori McCarney, Shelley White, and last but not least, our youngest member and honorary senior citizen, Andrea Huston. Along the way, we have had some great times, not only in training but also at numerous very enjoyable social gatherings. It has truly been a privilege and an honor to train with such a positive group of people, all of whom are not only dedicated athletes but also really fine human beings.

Throughout 2009, Teem Marr trained for several different events, eventually culminating in a wonderful trip to race in Ironman Western Australia in December. During the year, a few people left our original group, but we were joined by a couple of new members, Rose Paradise and Pomai Jones, who both turned out to be excellent athletes and great permanent additions to the group. Pomai, in fact, subsequently qualified for Kona in 2011, where he distinguished himself with a great performance.

Initially, the year 2009 did not get off to a great start for me. As a result of slacking off on the training and overindulging during the holidays, when we started training in January, my overall fitness level was at the lowest point that it had been since I had started doing triathlons in 2002. As a result, many of the workouts, particularly the biking and running, were really hard work at first. I found myself really struggling to regain the positive attitude toward training that had previously seemed to come so easily. Toward the end of January, Andrea and I entered Sharon's Run, a 10K event, which was held as a benefit for the Epilepsy Foundation of Hawai'i. At the time, Andrea was still nursing a broken hand from a biking accident a little earlier that month. Consequently, neither of us was in particularly good shape, but I was so out of shape that I struggled to even finish the race and ended up having to walk part of the way. It was an ignominious beginning to the year.

To add to my misery, a few weeks later I tripped and fell while I was out on one of our long Sunday morning training runs near Makapu'u and either cracked or seriously bruised a rib, which remained painful enough to keep me out of much of the action for a couple of weeks. Then, just when I thought I was ready to get back to some serious training, I started getting some pain in my right knee. Initially it wasn't too bad and I assumed it would go away after a while, but instead it gradually got worse to the point where I couldn't ignore it any longer. It finally came to a head when we were doing a swim/run workout at Kaimana Beach with Teem Marr one Saturday morning. I had just come out of the water and barely started the run when the pain became so sharp that I just had to stop and walk back to my truck. I knew at that point that, whatever the problem was, it wasn't going to get better on its own. A few days later, I had an appointment with my primary care physician who sent me for an MRI. It confirmed what both he and I had suspected—a torn medial meniscus. I was scheduled for arthroscopic surgery on April 15th. That obviously meant a lot more time away from training. At that point, I was completely frustrated with my situation. I just couldn't seem to get back on track.

Fortunately, the tide subsequently began to turn. My orthopedic surgeon did a great job on the knee, and, with the help of some physical therapy, I was able to get back to a full training schedule within a couple of months. During that time, I had to miss out on the Lanikai Triathlon, the Honolulu Triathlon and the Honu races, all of which I had originally planned to do. But the good news was, by the time my rehabilitation was complete, it was still early enough in the year to give me a good chance of being ready for Western Australia.

Incidentally, Honu 2009 turned out to be a great race for Teem Marr, as both Chuck Miller and Lori McCarney were able to qualify for Kona in their respective age groups. I was happy for them, as I felt they had both always been dedicated, hard-working athletes who really deserved to have the opportunity to race at Kona. As I indicated earlier, Chuck could actually have taken the Kona slot that I ended up getting in 2006, but he was not able to do so at that time because of other commitments. Consequently, I was particularly pleased that he finally got another chance to go to the world championship.

By the time I resumed serious training in June, I knew that I had a lot of catching up to do, and I think I earned a bit of a reputation in the group as someone who always wanted to do a little bit extra. For example, if the group was planning to start a ride at 7:00 a.m. on a Saturday morning, I would often get started at 6:00 a.m. before joining up with the group for the rest of the workout. That way I was able to get in a few extra miles to help make up for all the training that I had missed. Actually, I have often felt I needed to do a bit more than many of the other athletes that I have trained with, partly because I feared that I wouldn't otherwise be able to keep up with them and partly because I felt that doing a bit extra would give me more confidence that I could go the full distance in whatever race I happened to be training for. Perhaps I also still felt a need to compensate in some way for that same old "inherent mediocrity" as an athlete. I still had a way to go to get to a point of complete acceptance.

In addition, although I always very much enjoyed the camaraderie of the group, my focus at that time was still primarily on personal accomplishment, and secondarily on improving my performance whenever possible. After the disappointments of missing out on my marathon PR in 2007 and then having to pull out of the Brazil trip in 2008, I was absolutely determined to achieve my goal of setting a personal record in Western Australia, so I set about training for it accordingly.

A number of important changes took place in my life over the course of 2009. In March of that year, Joni and I had broken up after being together for over 6 years. Although we had a good relationship in many respects, and have since been able to remain friends, our lifestyles and priorities were very different, and those differences finally came to a head. On the other hand, things were going well with everyone in my family, so my mind was more at ease in that regard. The month of April 2009 saw the birth of my second granddaughter, La'i, who has proved to be a wonderful addition to our family. The net result of all these various developments was that I was once again able to devote more time and energy to training, and I threw myself back into it with renewed vigor.

Beginning in early June, I started to develop a training plan for the period leading up to the race in Western Australia, which at that time was 27 weeks away. I planned to use the same general format that had served me well when I was training for Kona, so I began setting up a tentative schedule for much of the summer, during which time I was doing a considerable amount of my training either on my own or informally with small groups of friends. This time, however, I did not lay out a detailed schedule all the way through to the race. That was because I knew I was soon going to be doing a lot of my training with Teem Marr once our Western Australia group formally got started later in the summer, and I wasn't sure exactly what the group schedule would be. Even before the group officially started, Tim began sending us a suggested training schedule each week, so I got into a routine similar to the one that had served me well in 2006, comparing what I had tentatively planned with the schedule that Tim had sent to us and then blending the two into something that I felt would suit my personal needs.

Once the group training formally started, I found that I was not motivated to be as diligent about laying out the details of my own training program for Western Australia as I had been for Kona in 2006. In addition, I became somewhat more flexible in the implementation of my plan, often making last minute modifications in order to coordinate plans with some of my Teem Marr comrades. This change in my level of diligence occurred partly because I was training with the group and, therefore, didn't really need to design my own training program. If I wanted to, I could just go out and do whatever was called for in the group's training schedule. In retrospect, however, I think that the change was also another subtle reflection of the change in orientation toward athletics that was slowly taking place within me. I was still passionate about training and still firmly focused on achieving the goal that I had set for myself in Western Australia. I was not, however, quite as driven as I had been when training for Kona in 2006. I was certainly going down under with the intention of racing to the very best of my ability, but I was also looking at the trip as an opportunity for a nice vacation with some good friends in an interesting and scenic part of Australia that I had never visited before. In contrast, when I went to Kona, although I was both happy and grateful that many of my family members and friends were there to support me, I wasn't looking at it in any way as a social trip or a vacation. My focus at that time had been strictly business.

To give myself some short-term goals to aim for, I decided to again enter the Dick Evans 112-mile road race on September 6th, followed as usual by the Waikiki Roughwater Swim the next day. I tried to get some of my friends from Teem Marr to join me in the Dick Evans race, but unfortunately there were no takers. I was going to be on my own for that one. I also signed up for the Honolulu Marathon Readiness Series, a series of five races leading up to the marathon in December, starting with the Norman Tamanaha 15K, which had been moved from its former schedule in March to about the middle of August. Signing up for all those events helped to motivate me to maintain a fairly rigorous training schedule during the summer. In addition to my regular ocean swims, Andrea and I joined a summer swim clinic with Boca Hawaii that met twice a week at Palolo pool. I also went on a series of increasingly long bike rides with the Teem Marr gang and some other friends, particularly Emy Ching, who always seemed to be ready and willing to join me out on the road. I also started riding Tantalus again regularly every week and maintained a consistent schedule of running. By the end of August 2009, I had almost forgotten about my knee surgery just four months earlier, and I was feeling fitter and stronger than I had done at any time since I developed the plantar fasciitis in July 2007.

Unfortunately, the Dick Evans race again turned out to be a bit of a disappointment for me, although certainly not as bad as it had been in 2007. With all the training I had been doing, I had hoped that I might be able to set a personal record for the event. However, that goal soon evaporated when a flat rear tire going up the hill on Kunia Road about 35 miles into the race put me right at the very back of the pack. After that, it was just a long day riding on my own. Andrea had planned to meet me at the final aid station in Kailua and ride with me back to the finish, but unfortunately she had some mechanical problems with her bike in Waimānalo, so I was on my own all the way. I had just come down the hill from Makapuʻu point and was only about a mile from the finish when I had another flat tire, this time on the front wheel. After a quick stop to consider my options, I decided to just keep riding rather than stay there and change the tube because I was so close to the finish and, by that time, I just wanted it over. I knew it was a bit risky, and I have to admit I did come close to losing control as I was going around the corner from Kalanianaʻole Highway into Kalama Valley. But I took it slowly and eventually made it across the finish line. After that experience, I decided to forget about the racing tires that I had put on the bike and stick with the puncture-resistant ones. Gator Skins are my favorite. I figure it's better to lose a minute or two to increased rolling resistance than to risk losing even more time to flat tires. The one positive thing about Dick Evans was that, despite the two flat tires, I was still able to finish the race well within the allotted time limit. I did feel disappointed that I had missed out on the personal record, but at the same time I felt very pleased with my effort because I knew I had given it my best shot under the circumstances. By that time, I was getting better at being able to tell myself that was all I could do, and I had every reason to feel satisfied with that. In addition, I still felt strong at the end, so I was happy and encouraged that I could feel my endurance coming back again. It gave my confidence a big boost as I looked ahead to the rest of the training for IMWA.

The Waikiki Roughwater Swim, which, as usual, took place the day after the Dick Evans race, was really tough that year. Before the start, we were told that there would be only a slight current against us, but I think they must have been messing with our minds. In reality, the current was so strong that there were times when I wondered if I was ever going to make it to the next marker buoy. I ended up being in the water for 2 hours and 45 minutes before I finally dragged myself up the sand to the finish line. In terms of time, it was the longest swim I had ever done in my life. Even when I had done a 5K swim in training a few years earlier it hadn't taken me that long. I swore that day that I would never do the Waikiki Roughwater Swim again—but read on.

I was able to keep training consistently for the rest of the year, and we had some excellent workouts with the group. One of the highlights was a trip to Kona in October, which allowed us to support Chuck and Lori in their contest with the infamous world championship course and, at the same time, put in a very hard weekend of training. Our workouts included, among other delights, a 90-mile bike ride on the Friday before the race and a 16-mile run on Monday after the race, both in scorching heat. I was very thankful for the assistance of our good friend, Eric Sanders, who volunteered to drive the sag wagon for us on both days. His support certainly made the workouts a lot less aversive than they would otherwise have been. Once again I was reminded that the support of friends and family makes the ordeals that are inevitably a part of endurance athletics so much easier to endure.

The Ford Ironman World Championship took place on the Saturday, which turned out to be a tough day for both Chuck and Lori, particularly Lori. They both put in excellent performances on the swim and the bike, but then had to deal with some major challenges on the run. Chuck had, for some time prior to the race, been having some problems with pain in his feet, which inevitably slowed him down considerably. Fortunately, he was able to keep going and finish the race in a very respectable time, although I know that his run was much slower than it would have been if he had been completely healthy.

Lori was not so fortunate. She had been having problems with pain in her back, which had suddenly come on about a couple of weeks before the race. She had desperately, but not entirely successfully, been trying to treat her back with chiropractics and massage. Although obviously in some discomfort by the time she left T2, she initially seemed to be running well enough to be able finish the race with plenty of time to spare. By the time she came back into Kailua town at around mile 10, however, her back was seriously starting to give out. I could see she was really struggling, so that the upper part of her body was bent forward at about a 45-degree angle as she shuffled along. I began to worry about whether or not she was going to be able to make it.

What ensued was one of the most amazing feats of determination that I have ever witnessed. A couple of hours later, long after the sun had gone down, I decided to go for a run out onto the highway to look for Lori and make sure she was able to continue. I'm not sure what I would have done if she had not been able to keep going, but heading out seemed better than just waiting in town for her. On the way out, around mile 24, I saw Chuck coming in, slowly but steadily, so I was relieved to know that he was definitely going to make it. I got all the way to about mile 21 before I finally saw Lori. I had been hoping that her back might have improved at least a little, but it had gotten even worse. By that time, she was bent over at almost a 90-degree angle, and just could not straighten up at all. I was utterly amazed that she had been able to keep going for so long in that condition. Despite her obvious discomfort, she simply refused to give up and kept moving forward as best she could, although the effort was so great that she was forced to stop for breaks at increasingly frequent intervals. For a while, I thought she would have just about enough time to make it to the finish within the time limit. The more time went by, however, the more she became almost doubled over and the slower her pace grew.

As we got closer to town, two other friends came along to check on Lori's progress. One was her chiropractor, Dr. Jesse Cracknell, who often volunteers his services at athletic events. The other was our good friend, Anne Perry, an excellent all-around athlete who subsequently went on to have a great race of her own in Kona in 2010. From the sidelines, we encouraged Lori to keep going, although she was so determined not to quit, I don't think she really needed any encouragement. By the time she got to the turn at the top of Palani Road, it was evident that she was going to have to pick up the pace if she were going to get to the finish line by midnight. Unfortunately, her body had nothing left to give, and her pace continued to decrease.

Refusing to give up, but with great difficulty, she painfully made her way down Palani Road and around the left turn onto Kuakini Highway. She was less than a mile from the finish line when midnight came and time expired. By that time, she was literally ready to collapse. All we could do was help her to lie down on the ground, completely exhausted. A few minutes later, the paramedics came for her. It was a heartbreaking ending to an absolutely incredible effort. Fortunately, Lori was able to bounce back amazingly quickly from her ordeal, and was soon back again in training with us all for the race in Western Australia. She never did really figure out exactly what went wrong with her back, and thankfully it has never happened again.

I'm happy to say that the rest of our training went by without any serious problems, and everyone seemed to be well prepared to take on the challenge that we were going to face in Western Australia. Around the end of November 2009, we left Honolulu on the long journey to the west coast of Australia, some of us going by way of Auckland and then directly on to Perth, and others going via Sydney. There was actually a large contingent of athletes from Hawai'i. In addition to those of us from Teem Marr, there was a group of around 20 athletes who had trained with Boca Hawaii, plus a few other Hawai'i-based athletes who had been doing their training alone. It was good to know that there would be so many familiar faces in the race.

By the time we arrived in Busselton, the little seaside town that is the venue for the race in Western Australia, I was feeling strong and confident, maybe a little overconfident once again. All of our training had gone extremely well, so I knew I had the necessary endurance, and I was convinced that I was going to have a good race. One of the reasons we had all chosen this particular race was because it looked like such a great destination, but another reason was because it looked like a relatively easy course, as iron-distance courses go. Consequently, it seemed like an excellent course for those of us who were aiming for a personal record.

The weather in Busselton during the days leading up to the race had been just what we expected, with early morning lows around 60 degrees and daytime highs in the low 80s—seemingly ideal for those of us from Hawai'i. In addition, when we rode part of the course prior to the race, the wind seemed relatively light and generally favorable for the race. Overall, the conditions looked excellent. Some time prior to the race, I had talked to one of our friends, Paul Patterson, an Australian who was returning to Busselton to do the race for a second time. It was Paul who had told me, based on his experience the first time around, that I would have the race of my life there. It seemed to me that all was set for Paul's prediction to come true.

On race day, the weather looked good initially, and the swim, in the clear blue waters of the Indian Ocean, went exceptionally well. It was the first time I had ever competed in the wet suit that I had originally bought in 2005. Combined with near perfect ocean conditions, the added buoyancy of the wet suit enabled me to come out of the water with the clock showing a time of 1:39. I would actually have been perfectly satisfied with that time, but then I realized that the clock registered the time that had elapsed since the professionals had started, which was 15 minutes before the age groupers. I had actually completed the swim in 1:24—by far my fastest ever swim over the 2.4-mile distance. You may recall that it had taken me as much as 32 minutes longer in Kona. I was thrilled that the race had got off to such a good start.

The first of the three laps of the bike course also went extremely well. With a time of under 2:10, I found myself wondering about the possibility of breaking 6:30 for my bike split. I had originally been hoping for around 7 hours, so I was really stoked at that point. In fact, I was so confident that everything was going to go well that I set my sights on the goal of breaking 14 hours for the race as a whole.

On the second lap of the bike course, however, things started to become more difficult. First, at about the 50-mile point, I finally had to stop for what turned into a rather lengthy bathroom break. Then, when I got back on the road again, I noticed that I seemed to be working a lot harder to maintain the pace of my first lap. The wind had definitely picked up since the start, and it seemed that, whichever way the road turned, the wind was never behind me. It constantly felt like either a headwind or a crosswind.

I also gradually began to notice that it was getting a lot hotter than I had expected it to be, although I don't think I realized the full extent of the heat at that point because I didn't seem to be sweating that much. I suppose I wasn't used to the dry heat of that area. I was more accustomed to sweating profusely, and hydrating accordingly, in the much more humid air that we get in Hawai'i. I thought I had been hydrating sufficiently up to that point, but, by the time I got to the start of the third lap, my legs were cramping so badly that I had to get off the bike and sit down for a few minutes before I could continue. Fortunately, I was able to stop near two of our friends who had come all the way to Australia to support us, Rick Keene, Lori's boyfriend who was always very supportive not only of Lori but also of our entire group, and Pomai Jones, who had started to do some training with us in the middle of the year but did not feel he was yet ready to do the race in Busselton. Drawing inspiration from those two friendly faces, I forced myself to get moving again, but the rest of the third lap was practically torture. My legs would start cramping again every time I tried to pedal beyond a relatively low level of intensity, so I was constantly having to back off on my effort. At one point, coming back into town against the wind, I couldn't believe I was down to less than 10 miles an hour on a completely flat road surface. I felt a huge sense of relief when I finally made it to T2 with a bike split of 7:15, roughly 45 minutes longer than the 6:30 I had been hoping for after that first lap. At that point, I never wanted to see a bike again.

It was when I dragged myself out of T2 and tried to start running that I really began to realize how hot it was. Somebody told me that it was in excess of 95 degrees on the run course, and I later heard that the temperature had actually reached well over 100 degrees in some places in the area around Busselton. I had taken in a lot of fluid in transition, but I was still cramping intermittently, so the best I could do was to run a short distance, then walk for a while, a pattern that I continued pretty much throughout the whole 26.2 miles. I must have consumed gallons of water and whatever sports drink they had at the aid stations, as well as a fair amount of cola, in order to stay hydrated. But, toward the end of the run my digestive system seemed to go on strike, and it even became difficult to force more than a few drops of water down. At that point, the only thing that really seemed to hit the spot was the saltiness of the Vegemite, which was available at some aid stations on a little wooden stick and at others on a small piece of bread. I couldn't manage to swallow any of the bread at all, so I would just lick the Vegemite off, and then throw the bread away. Not exactly the kind of thing you would do at a dinner party, but it helped to keep me going that evening.

After the sun had gone down it got a little easier to keep moving forward, and I wasn't cramping as much. However, I did feel fatigued, much more than I had during the run in Kona, so it was still very slow going. It seemed like a lot of the people I knew in the Hawai'i contingent were also having a tough race, judging by the looks on their faces and the remarks that we exchanged when we passed each other during the three out-and-back laps of the run course. Even Eric Glaus, a superb and highly experienced triathlete, who had sometimes assisted Tim with our coaching and who looks like he has the strength and athletic ability to be a mixed martial arts fighter, was obviously struggling. On the other hand, Eric's wife, Wendy, seemed to be one of the few people who breezed through the race without much difficulty. For myself, there were times when I really wondered if I was going to make it. At some points, I had to dig deeper than I had ever done before just to keep moving forward slowly.

As I finally approached the finish, I got a little bit of that adrenaline that always seems to kick in when you know you are almost home, but it was barely enough to allow me to pick up the pace just a little and try to look as fresh as possible as I exchanged high fives with some of the cheering spectators along the chute leading up to the finish line. I did feel a sense of exhilaration as I crossed the finish line and heard my name being called out as a finisher. It had been an extremely difficult day, but I had hung in there all the way to the finish, and I felt proud of that. At the same time, I was drained, much more so than after Kona, and all I really wanted to do was to stop moving and sit down in the recovery tent. My time for the marathon had been a little over 6 hours, my slowest ever for that distance. Although I actually did manage to achieve my primary race goal, with an overall finish time of 14:42, it had been a very humbling experience and it certainly taught me never to get overconfident when it comes to a race of that distance.

It turned out to be a tough race for almost everyone in the Teem Marr group. Rose Paradise, who is an Aussie now living in Hawai'i, was about the only one from Teem Marr who seemed to have had a good race all around, although even she complained of not feeling well for much of the race. Karen Sanders and Stephanie Marshall made it to the finish, but both seemed to be feeling pretty fatigued by the end. Likewise Lori McCarney and Chuck Miller, for whom Western Australia was their second iron-distance race in less than two months. I was happy for Lori that she was at least able to finish after her huge disappointment in Kona, although I know she felt that she was capable of doing a lot better. Chuck soldiered on to the finish despite continuing problems with his feet that again really slowed him down. Lilian Kanai was feeling so drained that she decided to pull out after getting off the bike.

My good training buddy, Andrea Huston, who faces the additional challenge of being a Type 1 diabetic, bravely struggled on to within less than 5 miles of the finish before she finally had to be brought back to the finish area by the medics. Andrea was very disappointed with her inability to finish. She had done one iron-distance event previously in Arizona, on another very hot day, so she knew was capable of finishing the distance, even under challenging conditions. In addition, she had worked hard in training for the race in Busselton, so she had been hoping to significantly improve her performance over Arizona. Consequently, there was unfinished business for her after the race. As I was writing a first draft of this part of the book, Andrea was in the process of preparing for the 2011 Ironman St. George in Utah. This race featured one of the most difficult iron-distance courses in the world, with multiple challenging hills on both the bike and run. She was participating in the race as one of the captains for the Triabetes team, a worthy organization that is dedicated to promoting physical exercise as an important tool in the management of diabetes.

I was definitely hoping that I would be able to report that Andrea had achieved her goal. But, with temperatures in the St. George area reaching well into the mid 90s on race day, she was forced to pull out before completing the bike course. The fact that about 20% of all the entrants, an unusually high percentage, were not able to finish the race that day is a testament to the difficulty of the course and the conditions. To her great credit, Andrea did not let it discourage her. Like all of our friends, she is a committed and determined athlete who does not give up. Since returning from St. George, she has continued training consistently, and I'm sure there will be further athletic achievements for her in the future.

In the aftermath of the race at Busselton, a few members of our group were dehydrated to the point of needing IV fluids to help speed their recovery. Fortunately, however, nobody suffered any lasting harm, and all of us were actually able to bounce back surprisingly quickly after the race. By the next day, in fact, we were all feeling good enough to go out and enjoy the excellent food and wine at our post race celebration at one the many great wineries in the Margaret River area. The icing on the cake for this trip was that everyone in our group was then able to enjoy a great vacation in various parts of Australia after the race.

The race in Western Australia provided another important learning experience for me. I know I came away with a much deeper appreciation of the fact that, although some courses may be more difficult or more challenging than others, there is never going to be any such thing as an easy iron-distance course. You just have to respect the distance no matter where the race takes place or how relatively easy the course looks. In addition, you can't expect that conditions are going to be the way you would like them to be ideally. Consequently, you need to be psychologically prepared to deal with the unexpected on race day, whatever that happens to be. I'm sure that I already knew these things intellectually, but there is nothing like personal experience as a way of ramming the point home.

I also came to the recognition that the accomplishment of setting a personal record was ultimately not as important as knowing that I had taken on the challenge and given it all that I had. By the time I got to Western Australia, I was coming closer to fully accepting the reality of my mediocre athletic ability. I certainly did not feel any need to compare my performance to that of others, and my focus for the race continued to be on personal accomplishment.

There was, however, still another issue that I had not even given a lot of thought to at that time, let alone completely come to terms with. The issue was that, in my athletic activities, I was still very much focused on specific goal achievement as the primary measure of personal accomplishment. Over the years, I had at least learned from some of my own experiences that, even if I did not achieve the goal I had set for myself, I could still give myself partial credit for having given it my best effort. Nevertheless, I still had a tendency to get down on myself on those occasions when, for whatever reason, I did not achieve my goal. At least at a subconscious level, I still viewed it as a personal failure. One of the things that happened in Western Australia was that I set myself up for some degree of disappointment when I adjusted my goals upward after the swim and the first lap of the bike course but then failed to achieve those new goals. After the race, I had mixed feelings about my performance, fortunately more on the positive side than the negative, but there was at least a trace of self-deprecation mixed with the sense of accomplishment. On the positive side, I definitely felt good about the fact that I was able to achieve my original goals for the race despite the difficult conditions. At the same time, however, in the back of my mind, that old thought that I should have been able to do better kept popping up from time to time.

It was not until I was writing this book that I began to seriously consider the implications of this issue. In the process, I began to reflect not only my own experiences in races but also on those of friends like Lori and Andrea who were forced to deal with major disappointments. In the process, I have come to a deeper understanding that goal achievement, while certainly very satisfying in some ways, is ultimately not as important as the process of simply taking on the challenge and doing the best you can under whatever the circumstances happen to be. When I considered Lori's almost superhuman effort at Kona or Andrea's courageous performances at Busselton and St. George, it occurred to me that from my perspective it was not at all important that they had not been able to achieve their original goals for those races. I had the utmost admiration for their efforts and in no way would I ever have viewed their performances as personal failures. In each of those instances, they had pushed themselves to their absolute limits. What more could one possibly ask of anyone? Surely anyone who did that could only be regarded as a winner.

Chapter 20

A Change in Focus

As 2009 turned into 2010, I found myself gradually re-evaluating my priorities. It was probably a continuation of some of the subtle changes that had been taking place, primarily at a sub-conscious level, during the previous year. At first, I began to notice that it was becoming increasingly difficult for me to keep motivating myself to maintain the volume of training that I had been doing during the months leading up to our trip to Western Australia and that I had actually been doing for much of the time throughout the previous 7 or 8 years.

Together with Andrea, I began the year with a focus on training for the Hilo International Marathon in March. I was able to get through all the training sessions that we planned, but some of the long endurance workouts seemed like hard work, and I just wasn't enjoying them as much as I had in the past. On Presidents' Day, for example, we did the Great Aloha Run from downtown Honolulu to the Aloha Stadium, a distance of just over 8 miles, and then pushed ourselves to run all the way back to the start of the race. I even managed to run an extra mile from where I parked my car to the start of the race, and then another extra mile back to the car at the end of our run. Up to a point, I was pleased that I was able to run over 18 miles and felt I could have kept going if I really had to. But it didn't feel like a whole lot of fun, and I could tell that my heart wasn't in it the way it would have been in previous years.

I found also that I wasn't really willing to make a commitment to any particular time goal for the race in Hilo. When we first talked about doing the event, I had vague thoughts about aiming for that elusive 4:20 marathon goal, which had been dormant since the Loch Ness marathon in 2007. As time went by, however, I knew that I wasn't willing to put in the amount of training that would have been required to get my running fitness up to the level at which I might have had a realistic chance of reaching that goal. Consequently, training became a matter of just doing enough to make sure that I could finish the race without too much difficulty.

The race in Hilo turned out to be another ordeal in at least one way. Don't get me wrong; it is a great event in almost every way. In particular, it features a beautiful course, particularly the first half, much of which travels along winding sections of the old road from the Hāmākua Coast down into Hilo town. I would highly recommend the race as a destination event. If I were to do it again, however, I would be sure to incorporate some regular downhill running in my training because the net elevation loss over the first 10 miles is over 500 feet, and the total elevation loss must be considerably more because of all the ups and downs along the way. As I went into the race, I did not feel that I had trained hard enough to commit to any specific time goal, so I just told myself that I would do the best I could and see what happened. I knew by then that I probably would not even come close to my old time goal of 4:20, but I did find that I was able to run surprisingly well for about two thirds of the race. I actually seemed to be on track for about a 4:30 finish up until around mile 18, when my quads gradually started to tighten up. Initially, I couldn't understand why that was happening, but then it suddenly dawned on me that it was probably because of all the downhill running during the first half of the race. My legs just weren't used to that. My pace became progressively slower, and it became harder and harder to keep running, although I just couldn't allow myself to walk except for brief distances at the aid stations. Eventually, I crossed the finish line in a time of about 4:50, by which point I was telling myself that I had no desire to do another marathon for a long time. One of the good things about the Hilo marathon is that the athletes are given free beer after the race. I was very grateful for mine that day.

A little later in the year, I did have another of those "icing on the cake" moments at the Lanikai Triathlon in April. In my first year in the 65 to 69 age group, I was able to finish in first place. By now you will not be surprised to learn that there were, however, only three of us in the age group. Despite that success, my heart still wasn't in the training as much as it had been in the past. Subsequently, I became less consistent in my attendance at training sessions. Although I trained hard at times, I also found myself slacking off at other times. The consequences ultimately became very clear at Honu, where my performance was rather disappointing in comparison with what I had hoped, in vain, that it might be.

At least in part because I hadn't put 100% into the training, I didn't enjoy the race at Honu as much as I had done in the past. I had taken on the challenge, and I had a specific time goal in mind as I usually did. But, because of my lack of complete commitment to the training process, I really wasn't able to perform at the level at which I thought I was capable. Not surprisingly, the sense of accomplishment was muted at best. All three segments of the race seemed to be really hard work, and, by the time I finished I again found myself thinking that I had no great desire to put myself through this ordeal again in the immediate future.

It so happened that there was an interesting, and perhaps ironic, turn of events at Honu. Despite my disappointing performance, it turned out that I was the second registered Hawai'i resident finisher in my age group, coming in a long way behind perennial top dog, Ed LeTourneau. I had naturally assumed that Ed would take the Hawai'i resident slot for Kona because he had told me earlier in the year that he probably would. After finishing the race at Honu, however, Ed apparently decided not to take it. I was next in line, but I was not even aware of it at the time. After the race, I was feeling hot, tired, and grouchy, and I had not bothered to wait around for the award ceremony and the announcement of the Kona slots. I just wanted to get back to the condo that I was sharing with Karen and Eric Sanders, jump into the shower, and take a good, long nap. On the way back to our rented van, I was so spaced out that I even fell off my bike when I foolishly tried to ride over the cinders of lava in the makeshift parking lot. Had I stayed at the finish for the awards, I could have taken the slot and gone to Kona for a second time. Because I had left, however, I was blissfully unaware, as I took a much-needed nap, that the slot had rolled down to me.

Later that evening when we talked on the phone, it was Lori McCarney who informed me that the Kona slot had rolled down to me. My initial reaction was not so much one of regret or disappointment for having let the opportunity pass, as it certainly would have been under the same circumstances in previous years, but guilt. I realize now that I had no obligation to take the Kona slot and, therefore, no real reason to feel guilty, but that was my immediate reaction at the time. The guilt came up at least in part because I knew very well that Lori desperately wanted to go back to Kona to take care of her unfinished business after her disappointment of the previous year. I wished that I could somehow have gotten the slot back and passed it on to her. I knew, however, that Kona slots cannot simply be given away, so that would have been impossible, even if I had been there to take it. The guilt was also related partly to the fact that I knew there were many other athletes who would probably have exchanged everything they own for that opportunity to go to Kona. I imagined that, if they had known, they would all have been cursing me for allowing an opportunity like that to pass.

My sense of guilt finally dissipated when I learned that the slot had eventually rolled down to Troy Keipper, a younger athlete who had been training with Boca Hawaii. I knew that Troy had consistently been training hard for several years, so he was certainly deserving of the opportunity. I must admit that I did sometimes wonder what it would have been like to go back to Kona. In retrospect, however, I am actually very glad I wasn't there when the slot rolled down to me. If I had been there, it is likely that I would have felt obligated to take the slot, but I know that I would not have been able to commit myself to the training process the way I had done in 2006. My attitude toward training for both the Hilo Marathon and Honu earlier in the year had clearly confirmed that, if I had taken the Kona slot, I would not have been able to do justice either to the event or to myself. Under the circumstances, it was entirely appropriate that the slot went to someone who was going to be more committed to the process than I could possibly have been at that point in time.

About six weeks after Honu, a group of us from Teem Marr flew up to California to participate in the Vineman 70.3 race in the Sonoma County area. For a number of us, this had been our primary goal race for the year. But, as race day approached, I found, even more than in Western Australia, that I was focused more on the vacation aspect of the trip than on the race itself. When we arrived in Healdsburg a few days before the race, after a tiring overnight journey from Honolulu, the temperature in the middle of the day was a debilitating 105 degrees or more. After we checked into the comfortable vacation home that I was sharing with Jeff and Shelley White, Susan Seah, and my trusty training buddy Andrea, I lay exhausted on the bed at 3:00 in the afternoon seriously thinking about pulling out of the race if the weather conditions were going to be so hot. In previous years, I would never have even entertained such a thought.

Fortunately, the weather was not so extreme on race day, with the temperature reaching a high of "only" about 90 degrees during the middle of the day. Vineman is held in a beautiful area with rolling hills, scenic river valleys, and wide expanses of vineyards and other farmland—another great destination event that I would highly recommend. I felt that I was reasonably well prepared for the race, based on the volume of training that we had done, but I didn't have a lot of motivation to push myself to the limit. By that time, I was definitely more into vacation mode than race mode in many respects. As it turned out, however, I really enjoyed the event—almost as much as I enjoyed the great food and wine that we happily consumed both before and after the race. Because the course was relatively easy in comparison to Honu, I was even able to set a personal record for the 70.3 distance, with a time of about 6:43, even though I wasn't pushing as hard as I might have been able to do if had put more effort into the training. In any event, that was my big achievement for the year. I was happy with the personal record, and I came away from the event feeling perfectly satisfied that I had done the best I could under the circumstances.

After Vineman, I was basically done for 2010 as far as races were concerned. As the year went by, I became aware that I was becoming less and less consistent in my training. I was finding reasons to skip workouts more frequently than I had done in the past, and I often wasn't motivated to try to make them up. It wasn't that I wanted to give up training completely by any means. I was still very much committed to maintaining a high level of physical fitness, and I still greatly enjoyed training with my good friends in Teem Marr, who had in many ways become an important part of my extended family. On the other hand, I had finally reached a point where I didn't want to perpetually have to maintain the high volume of training that was required for long distance endurance events. For a while, I had been telling myself that it was not really the volume of training that was the issue, but the pressure of constantly being on the go, from one activity to another, in all the various areas of my life with little opportunity to simply relax and take life at a leisurely pace. I imagined that, if only I could focus on the training and not have so much going on in other areas, then I wouldn't feel as much pressure. Although that was not a very realistic scenario, I'm sure that it would have been true to some extent. As I began to reduce my professional workload and move toward semi-retired status, however, I realized that the volume of training was indeed a large part of the issue also. I just didn't want to be continually committed to devoting 20 to 30 hours of every week to training and related activities. I wanted and needed to be able to use some of that time for other purposes. In addition, I no longer wanted to be psychologically locked into the ongoing goal of trying to improve my performance in some way in race after race. In short, my priorities were changing. Personal accomplishment and improving my performance were motives that just didn't seem to be as important to me as they had been in previous years.

As I looked back over the years since my first triathlon in 2002, I was very much aware that I had achieved things in my athletic endeavors that I could never even have dreamed of before I started participating in triathlons. I had gone from being a naive, novice triathlete, who was not at all confident that I had the ability to finish even a short, sprint distance triathlon, to being a somewhat seasoned veteran of a considerable number endurance-based athletic events. Along the way, I had participated in numerous triathlons of various distances, as well as several marathons and long distance bike events, and a number of long open-ocean swims. I was particularly proud of the fact that, despite my indubitably mediocre ability as an athlete, I had been able to finish five half-iron- distance races and two full iron-distance races, including the World Championship in Kona. In the process, I had, on numerous occasions, been able to savor the experience of transcending my inherent mediocrity during the course of what had been an incredibly exciting and rewarding journey to my personal Extremistan. In the process, I had brought not just one but several of those highly positive "Black Swans" into my life. By the time Vineman was over in July 2010, I felt extremely satisfied with what I had been able to accomplish. I honestly did not feel that I had anything else to prove to myself, or to anyone else for that matter. Sure, I told myself, I could aim for another PR in a 70.3 or even a full 140.6 race, but somehow those types of goals didn't really seem to be that important to me at that point in my life.

On the morning of Labor Day 2010, perhaps as a round about way of proving a point to myself, I decided on the spur of the moment to enter the Waikiki Roughwater Swim, despite the fact that I had not been swimming more than 2000 meters per week for at least the whole of the previous month. Under those circumstances, I had absolutely no intention of trying to set a personal record or even of trying to finish in any particular time. I didn't even care about performing to the best of my ability. It was a beautiful day, and I just thought that it would be really nice to go for a long swim in the warm, and relatively calm, waters off Waikīkī Beach. As it turned out, I actually wasn't all that far outside my personal record for that particular event. In fact, I ended up finishing well over an hour faster than I had done the previous year. Actually, there's no great significance to that. The only thing it really proves is what a huge difference the ocean currents can make in that event, depending on whether they are favorable or not! Best of all, because of the change in my mindset, I was really able to relax and enjoy the swim much more than I would have done if I had been more focused on improving my performance or achieving a specific goal.

During the first few months of 2011, I continued training quite consistently with Teem Marr, and actually did do some fairly long bike rides with Andrea during her training for Ironman St. George in May, but I never had any great desire to be doing the race with her. I was happy to just go along as a supporter and to enjoy another excellent vacation in the process.

Then, in July of 2011, together with about half a dozen good friends from Teem Marr, I ran the San Francisco Half Marathon. I tried to make a point of doing enough training to be ready for the race, but I must admit that even some of those workouts required more effort than I really wanted to put out. I did not have any specific goals in mind for the race. To tell the truth, I went to San Francisco with the intention of doing the race just for fun and as an excuse for a vacation with my friends. I simply told myself that I would do the best I could and be satisfied with whatever happened on race day, and that is exactly what I did. There was no pressure to perform, and I had a very enjoyable time all around.

After returning from San Francisco, I decided not to set any major athletic goals for myself in the near future. I did enter a few short distance athletic events in the ensuing months, just to give me an incentive to maintain some degree of consistency in my training, but I had no great desire to enter any long distance events. During that time, I became increasingly aware and acceptant of the change in my priorities that had been taking place over the previous year or so. I continued training fairly regularly with some of the gang from Teem Marr, particularly Jodie Hagerman and Karen Sanders, and sometimes with other friends like my long time running buddy, Emy Ching. In addition, I certainly remained firmly committed to a lifestyle that would promote lifelong health and fitness, both physical and psychological. The thing that I started doing differently was choosing to do only as much training as I really felt like doing, and giving myself more permission to take days off whenever I felt like doing so.

As the year 2012 begins, I am continuing to enjoy this flexibility. It has allowed me to devote more of my time to other activities, such as getting some projects done at home—not to mention writing this book! In addition, over the course of the last year, I probably went to more shows on Saturday nights and read more books not related to either my work or my athletic activities than I had done during the previous decade. I also had the time to enjoy other outdoor activities such as hiking on a more regular basis. For the immediate future, my focus will simply be on maintaining physical fitness and enjoying the camaraderie of my training buddies. Maybe at some point in the future, I will become more accomplishment-and performance-oriented again. I really don't know.

Because I am clear about my current focus, I find that I am very much enjoying all of the shorter workouts that I now do. An hour, or even just half an hour, of running or working out on the turbo trainer is enough to leave me feeling invigorated without being physically drained in the way I not infrequently was after some of those six hour plus bike rides and three hour plus runs that training for iron-distance events inevitably involves. In particular, I have been making good use of my old Trek 2500, which now sits pretty much permanently on a turbo trainer on the lanai of my house, looking out toward Diamond Head, so it is available whenever I need it for what is always a pleasant and scenic workout at home. Incidentally, back in 2003 when our training schedule first began to include turbo trainer workouts, I was not at all enthusiastic about having to pedal for any extended period of time in a stationary position. Over the years, however, I have come to appreciate the value of the turbo trainer because it can allow me to get a quality workout in a highly time-efficient manner. On days when I am pressed for time, I can just get on the turbo trainer without having to drive anywhere. For example, one of my favorite short and simple workouts on the turbo trainer is to warm up for 5 minutes, followed by a fairly intense main set of 20 minutes in my hardest gear, with 5 minutes cool down at the end. By the time I'm finished, I feel like I've had a solid workout, and the whole thing, including preparation and clean up, has taken me well under an hour.

When I think about how much time I want to devote to training now, I am sometimes reminded of Dr. Kenneth Cooper's classic book, *Aerobics*, which is credited by many observers as one of the pieces of work that provided the initial impetus for the huge growth of interest and participation in various forms of aerobic exercise since the late 1960s. I originally read the book almost 30 years ago, and it was certainly one of the things that originally motivated me to start exercising more regularly. When I recently perused the book again, it occurred to me that although the book might be considered a bit dated now, in many ways much of its content is still as relevant as it ever was. One of the points that Dr. Cooper makes is that it takes only a relatively modest amount of aerobic exercise, such as 12 minutes of high intensity running 4 days per week, to maintain a very high level of physical fitness. It is probably true that many health and fitness experts would now tend to recommend somewhat more than that. Perhaps a total of around 3 or 4 hours of moderately vigorous exercise over the course of a week might be considered more appropriate as a goal to shoot for. Nevertheless, as Cooper himself implied, if you are doing the amount of training that has to be done for any type of extreme endurance event, you are never going to be doing it solely for physical fitness. Preparing yourself for such an event inevitably involves a far greater volume of training than you will ever need for that purpose alone. As a recreational athlete, if you are going to put in the amount of time that is needed to train for endurance events, you need to have that burning desire not just to be physically fit, but also to accomplish something extraordinary. As I have indicated, I just don't have that that burning desire right now.

Although my priorities have changed over the past couple of years, I can still say without a doubt that I am very glad that I made the decision to enter that first triathlon back in 2002. It set me on a course that has changed my life in a number of important, perhaps critical, ways. I am much fitter and healthier physically. I think that I handle stress more effectively now. In general, I feel better about myself. I can now honestly define myself as an athlete, and I am proud of my athletic accomplishments, particularly my two finishes at Kona and Busselton. At the same time, I can more openly and honestly admit to my own inherent mediocrity as an athlete and even take pride in that mediocrity. It has not prevented me from accomplishing some things that are, at least by my own standards, quite extraordinary. It would, in fact, not be inaccurate to say that in many ways it is that very mediocrity that has allowed me to experience those accomplishments as extraordinary.

For the foreseeable future, the fact of the matter is that I am not planning to do anything particularly extraordinary in my athletic activities, even by my own mediocre standards. I do know, however, that whatever direction my life does take in the future, the extraordinary memories that I have made over the years since my first encounter with triathlon will always be with me. I am also very confident that some of the extraordinary friendships that I have made in the process will endure for many years to come. When all is said and done, perhaps that is really the best reward of all.

Kona 2006: out of the water.

Kona 2006: on to the bike.

Kona 2006: ready to run.

Kona 2006: mission accomplished!

Kona 2006: Brian, Jen and Hina.

Kona 2006: Brian and Laurie celebrate!

Busselton 2009: almost there – what a relief!

Vineman 2010: the joy of crossing the finish line!

Part Three: Endurance Training For The Recreational Athlete

Chapter 21

A Brief Background

I sincerely hope that my account of my athletic endeavors has left you with the thought, "If this guy can do it, I can do it too." If you have never done an endurance triathlon before, and you are now thinking that maybe you are up for the challenge, you may also be asking yourself, "Okay, so how do I go about it?" I hope this final part of the book will help to get you started on the process of answering that question.

I have aimed this part of the book primarily at those of you who identify yourselves as recreational athletes, and more specifically at those of you who are interested in learning more about training for endurance triathlons, particularly iron-distance events, although the same principles could easily be applied to half-iron, Olympic, or even sprint distance events. If you are also able to identify with all that I've said about the theme of mediocrity, welcome to the club! In writing it, I have purposely taken what may be seen as more of a didactic rather than a narrative approach, although I have attempted to keep the tone relatively informal and to illustrate the ideas that I present with experiences of my own.

Let me first say a little about how this part of the book came into being. When I began my training for Kona in June 2006, I was faced with a new challenge in terms of planning a training program. Over the previous four years, most of my training had been done in organized groups, first with Brian Clarke and then with Boca Hawaii. In the group format, the training schedule had been laid out for me on a week-by-week basis, so there was relatively little active planning required on my part. Basically all I had to do was show up and follow the schedule that I had been given. You could say that it was essentially a no-brainer. In my preparations for Kona, however, there was no formal training group that I could join. Thus, for the first time since getting involved in the sport of triathlon, I found myself in a position where a good deal of my training had to be done alone. In addition, although I received a lot of helpful guidance from Raul, I was ultimately responsible for setting up my own training schedule. Consequently, I thought that I had better take some time to figure out how I was going to approach my training for the race. I wanted to have a better understanding of why I was going to be doing what my training plan called for me to do. I reflected on all that I had learned from various sources throughout my experiences with endurance sports. In the process, I began trying to formulate a simple conceptual framework for a training program, particularly for the upcoming race in Kona, but also for endurance athletic events more generally. I wanted it to be logical and coherent so it would make sense to me, but I also wanted to keep it as simple as possible. Initially, I wasn't thinking about including my ideas in a book. I was just trying to put together some ideas for my own benefit. As that conceptual framework began to take shape in my mind, however, it occurred to me that perhaps the ideas could be of some use to other recreational athletes who might have some interest in learning how to train for endurance triathlons. Consequently, I eventually made a decision to share some of those ideas in this final part of the book.

Before proceeding, I want to reiterate that this part of the book is most definitely not intended to be a comprehensive guide to training. There is a wealth of material on "triathlon training" out there. My goal is to provide some basic conceptual tools that can help you, as a recreational athlete, begin to develop your own training program. There are many aspects of training that I don't address, and many additional details that you will need to attend to in order to successfully get through a training program. But I hope that the ideas in this part of the book will at least help to simplify and demystify the training process.

I must also emphasize that I absolutely do not take any credit for the development of the concepts and ideas that I present here. As I confessed in the introduction, I am eminently unqualified as an athletic coach. The most I can say is that I have now had a fair amount of what might reasonably be described as "on the job training." My hope is that it may be of some help to you if I share with you some of the ideas that I have picked up along the way. Although I have taken the liberty of slightly modifying some of those ideas as a result of my own experiences, the basic concepts are not of my own making. They are derived particularly from all that I have learned from numerous coaches, books, training buddies, and other sources. In particular, I would like to acknowledge the contributions of the various head coaches with whom I have trained, particularly Brian Clarke, Raul Boca, and Tim Marr, as well as all of the assistant coaches in their respective programs with whom I have had the pleasure of training. I have learned something of significance from each and every one of them. In addition, the ideas contained in a number of excellent books, particularly *Going Long* by Joe Friel and Gordo Byrn, as I mentioned early on, and *The Perfect Distance: Training for Long-Course Triathlon* by Tom Rodgers, have been extremely helpful in developing a clearer conceptual overview of the training process.

My only contribution to this part of the book is that I have tried to put some of the ideas that I have learned from others into a conceptual framework that meets my own needs as a recreational athlete. In keeping with one of the overall themes of the book, I have attempted to keep things as simple as possible. I have stated before that, at a fundamental level, there is a beautiful simplicity to athletics. Ultimately, finishing a race, or even just a workout, simply involves using our natural physical abilities to keep moving forward until we eventually get to the finish line. There is nothing really complicated about that. I have the utmost respect for all of the coaches and other experts who direct their energies toward finding ways of helping competitive athletes perform to the absolute best of their ability and sharpen their competitive edge, and an equal amount of admiration for the awesome performances of those athletes. For competitive athletes, a few seconds, even a fraction of a second, may make the difference between a podium place and being an "also ran." Consequently, it is imperative for a competitive athlete to do whatever it takes to bring about every possible increment in improvement in performance. As a recreational athlete, however, I must say that I have sometimes found training programs geared toward competitive athletes to be overly detailed and complicated for my own needs. I would even go so far as to say that, occasionally, some of the things I read or was told did not seem to make complete sense from my point of view as a recreational athlete. I can't help but think that if we make the training process more complicated than it needs to be, we may actually end up taking some of the simple pleasure out of our participation in athletic activities.

In developing the conceptual framework that I want to present, I was, therefore, guided by the notion that, the more simple the guiding framework, the easier it should be to design and follow a training program. Accordingly, this part of the book is not about subtle refinements that can help you to fine tune your performance; it is about bare bones, basic ideas—a lowest common denominator, if you will. The guiding principle has simply been to keep it simple!

The next chapter addresses the issue of setting priorities and goals for yourself. I hope it will help you to make a more educated decision about whether to take on the challenge of doing an endurance triathlon. The subsequent chapter presents a conceptual framework that includes the basic ingredients of an endurance training program for the recreational athlete. The final chapter focuses on how you can use that conceptual framework as a basis for developing a training plan that meets your individual needs.

Chapter 22

Setting Priorities and Goals

Setting Priorities: Knowing Why You Are Doing It

Before you make a final decision to enter and train for any athletic event, be it an iron-distance triathlon or a 5K fun run, it is worth taking some time to reflect on the reasons you will be doing whatever it is that you plan to do.

There are many specific reasons why people choose to participate in athletics. I conducted an informal poll of my fellow athletes in Teem Marr, asking them to list all of the reasons why they participate in athletic activities, including both training and racing. As I expected, the results indicated that most people have multiple reasons for participating. A review of all the responses suggested that virtually all of the specific reasons that my athletic comrades gave could be divided into a small number of general categories. These categories can be regarded as being somewhat distinct from each other, although there is probably some degree of overlap among them. They should not, therefore, be thought of as being mutually exclusive categories. The seven categories that emerged can conveniently be defined as follows:

1. *Competition*: Your focus is on competing against other athletes, and you are trying to place as high as possible in the races that you are entering.
2. *Performance enhancement*: Your focus is on performing to the very best of your ability, but not necessarily on competing with other athletes.
3. *Personal accomplishment*: Your focus is on some specific personal goal, such as finishing a challenging event or setting a personal record.
4. *Physical health and fitness*: Your focus is on improving or maintaining your physical fitness and/or your overall physical health. For some athletes this may include weight management or other aspects of personal appearance.
5. *Mental health*: Your focus is on the mental health benefits of athletics, such as stress management, improving self-esteem, and mood enhancement.
6. *Socialization/friendship*: Your focus is on the social aspects of athletics, such as the camaraderie, friendship and support of fellow athletes, or meeting new people.
7. *Fun/enjoyment*: Your focus is on the simple enjoyment and pleasure that you get from participation in athletics.

If, like me, you define yourself as a recreational athlete, you are likely to find that several of these categories are important to you to some extent. You are also likely to find, however, that the relative importance of each of these categories will vary from time to time, depending on many other different factors that impact your life. At any particular point in time, you can assess the relative importance of the above categories by simply rating each category on a scale from 1 to 10, with 0 being "not at all important" and 10 being "extremely important." The resulting list of numbers should give you a clear picture of the relative importance of each category and, thus, the particular order of your priorities at that particular time.

The point of this rating exercise is that, if you can be clear about the order and the relative importance of your priorities, it will help you to determine your individual approach and attitude toward both training and racing. For example, if you recognize that your top priorities at a particular point in time are maintaining physical health and socializing with friends, as mine are currently, your approach and attitude toward both the training process and any races that you decide to enter are likely to be very different from someone whose top priorities are competition and improving performance.

I want to say a few words about competition, in particular, because many people automatically view a race as an event in which athletes compete against each other. For the recreational athlete, however, it doesn't have to be that way. I can't say that competition with other athletes is completely insignificant for me, but it has never been particularly high on my list of priorities. Furthermore, I would respectfully suggest that, for most of us Mediocristanis, it is probably not wise to make competition a top priority because doing so is likely to be a recipe for a considerable amount of disappointment and frustration. I must say, however, that, although I generally do not consider competition to be a high priority, I have noticed that the competitive drive sometimes tends to emerge almost automatically during the course of a workout when I am training with a group of friends. For example, I may start out on a long bike ride with the intention of taking it relatively easy. Before we have gone very far, however, a few people in the group start to push the pace and maybe begin to pull away from the rest of the group. Without really making a conscious decision to do so, I sometimes find myself compelled to try to keep up with the pace that they are setting because I don't want to get left too far behind if I can help it. The end result is that, before long, I find that I am training at higher level of intensity and expending a lot more energy on the workout than I had originally planned to do. On the one hand, this kind of friendly, and often unspoken, competition can be beneficial in improving your performance if that is one of your priorities. On the other hand, if you are really clear that competition and performance enhancement are not that important to you, then allowing yourself to get caught up in this type of scenario is likely to mean that you end up working a lot harder than you really want to. This is a factor that could potentially contribute to burnout and possibly lead to injury, particularly if you are doing it repeatedly.

Aside from competition, all of the other categories have always been important to me to some extent, although the relative importance of each has certainly varied considerably from time to time. When I was training for Kona in 2006, personal accomplishment was clearly at the top of my list and certainly would have had a rating of "10" if I had been using this scale at that time. I was primarily motivated by the desire to accomplish the goal of finishing that 140.6-mile distance for the first time. I also wanted to perform to the best of my ability, but specific time goals were not as important to me as just making sure I could get to the finish line within that 17-hour time limit. Consequently, performance enhancement would have been in second place, probably with a rating of about "8." The other categories were not entirely unimportant to me, but they were considerably lower on my list of priorities at that time. For example, the training inevitably yielded significant benefits for my physical fitness, but at that time I was doing much more training than I would have needed to do if my top priority had simply been maintaining my fitness. I suspect that most recreational athletes who choose to take on the challenge of an endurance triathlon will have a similar order of priorities, but, of course, only you can decide what the right order will be for you.

Once you are clear about your priorities, you can then make a logical decision about whether or not you want to enter a particular event. Basically, you will need to ask yourself how much time and energy you are willing and able to put into your training before you decide to enter that event. If you are going to take on the challenge of doing any endurance athletic event, it is important that you are willing and able to commit yourself 100% to doing whatever it takes to prepare you for that challenge. If you are certain that you are indeed willing and able to make that commitment, go for it. If, however, you are not certain that you can make the necessary commitment, you should consider aiming for a shorter distance event that does not demand as much of your time and energy. When you are able to make the necessary commitment, then you can take on the challenge of an endurance event.

Once you have made the decision to enter a particular event, being aware of your priorities will help you to decide how you are going to approach that event. There may be times in your life when your primary focus is on socializing with friends or just maintaining a healthy level of physical fitness. There is absolutely nothing wrong with that. Those are, in fact, my personal priorities right now. However, if you are a recreational athlete making the decision to take on the challenge of an endurance triathlon for the very first time, I believe that your approach to training must involve a primary focus on doing whatever it takes to develop the endurance that you will need to accomplish your goal of getting all the way to the finish line. That was certainly the approach I took when I was training for Kona in 2006.

Setting Specific Race Goals

Okay, so you have decided that you are going to enter a particular event and you are clear about your priorities and your reasons for doing it. The next step is to define specific goals for that event. It is usually best to set at least some tentative goals prior to the start of your training program, but it is also important to be willing to modify those goals if necessary as your training progresses. While it is natural to want to set goals that are challenging, you are likely to maximize your chance of succeeding and fulfilling that sense of accomplishment by setting goals that are also realistic. If you are not sure what is realistic for you, talk to some experienced athletes and to friends who have some knowledge of your ability level. Their input can help you set some initial tentative goals for yourself. You can then adjust them up or down as necessary as you go through your training so that you eventually have a set of realistic goals by the time you get to race day.

I have learned from a number of coaches and fellow athletes, as well as from personal experience, that, for any race, the preliminary goal should always be to get to the starting line healthy. If you are not able to do that, then obviously all your other goals are likely to be out the window. There are three major types of medical problems that can potentially derail even the most detailed and comprehensive training program—infectious illnesses, repetitive strain injuries, and traumatic injuries. The old saying, prevention is better than cure, should be the watchword for all of these types of problems.

We all know that it is difficult to completely avoid common infectious illnesses such as colds or flu. In many cases, these conditions may not be serious enough to completely disrupt a training program, but there are no guarantees. A severe upper respiratory infection during the week immediately prior to a race may leave you with no option but to pull out, as I had to do in the case of the 2004 Honolulu Triathlon. The risk of contracting these conditions can be minimized by getting flu shots every year and by taking commonly recommended preventive measures such as avoiding contact with people who are obviously contagious and washing hands regularly. In addition, you can be proactive in terms of maximizing the efficiency of your immune system by maintaining healthy nutrition throughout the training program and by making sure that you consistently get sufficient rest to allow for recovery between workouts. Nevertheless, it's obviously a rare individual who doesn't come down with one of these ailments at least occasionally. If you do happen to get sick, don't try to resume training too quickly or you may risk a relapse. Take enough of a break to allow for a full recovery.

You can minimize the risk of repetitive strain injuries by avoiding overtraining, learning good technique in all three sports, and making sure you have appropriate equipment that fits you well. The guidance and assistance that you can get from qualified coaches and other experts can be helpful in all of these areas. I recognize now that the plantar fasciitis I developed in 2007 was probably the result of overtraining, and I'm inclined to think that it could have been avoided if I had not been so intent on cramming as much training as I possibly could into the time that I had available without regard for the potential consequences.

Training for any athletic event inevitably involves the risk of traumatic injury, as I have learned the hard way from personal experience. These types of injuries are probably more difficult to prevent than infectious illnesses and repetitive strain injuries because they typically result from accidents that, by definition, occur unexpectedly, as with my bike crash during our training for Ironman New Zealand. Nevertheless, the risks can certainly be minimized by learning and following safety-first procedures, particularly on the bike. For example, if the weather looks bad, maybe it's more prudent to spend a couple of hours on the turbo trainer rather than risk cycling on the road in potentially hazardous conditions. Furthermore, I am still amazed at the number of cyclists I see riding on the road without a helmet. Don't leave home without one! The large cracks in the helmet that I was wearing on January 2, 2006 tell me that I would probably have sustained not only a fractured skull but also serious brain damage if I had not been wearing that helmet when my head hit the ground.

Assuming that you can get to the starting line healthy, how should you go about setting specific goals for the race? I have found that it is a good idea to establish a hierarchy of goals rather than to focus solely a single goal. Many unexpected things can happen not only during training but also during the race itself. By establishing a hierarchy of specific goals, you minimize the risk of disappointment and failure. When I started preparing for Kona in 2006, I was exquisitely aware of the fact that I had absolutely no previous experience of attempting to cover a distance of 140.6 miles under my own power in a single day. I wasn't completely sure of what I could expect from myself on race day, let alone from factors outside of my control, such as weather conditions or flat tires. Consequently, I took a somewhat cautious approach toward the goals that I set for myself. I wanted my primary goal to be something I felt confident that I was realistically capable of accomplishing, even if I did encounter a few setbacks along the way. If I could achieve that primary goal, I would be very satisfied with my performance. At the same time, I wanted to set some additional goals in order to give myself an incentive to perform to the best of my ability. I therefore defined my hierarchy of goals for the race as follows:

Primary Goal:	Finish the race under the 17-hour time limit.
Second:	Under 16 hours would be icing on the cake.
Third:	Under 15 hours would be a double layer of icing.

After finishing the race in Kona, and accomplishing two out of those three goals, the focus for my next race over that distance in Western Australia became more specifically performance oriented because I really wanted to see if I could improve my finish time. At the same time, I recognized that I still needed to be able to feel satisfied with a simple finish, in case I could not, for some unforeseen reason, make the finish time that I ideally hoped to achieve. Accordingly, the set of goals for the race in Western Australia was defined in slightly different manner:

Primary Goal: Finish the race under 15 hours.
Second: Under 14 hours would be icing on the cake.
Back-up goal: Under the 17 hour time limit would be fine.

Beware of the temptation to mentally adjust your goals during the course of the race. Because I allowed overconfidence to creep in, that is what I did during the early stages of the race in Western Australia. The end result was a certain degree of disappointment. On the one hand, I was happy that I was able to achieve my original primary goal under relatively difficult conditions. On the other hand, because I did not manage to achieve those mentally adjusted goals, I ended up with the nagging thought that I had failed in some way and that I should have been able to do better. I really didn't need to be so self-critical. If I had just stuck with my original goals and been satisfied with achieving them, I would have avoided that disappointment.

When preparing for a triathlon, in addition to setting goals for the race overall, you may want to consider setting specific goals for the swim, the bike, and the run. In training for Kona and Western Australia, I did not actually do this. I had some vague ideas about how I wanted to perform in each of the three sports, but my main focus was on the overall goal, and I didn't want specific goals for parts of the race to distract me from that overall focus. I can certainly see, on the other hand, the potential value of breaking your overall goal up into separate goals for the three different components of the race in order to facilitate achievement of your overall goal.

Chapter 23:

A Simple Conceptual Framework

Now that you are clear about your priorities and you have a set of specific goals in mind for the event you have chosen to enter, you are ready to start thinking about how you are going to approach your training program. In this chapter, I describe a simple conceptual framework that can help you to design a specific training program for yourself in a systematic way.

Areas of Focus

If you are a recreational athlete who is planning to do an iron-distance event for the first time, as I was in 2006, your highest priority is likely to be the personal accomplishment of just finishing the event. You may decide that you want to aim for a certain time goal, but I think that for the majority of first-timers, the most important thing is just getting to that finish line. If this is true for you, there are typically going to be three main areas of focus for your training program—*endurance, endurance*, and *endurance*.

There are actually two additional areas to which you may also wish to focus some of your attention—*technique* and *strength*. Other areas of focus, such as *speed* and *power*, are obviously going to be important for the competitive athlete, but I'm going to suggest that most recreational athletes don't need to be too concerned about these areas. If you focus primarily on building *endurance*, you will automatically see some gains in areas like *speed* and *power* over the course of your training. Again, the aim is to keep the training process as simple as possible.

Endurance

Endurance can be informally defined as the ability to keep moving forward over an extended period of time without collapsing, passing out, voluntarily dropping out, or otherwise coming to a complete halt. An iron-distance race can be viewed as a quintessential endurance event and, many people would add, a rather extreme one at that. Because of the distances involved in such an event, it is obvious that the primary focus of a training plan, particularly for recreational athletes, must be on developing a *very high* level of endurance. There's just no getting away from the fact that 140.6 miles is a very long distance to cover under your own power. Moreover, as triathletes, we have to develop a high level of endurance not just in one sport, but in all three sports. I know from my own experience that this initially seems like a daunting challenge, to say the least, but the good news is that there is absolutely nothing complicated about it. The fact of the matter is that a high level of endurance can be built by just about anyone over a long enough period of time. I mean no disrespect whatsoever to the experts when I say to you that, if your main goal is just to experience the accomplishment of finishing your first iron-distance triathlon, then training for it is not rocket science. In fact, at the most basic level, there are essentially two simple but key principles that you will need to follow in order to develop the level of endurance that will allow you to achieve your goal.

1. Focus on building your endurance by gradually and systematically increasing the volume of your training over the course of the program.

This first principle is really a matter of common sense. Almost all training programs follow this principle one way or another. Once you have chosen to take on the challenge, your primary task will obviously be to build your endurance up to a level at which you are capable of finishing the race. Equally obviously, this cannot be done overnight. This first principle simply says that building the necessary endurance is best done in small increments over an extended period of time. This gradual approach will allow your body to progressively adapt to the increasing demands that you will be placing on it throughout your training. As time goes by and your endurance progressively grows, you will repeatedly be amazed that you are able to handle a volume of training that would have seemed impossible earlier in the training program.

2. Make a commitment to be relentlessly consistent in following the schedule of your training program.

I hope that by now I have clearly made the point that you absolutely do not have to be an outstanding athlete to achieve the goal of finishing an iron-distance triathlon. Mediocre ability will do just fine. It certainly has worked for me. You do, however, have to be willing to commit yourself 100% to the accomplishment of that goal. You will need to be relentless in applying your mediocre ability to the pursuit of that goal. Then, when race day comes you can truly give it your best shot. That means consistently following through with whatever your training program calls for you to do. As a general rule, make it a priority to go out for all of the workouts on your schedule unless there are absolutely unavoidable reasons for missing a workout.

If you have made the decision to take on the challenge, you already know what needs to be done in order to get to the finish line. When race day comes around, you have to be physically and psychologically prepared to swim 2.4 miles, bike 112 miles, and run

26.2 miles. That's all there is to it. It is definitely a challenge that will require you to put in a great deal of hard work, but it is not complicated. If you are able to keep these two simple principles in mind as you plan your preparation for the race, you will find that much of the specific content of your training schedule will logically fall into place as a matter of common sense.

There are a couple of other issues related to the topic of endurance that I would like to briefly address. Some people make a distinction between aerobic or cardiovascular endurance (i.e., the ability to maintain a certain level of cardiovascular output over a period of time) and muscular endurance (i.e., the ability to maintain a certain level of musculoskeletal activity over a period of time). It may be important for the competitive athlete who is particularly concerned with maximizing speed throughout the race to make a clear distinction between these two forms of endurance and to focus certain components of training on one or the other. However, because we are trying to maintain the theme of simplicity, I am inclined to think that the distinction may not be that critical for the recreational athlete for two reasons. First, the recreational athlete usually does not have that singular focus on maximizing speed that the competitive athlete must have. Second, the two forms of endurance inevitably go together to some degree. You cannot really focus your workouts exclusively on building aerobic endurance without also building some degree of muscular endurance, and vice versa. Consequently, if you focus simply on building endurance by following those two key principles, then you will automatically see significant gains in both the aerobic and muscular components.

My older daughter, Jen, who has a considerable amount of experience herself as an endurance athlete through her involvement in outrigger canoe paddling, made the valuable suggestion that I also make mention of the critical importance of mental endurance. Training for any endurance athletic event inevitably means developing the will and determination to push through a certain amount of pain and discomfort in order to finish all your workouts, not to mention the race itself. It is critically important to develop the mental endurance to keep your body moving forward, even when you feel like quitting. In the process, you will repeatedly be surprised at what you are capable of doing if you can just find a way to keep going. As you progress further along in your training program, there are inevitably going to be times when you find that some of those long training sessions are really an ordeal, so it is essential that you find ways of getting yourself through them. There are an infinite number of mental techniques that you can use to do that. It doesn't matter which one you use. There is no single correct technique. Focus on your breathing, sing to yourself, find positive ways of talking to yourself, keep counting backwards from one thousand, let your mind wander where it will, focus on just enjoying the scenery along the way. Simply find out what works for you, and use it to develop that mental ability to keep moving toward the finish line, no matter how much your body is screaming at you to stop.

In addition to the primary focus on endurance, there are two secondary areas of focus that will ideally require some of your attention during your training—technique and strength.

Technique

I'm only going to make a few general comments about the importance of good technique. Remember, I'm no expert, so I'm not even going to try to give you any specific advice about how to improve your technique. The basic point is that none of us can ever hope to achieve perfection in technique, particularly those of us who got into the game relatively late in life. Consequently, we are always going to have reasons to keep working to improve our technique in all of the three sports. Even though, as a recreational athlete, you may not be focused primarily on maximizing speed, improvements in technique mean greater efficiency in performance, which, in turn, means less energy used per unit of distance traveled.

Improving technique is one of the areas in which instruction and guidance from a good coach is likely to be most helpful, particularly if you are a relative newcomer to the sport. In addition, there is an almost limitless supply of books and online resources that can provide many useful tips on how to fine-tune your technique. For novice athletes, there may sometimes be a need to focus specifically on some aspect of technique during certain training sessions. More generally, we can all benefit from learning to consistently focus on maintaining good form during our workouts, especially when we are tired, because that is when our technique is most likely to deteriorate.

It is no secret that technique is especially important for the swim. Consequently, it is likely to be the sport in which improvements in technique will result in the greatest percentage improvement in speed and time. However, do not neglect the value of good technique in the bike and run. You certainly don't need to have excellent technique in order to finish an endurance event, but ideally you do want to learn how to use your energy as efficiently as possible in all three of the sports in order to maximize your capacity for endurance. If you know that you need to do some serious work on certain aspects of your technique, particularly in the swim, you may want to consider seeking individual coaching from a professional, if you have the time and resources to do so.

Strength

Building *strength*, particularly in the core of the body, can be helpful to some degree in building endurance and also in developing the ability to maintain a higher level of intensity in your workouts. If time permits, it's not a bad idea to plan at least one workout focused specifically on building core strength each week. In addition, some training programs recommend trying to incorporate at least a brief strength training component into every workout whenever possible. On the other hand, if you find that your time is really limited or your supply of energy is getting low, I am inclined to believe that the strength training should probably be the first thing to go because it is likely to contribute less than your other workouts to directly building the endurance that is the primary thing you will need to finish the race.

Over the years, I have at times included a strength component in my training on a fairly regular basis, but I must admit that I have not always been as consistent with it as I might have been ideally. If you do want to include a strength component in your training, and you are not sure exactly what types of exercises to do, this is another area where you may want to consider getting some expert advice.

Workout Parameters: Basic Concepts

Before I introduce the basic concepts, let me initially make one fairly obvious but important point. When you are training for any triathlon, you will need to keep in mind that, in order to fit the necessary amount of training into each week, most of your training sessions will consist of combinations of two workout components: swim/bike, swim/run, or bike/run. In the discussion that follows, I use the word "workout" to mean one component of a training session that may include two or even three components.

If we keep in mind that the primary area of focus of an iron-distance training program for the recreational athlete is building endurance, based on the two key principles noted above, a simple conceptual framework that describes the parameters of your workouts can be developed around three basic concepts—*duration, intensity,* and *frequency*. This framework can then serve as a guide to the development of a detailed training schedule.

Duration and intensity are the two most important concepts because they can be viewed as forming the essential parameters of each individual workout. Any given workout can be described simply in terms of these two variables. Together, they will determine how long and how hard a particular workout is going to be for you. The third concept, frequency, simply refers to the number of workouts that are performed over a given period of time, such as one week. It is not one of the parameters of an individual workout, but it does become one of the parameters of your weekly training schedule.

If you want to develop the endurance that is necessary to accomplish your goal, you have to be willing to pay your dues by putting in a series of increasingly long workouts. That inevitably means an emphasis on duration in many of your workouts. It does not mean, however, that you are only going to be concerned about the duration of your workouts. Effective and efficient training always involves finding a balance between duration and intensity. As a general rule, there is going to be an inverse relationship between these two variables—the longer the duration of a workout, the lower the intensity. Conversely, the shorter the workout, the higher the intensity will be.

There are two additional concepts that can be derived from combinations of these three basic concepts. These additional concepts are *total workload* and *volume*. Both of these concepts can be thought of as providing, in rather different ways, a measure of the amount of work you plan to do, or have done, either during a specific workout, during a complete training session, or over a particular period of time, typically one week.

All of these five concepts should be self-explanatory to some extent, but a little elaboration is necessary to develop the conceptual framework. In order to maintain the theme of simplicity, I will emphasize measurement of these variables on a subjective rather than an objective basis.

Duration and intensity, as well as total workload, can all be measured relatively easily on a subjective basis using simple 5-point scales, each of which is described in more detail below. After seeing a number of different methods of measurement used by various coaches and authors, I have settled on the use of 5-point scales because I find that they are relatively simple and easy to keep in mind, particularly while I am out there riding the roads or pounding the pavement. Complex thinking is not something that is particularly easy for me to do when I am putting all my energy into the physical exertion of the workout. Frequency and volume are simple concepts that do not really require the use of any form of measurement scale.

Duration

Duration can be measured in units of either time or distance. It is debatable whether it is better to use time or distance for training purposes. I have used both during training over the years. I typically use distance more than time, but, from a practical standpoint, it may sometimes be essential for the busy recreational athlete to plan many training sessions in terms of available time. For example, if two hours is all the time you have to spare for a bike ride between the end of your workday and whatever you have to do next, then you really don't need to be concerned about the exact distance that you are going to ride. Just go out and put in the time that is available to you. Ultimately, however, when it comes to preparing for an iron-distance event, I believe that it is important psychologically to feel confident that you have the ability to complete all of the distances involved in each of the three sports. Consequently, I'm going to suggest that even if you plan most of your workouts in terms of time, it is a good idea to base some of your longer workouts on distance rather than on strict time guidelines. I know that when I went to Kona, I wanted to be confident, based on my actual experience in training, that I could comfortably swim at least 2.4 miles, bike at least 112 miles, and run at least 26.2 miles.

Duration is obviously the variable that can most easily be measured on an objective basis if you wish to do so. Time can be easily measured with a watch, which most athletes wear, or a clock of some kind, such as the ones that often can be found on swimming pool decks for use with swim intervals. Similarly, distance can easily be measured objectively with an odometer or GPS device. In addition to these objective measures, however, I found it helpful for the development of the conceptual framework to roughly conceptualize ranges of duration on a subjective basis. You will see why a little later when we get to a discussion of types of workouts. This can be done using a simple 5-point scale that includes terms ranging from Very Short to Very Long, and which is based, at the high end of the scale, on iron-distance race durations for each sport. In this particular scale, I have taken time as the unit of measurement. A similar scale could easily be constructed using distance as a measure of duration if you prefer.

Before introducing the scale, I do want to make a few observations about the relative nature of subjective measures such as this. Our subjective perception of duration is likely to be influenced by several different factors. First, the ranges of both time and distance involved in your workouts will obviously vary significantly from one sport to another. For example, a 1-hour swim might be considered relatively long, even for a slow poke like me who is not able to cover a great deal of distance during that time, whereas a 1-hour bike ride would certainly be considered short in the context of training for an iron-distance event. Second, if you are measuring duration in terms of time, different ability levels must also be taken into account. Another of the brutal facts of life when it comes to athletics is that the slower you are, the more time it is going to take you to cover a particular distance. For example, for an 8-mile run, someone who is able to maintain a 7-minute-mile pace will cover that distance in just under 1 hour; however, it will take someone who runs at a 12-minute-mile pace over an hour and a half to cover that same distance. Third, and somewhat incidental to the current focus on training for endurance triathlons, the training context is obviously likely to influence our perception of duration. For example, a 4-hour run would be considered a relatively long workout by my standards, even when training for an iron-distance event, but it would have been relatively short for über-athletes like my friends Brenda Yim and Ryan Seto when they were training for a 100-mile ultra-marathon. With these caveats in mind, and based on my own admittedly mediocre pacing ability, the following scale can be considered a rough guideline for measuring duration in terms of time.

		Swim	Bike	Run
1	Very Short:	15 minutes	1 hour	30 minutes
2	Short:	30 minutes	2 hours	1 hour
3	Intermediate:	45 minutes	3 hours	2 hours
4	Long:	1 hour+	4 hours+	3 hours+
5	Very Long:	Up to iron-distance durations or more		

Intensity

Intensity can be defined simply as how hard you are working, or how much effort you are putting out, at any given point in time. It might also be called "work rate." In contrast to duration, which will tend to progressively increase over the course of your training program, the level of intensity in any particular type of workout will remain relatively constant from week to week. On the other hand, the level of intensity will vary considerably from one type of workout to another, as we will see a little later.

As with duration, intensity can be measured objectively, in this case with a device such as a heart rate monitor or a power meter. On the other hand, it can also be measured subjectively using a simple scale of *perceived* intensity. Alternatively, some coaches may call this "perceived exertion" or "perceived effort." I recognize that devices such as heart rate monitors and power meters may be critically important tools for the competitive athlete, and some recreational athletes may also find them to be quite helpful. If you are into high tech gadgets, then by all means go for it. However, I will say that, after utilizing a heart rate monitor for some time, I have come to prefer using just a subjective measure of perceived intensity for several reasons. This is partly for the sake of simplicity. It is one less piece of material gadgetry to have to purchase and maintain, to have to remember to take along with me, and to be concerned about more generally. It is also partly because using a subjective measure forces me to pay close attention to how my body is feeling during a workout. I firmly believe that becoming attuned to how your body feels is critical in making your training program not only as effective but also as enjoyable as possible.

Intensity can also be conveniently measured on a subjective basis using a simple 5-point scale, in this case utilizing terms ranging from Very Low to Very High. Again, the following can be considered rough guidelines:

1. Very Low: 50–64%
2. Low: 65–74% (typical iron-distance race pace)
3. Medium: 75–84%
4. High: 85–94%
5. Very High: 95–100%

In order to provide some mental anchor points, I think of this scale as being based on a perceived level of intensity in which 0% would be equivalent to lying down at rest and the 50% level might correspond to a brisk walking pace. I'm going to assume that most, if not all, of your training will be done at somewhere above the 50% level, although I must emphasize that there is absolutely nothing wrong with doing a mixture of walking and running on your longer workouts if you feel more comfortable with that. Toward the lower end of the scale, I like to think of the 55% level of intensity as being roughly that level at which I feel confident that I could keep going relatively easily and comfortably for as long as necessary without being greatly concerned about the duration of the workout. In other words, this might be roughly the equivalent of a very slow jogging pace. At the top end of the scale, the 100% level would roughly correspond to an all-out effort over a very short distance, such as a 25-meter swim, a 500-meter bike sprint, or a 100-meter run. Although these are very short distances, if I go all out, I really need to take a break to recover.

I have found that paying attention to my breathing pattern is an easy way to give me a pretty good indication of my intensity level. For example, when I am running, what I call "2-beat breathing," that is two strides breathing in and two strides breathing out, roughly corresponds to the High level of intensity. Similarly, "3-beat breathing" roughly corresponds to the Medium level and "4-beat breathing" to the Low level of intensity. Almost all your endurance triathlon training will probably fall somewhere within these three levels of intensity. Finer distinctions can also be made between, say, "relaxed 2-beat breathing" and "pressured 2-beat breathing," with the latter coming closer to the Very High level of intensity. This general principle of using your breathing as an indication of intensity level can be extended to biking relatively easy by focusing on your rate of breathing in relation to your pedal cadence or by simply counting in your head as you breathe. I find it a little more difficult to apply to swimming because I usually prefer to breathe once every stroke cycle, even when I am swimming at a relatively low level of intensity. The same idea could, however, be applied in principle to swimming, particularly if you are able to comfortably breathe bilaterally or once every two or three stroke cycles.

In addition to using breathing as a measure of intensity, maintaining a mental focus on your breathing pattern can add an almost meditative component to your training. For example, I will, at times during turbo training sessions, close my eyes and maintain an ongoing focus on my breathing. Then, after eventually opening my eyes to look at my watch, I often find that I am quite surprised at how much time has gone by. This type of workout then becomes a form of mindfulness exercise that can help to make the training particularly valuable as a stress management tool. Furthermore, I think that maintaining a consistent focus on your breathing during all of your workouts can be helpful in making your athletic performance as efficient as possible.

The more training that you do and the more that you pay attention to the way you feel during training, the easier it becomes to estimate perceived intensity level. With practice, you can get to the point that you can begin to make meaningful distinctions in your mind between, say, an 80% intensity level and an 85% level. There is a lot to be said for learning to stay in touch with your own body as a way not only of assessing intensity but also becoming aware of your own limits. For example, if at any particular time you feel that the Very Low intensity range is as much as you can realistically maintain throughout one of your long workouts, then that is just fine. There may be other times when you feel capable of testing your limits, in which case you can focus on working harder for part of your workout.

It should be noted that the five levels of intensity must be viewed as highly subjective and definitely do not imply any particular pace. At a High level of perceived intensity, for example, I may be running at a pace of about 9 minutes per mile. At the same perceived level, however, another athlete might be running at a 7-minute-mile pace and yet another athlete at a 5-minute-mile pace.

Intensity may also, to some extent, be thought of as being relative to the type of event that one is training for. For example, a 10K tempo run at a Medium perceived level of intensity might be viewed as one of the more intense workouts in the context of an endurance triathlon training program, in which, for the recreational athlete, there is likely to be a singular focus on simply building endurance. On the other hand, the exact same workout might be viewed as one of the less intense workouts in the context of training for a shorter event such as a sprint distance triathlon, in which there is likely to be somewhat more of a focus on maximizing speed.

In all of your workouts, and of course in the race itself, intensity management, which involves appropriate pacing, is an important issue for two reasons. First, it is critical to appropriately ration your energy expenditure in order to avoid "running out of gas," particularly on the longer workouts. Second, effective management of your intensity level will allow you to derive the maximum amount of adaptive benefit from your workouts.

Frequency

Frequency simply refers to the number of workouts that you perform over a given period of time, such as one week. It is obviously a simple concept that does not require measurement on any type of scale. For an endurance event in a single sport, such as a marathon, training programs generally call for a minimum of 3 workouts per week, and often as many as 6 workouts per week, which can be quite time consuming. Training for an endurance triathlon, which involves training for not just one but three sports, is obviously going to require particularly good time management to fit in all of the necessary workouts. In order to get an adequate amount of training in each sport without putting excessive demands on your time, I would recommend that you plan on a minimum of three workouts per week in each of the three sports, for a total of nine workout components.

Total Workload

The concept of *total workload* can be used as a perceived indication of how hard you plan to work, or have worked, in your training. Total workload can be subjectively assessed over the course of a particular workout component, or over the course of a combination training session involving two or more sports. This concept roughly corresponds to the total amount of energy or effort expended during your training session. Total workload is related to both duration and intensity, although, unfortunately, it is not a simple linear function of these two variables. Consequently, there's no easy way of measuring it objectively, and I'm afraid I'm not a good enough mathematician to be able to offer you a simple equation for calculating it. As a general rule, the longer the duration and/or the higher the intensity, the harder the total workload is going to be.

My subjective impression is that total workload tends to be somewhat more a function of intensity than duration, particularly as you develop a higher level of endurance and can, therefore, better tolerate longer workouts. For example, I find that I usually perceive a workout composed of High intensity intervals as being a pretty hard workout, even though the total duration of the workout may only be in the Short to Intermediate range. On the other hand, there's no denying that those Long duration, Low intensity workouts, which are the backbone of any endurance triathlon training program, are likely to be perceived as being challenging in terms of total workload. After a 100-mile bike ride or a 20-mile run on a hot summer day, even at a Low level of intensity, I think you'll know what I mean. Incidentally, be aware that heat is a factor that can add significantly to your perceived level of total workload, so be prepared to take that into account if you are training in relatively high temperatures. Your perception of how hard you have worked during a particular workout may also be influenced by a number of other factors such as how well rested you are, how well you have maintained your hydration and nutrition both before and during the workout, and your perceived energy level on that day.

Like duration and intensity, total workload can also be roughly measured on a subjective basis using a simple 5-point scale, in this case from Very Easy to Very Hard.

1. Very Easy
2. Easy
3. Moderate
4. Hard
5. Very Hard

If a training session consists of a workout in a single sport only, a Hard level of total workload might, for example, be the product of a Long duration/Low intensity workout, such as that 100-mile bike ride or 20-mile run that I mentioned above. Conversely, a Short or Intermediate duration/High intensity workout consisting of intervals or hill repeats might also be experienced as being at the Hard level of total workload.

Remember, however, that, when you are training for an endurance triathlon, most of your training sessions are likely to involve combinations of more than one sport. By their very nature, these combination workouts are rarely likely to be perceived as being Easy or Very Easy overall, even if one of the components is in the Easy range. So be prepared for the total workload for almost all of your training sessions to be in at least the Moderate range, with many of them being in the Hard to Very Hard range. For example, an Easy swim workout followed by a Hard run workout on the same day is likely to be perceived as a Hard training session overall. Similarly, a Hard swim workout followed by a Hard bike workout will probably be perceived as a Very Hard training session overall. Training for endurance triathlons obviously involves being willing to do a lot of hard work, but the good news is that all those hard workouts will pay off in the end when it comes to race day.

This same scale can also be used to measure your perceived workload over the course of a longer period of time such as a whole week. This can then be defined as "total weekly workload," which can be thought of as the perceived cumulative total of the workloads for all of the workouts performed during a particular week. As we have seen, when training for an endurance triathlon, there will inevitably be a lot of challenging days because of the number of combination workouts. In addition, because of the focus on building endurance, every week of training will need to include at least one relatively long duration workout in each of the three sports. Consequently, it is virtually inevitable that there will be times when you feel fatigued as a result of the workload. It is important, however, not to try to cram too many hard days into one week. Always remember the importance of getting sufficient rest between workouts. This is a point that I will emphasize repeatedly. As a general rule, the harder the total workload of any particular training session, the more rest you are likely to need before your next workout. Similarly, the harder your total weekly workload, the more likely it is that you will need to take a day or two off in order to fully recover.

In the early weeks of your training program, the total weekly workload may be perceived as being in the Easy to Moderate range, depending on your starting level of fitness. You can then plan to gradually progress to the Hard range and eventually to the Very Hard range over the course of your training program. However, I would strongly recommend that you plan to make one week per month somewhat easier than the other weeks during that month in order to allow some time for more complete recovery and consolidation of the gains in fitness that you have made as a result of all those hard workouts that you have been doing.

Volume

Volume is another way of measuring how much work you have done in your training. It can be defined simply as the total amount of training that is done over a specific period of time like one week. Like duration, volume can be measured either in time or distance and can, in fact, also be thought of as "cumulative duration." Volume is a simple linear function of duration and frequency, and can be calculated as the sum total of the duration of all of the workouts during a particular week. Volume can be calculated for each of the three sports individually, using either time or distance as the unit of measurement. Using time as the unit of measurement, volume can also be calculated in terms of the total number of hours that you have put into all of the workouts in all of the three sports combined. This will give you a clear picture of how much time you are devoting to your training as a whole. Like frequency, volume is a simple concept that does not really require measurement on any type of scale. You could, however, easily adapt the duration scale above for the measurement of volume if you wanted to.

Notice that, in contrast to total workload, the concept of intensity does not enter into the equation for volume. Consequently, although there is likely to be some correlation between weekly volume and total weekly workload, as both are indicators of the amount of work performed, that correlation will probably be considerably less than perfect. This distinction can be quite important in subjectively assessing how hard you have worked over a particular period of time. For example, your perception of the total weekly workload involved in a particular weekly volume of training might vary from the Moderate to the Very Hard level depending on the intensity of the various workouts performed. If, for some reason, all of your workouts during a particular week are performed at a Low level of intensity, then the total weekly workload might be perceived as being at no more than a Moderate level, even if the volume is fairly high. On the other hand, if some of those same workouts are performed at a High level of intensity, then the total weekly workload might be perceived as Hard or even Very Hard, although the weekly volume is the same. Remember that the amount of rest and recovery that you need is likely to depend in large part on how hard you perceive you have worked. That may involve taking both total workload and volume into account.

Types of Workouts

Now that you have a basic conceptual framework as a guide, you can begin to consider the different types of workouts that you will want to include in your training program. In general, remember that it is important to be clear about the purpose of every workout in order to get the maximum benefit from your training program. Make every workout count, and know what you are expecting to put into and get out of each workout. Work hard on days that are supposed to be hard, but be sure to rest adequately between workouts in order to maximize the adaptive benefit of each workout. Avoid "junk" workouts that are done just because you feel that you ought to be doing something, particularly on days when your energy level is low. Such workouts provide no real training benefit, and they may contribute to the development of excessive fatigue or burnout.

We have seen that the parameters of any particular workout component can be described in terms of duration and intensity. If we subjectively measure these two variables using the scales described on previous pages, each of which has 5 levels, we can see that there are theoretically a total of 25 (5 x 5) possible combinations of levels. That sounds way too complicated to me, so let's make it much more simple. For practical purposes as recreational athletes, we don't need to consider 25 different options. All we need to know is that we can get a certain amount of work done in multiple ways by varying the relative degree of focus on the duration and the intensity of a workout. I'm going to suggest that virtually all of your workouts can be done at one or another of only four basic combinations of levels.

1. Long duration/Low intensity: Let's call these *endurance workouts*.
2. Short duration/High intensity: Let's call these *intensity workouts*.
3. Intermediate duration/Medium intensity: Let's call these *tempo workouts*.
4. Short duration/Low intensity: Let's just call these *easy workouts*.

These four types of workout are discussed in more detail in the following sections.

Endurance Workouts

You will again recall that the primary focus of an iron-distance training program for the recreational athlete is building a *very high* level of endurance. While all of your workouts will be focused on this goal to some extent, it is these Long duration/Low intensity workouts that are the foundation of your training program. Some coaches may refer to these as "long, slow distance" or "LSD" workouts. In terms of pace, these workouts are always going to be relatively slow, although the specific pace may obviously vary considerably from person to person. As an extreme example, when training for a marathon, the top Kenyan long distance runners are going to maintain a pace that is well over twice as fast as mine. In fact, I can't even run 100 meters at their marathon pace. It is important, therefore, to get a realistic estimate of the particular pace you will be able to maintain throughout your long workouts in each of the three sports. This should become readily apparent after you have done your first few workouts. Once you are able to get a good feel for the pace that you can comfortably maintain over the long haul, you can plan on doing all of your endurance workouts at approximately that pace. This pace may gradually increase as you level of fitness increases, but it doesn't have to if your primary goal is just to finish. By the time you have built up a solid base of fitness, this pace will correspond roughly to your anticipated race pace.

Throughout your training program, you should definitely plan on making one workout per week in each of the three sports an endurance workout. A short warm up and cool down can be included as an integral part of the workout. In accordance with the first of our two key principles, you should plan to progressively increase the duration of these workouts throughout your training up until the time when you begin your taper about three weeks before the race. By the time you reach the peak of your training, the duration of these workouts should be up to, or close to, the full iron-distances in each of the three sports. Thus, you can expect that your endurance workouts will account for an increasingly large proportion of the volume of your training as you progress through your training program.

Over the course of your training program, you can maintain a relatively constant level of intensity in these endurance workouts. For recreational athletes, the intensity level for these workouts in the context of endurance triathlon training will typically be within the Low range, corresponding to about 65 to 75% of your maximum intensity level, or possibly the Very Low range if that is more comfortable for you. Accordingly, I generally plan to maintain 4-beat breathing for most of these workouts. There may be short periods during these workouts when your intensity level will go up to the Medium range or even higher, such as when you are climbing hills on the bike or run. However, the primary emphasis in endurance workouts is on developing the ability to maintain a relatively low level of intensity for an increasingly long period of time.

Because of their long duration, the total workload in these endurance workouts will be perceived as being in about the Hard to Very Hard range, particularly as you get toward the peak of your training. I find, however, that I usually don't perceive the endurance workouts for the swim as being quite as hard as those for the bike and run, probably because they simply do not take as much time.

It is obviously important to build endurance in all three sports, but building endurance on the bike is particularly important, as it is by far the longest of the three sports, in terms of both distance and time. So, if you do make that decision to enter an iron-distance event, be prepared to put in a lot of hours on your bike

If you already have some experience doing triathlons up to Olympic distance, you should probably plan on beginning your training program with one endurance workout per sport per week of approximately Intermediate duration, or possibly a little shorter, depending on your current level of fitness. In terms of distance, this might correspond to the distances involved in Olympic distance triathlons in each of the three sports—1500 meters for the swim; 40K for the bike; and 10K for the run.

If you are beginning from a lower baseline with less experience, the duration of your initial endurance workouts can be adjusted downward accordingly. By all means, start your training at whatever duration you feel comfortable with, even if it is at the Very Short level initially, and don't feel that you should be doing any more than that until you are absolutely sure that you are ready for it. You will have plenty of time to build your endurance as long as you are consistent in the implementation of your training plan. Regardless of your initial baseline, the general principle is to gradually and progressively increase the duration of these endurance workouts from your own personal starting point to the Long and eventually to the Very Long levels.

Intensity Workouts

The second type of workout that you will need to include in your training program is the *intensity workout*. These workouts typically involve a much shorter duration but a significantly higher level of intensity than the endurance workouts. They should usually begin with a short warm up at a lower level of intensity before you begin the main set, and finish with a short cool down after the main set.

For endurance triathlon training purposes, the duration of your intensity workouts will typically be in the Short to Intermediate range, with the intensity going up to the High level, which corresponds to at least 85% of your maximum intensity level, during the main set. Accordingly, I usually plan on maintaining a 2-beat pattern of breathing for the main sets in these types of workouts. In my experience, the total workload for these types of workouts will typically be perceived as being in the Hard range, despite their relatively short duration. As a general rule, remember that the higher the intensity level, the more likely it is that you will perceive a workout as being aversive in some way.

In contrast to endurance workouts, you will not need to keep increasing the duration of these workouts throughout your training. The duration of these workouts can gradually be increased somewhat as your level of fitness improves over the early stages of your training program, but the good news is that the proportional amount of increase in duration does not need to be anywhere near as much as it will be in the endurance workouts. As a rough guide, once you have reached a level of fitness at which you feel you have the necessary endurance to comfortably finish the distances involved in each component of an Olympic distance triathlon, the duration of these intensity workouts can be kept fairly constant over the remainder of the training program.

There are several different sub-types of intensity workouts. The main set may often include some form of interval training, in which a relatively short distance is repeated numerous times at a relatively high level of intensity with short recovery periods either at a lower level of intensity or at rest between each interval. An effective variation on the interval workout can be some type of "fartlek" workout, in which the intensity level is varied in either a systematic way or a random way during the course of a continuous workout, depending on what you feel capable of doing on a particular day. You may also want to consider including some hill work in your intensity workouts on both the bike and run, particularly if you know that parts of the race course are going to be hilly. My weekly bike workout on the hill at Tantalus was one of my favorite workouts when I was training for Kona and for Western Australia. I have often heard it said that hill work is the equivalent of speed work in disguise, because it allows you to get a similar high intensity workout without putting as much stress on your body.

Because the main area of focus of the training program for recreational athletes is building endurance, you may be wondering about the purpose of intensity workouts. Although shorter workouts at a higher level of intensity are often used primarily as a way of increasing speed, particularly for competitive athletes, there is a mounting body of research that suggests that working out at higher levels of intensity can also contribute to building endurance. As a bonus, although, as recreational athletes, we are not primarily concerned about speed, these types of workouts can also help us to increase our sustainable pace during our longer workouts, and during the race itself. Consequently, the more that you become focused on achieving a specific time goal and optimizing race performance, the more important that intensity workouts are likely to become for you.

A particular advantage of intensity workouts is that they are relatively economical in terms of time, as compared to those long endurance workouts. You basically get "more bang for your buck" as it were. This economy of time may be particularly important if you are a typical recreational athlete like me with a limited amount of time available for training purposes. In addition many coaches now emphasize the importance of quality (i.e., higher intensity), as opposed to sheer volume when training for endurance sports, which obviously means putting more of an emphasis on intensity workouts. I'm inclined to agree with this approach, even for the recreational athlete. In fact, when training for Western Australia in 2009, I did put somewhat more emphasis on intensity workouts and less emphasis on those long endurance workouts than I did when I was training for Kona in 2006. If I ever do decide to train for another iron-distance event, I will probably extend that tendency even more in order to economize on time.

I would recommend that, as with the endurance workout, you plan on doing one intensity workout per sport per week. As indicated above, this could include intervals, a "fartlek" type of workout, some hill work, or some variation of these types of workout, depending on what you feel is going to be most beneficial for you.

Tempo Workouts

The third type of workout that you will need to include in your training is the so-called *tempo workout*. The duration of these workouts is generally not as long as the endurance workouts. The intensity level is somewhat higher, although not up to the level of the intensity workouts. In other words, they can be considered intermediate between the endurance workouts and the intensity workouts. Like the intensity workouts, tempo workouts should also usually begin with a short warm up at a lower level of intensity and finish with a short cool down. After the warm up, I try to maintain a 3-beat breathing pattern in these types of workouts. In my experience, these workouts are typically perceived as being at about the Moderate level of total workload.

In the context of training for endurance triathlons, tempo workouts will generally involve a Short to Intermediate duration at approximately a Medium level of intensity, which is about 75 to 84% of your maximum intensity level. Consequently, they are typically done at a pace that is somewhat faster than your anticipated race pace. As with the intensity workouts, you will not need to keep increasing the duration of these workouts. Again, as a general rule, once you have reached a level of fitness at which you feel you have the necessary endurance to comfortably finish an Olympic distance triathlon, the duration of these workouts can be kept fairly constant over the remainder of the training program.

These workouts are also relatively economical in terms of time as compared to the long endurance workouts, and they contribute significantly to the volume of training that you need to accumulate each week without requiring you to work as hard as you do in the intensity workouts.

Incidentally, I really don't like the term "tempo" because it is not a particularly descriptive term, and its meaning is not readily evident. In common parlance, "tempo" is something that can be either fast or slow, as in a piece of music. Consequently, the term doesn't really tell you much about the nature or purpose of the workout. In addition, although it is a term that is commonly used by coaches, definitions of what actually constitutes a tempo workout seem to vary somewhat from one coach to another. I had thought of using a different term such as "maintenance workout" because it seems to me that the primary purpose of these types of workouts is to help you maintain whatever level of endurance you have developed, rather than to actually increase your endurance. However, I eventually decided to stick with the term "tempo" simply because it is so commonly used.

Easy Workouts

I couldn't think of a particularly appropriate name for the fourth type of workout, so I eventually settled on the term *"easy workout."* I think of an easy workout as one that is done at or less than your anticipated race pace, that is, at no more than a Low level of intensity, and usually for a relatively Short duration. When training for endurance triathlons, do not expect to be doing a lot of easy workouts. In fact, these workouts do not really need to be included as an essential part of your schedule. There are, however, three ways in which easy workouts may sometimes be included in your training program.

First, after your long endurance workout on the bike, you should always try to include at least a short run in order to get your legs used to running after a long ride bike ride. These runs will often take the form of a tempo workout. However, on days when your energy is severely depleted after the long ride, you may need to scale back the run to an easy workout.

Second, you may sometimes want to do what is often described as an *active recovery workout* on days when you are still feeling drained after you have done a Hard or Very Hard training session the previous day. These types of workouts can sometimes be a particularly beneficial alternative on those days when you just do not feel up to doing anything as demanding as your scheduled tempo workout or intensity workout. Almost inevitably, during the course of your training program, there will occasionally be days like that.

Third, it is also fine to go out for an active recovery workout on your scheduled days off if you feel up to it. The primary purpose of these workouts is not to contribute directly to building endurance but to help promote recovery. I have often found that doing one of these short easy workouts actually helps to get the blood flowing and make me feel a little better than I would have done if had taken the day off completely. On the other hand, there are some days when I really feel that I need to just take a whole day off and do nothing but rest. It is important to learn to listen to what your body is telling you that it needs.

The Weekly Schedule

In order to build the necessary endurance in each sport when you are training for an iron-distance event, I have suggested that you plan to do at least three workouts per week for each sport—swim, bike, and run. This obviously amounts to a minimum total of 9 planned workout components each week. In addition, I have suggested that you consider including at least one core strength workout per week, if time permits, which would increase the total to 10 workout components per week. For each sport, the weekly training schedule should typically include one endurance workout, one intensity workout, and one tempo workout. As indicated in the previous section, you may sometimes want or need to either substitute or add an easy workout depending on how you feel on any given day. Could you get away with less than 9 workout components per week in case you just can't fit that many workouts into your training schedule?

Yes, I'm sure some people could. However, if you want to ensure that you are adequately prepared for the race, I would strongly recommend aiming for that minimum of 9 workout components each week whenever possible.

If you are going to fit a minimum of 9 workouts components into your schedule, you should, as a general rule, be prepared to train at least 5 days per week. Remember that most of your training sessions will take the form of combination workouts, which will consist of two components per day (swim/bike; swim/run; bike/run). Occasionally, you may want to include a practice triathlon in order to get some experience of doing all three sports on the same day. If your schedule permits, I'm inclined to suggest that it is better to spread your workouts over 6 days instead of trying to fit them all into 5 days. In that case, one or two of your training days can be somewhat easier in terms of total workload, and you will still have one day off completely. On the other hand, there is certainly something to be said for training only 5 days per week so that you can take two full days off for rest and recovery. You can decide what works best for you.

In my experience with triathlons, I have found that it tends to be a lot easier to transition from the swim to the bike than from the bike to the run, particularly in the early stages of training. Consequently, I think that the "brick" (bike/run) workouts are particularly important in order to get your leg muscles accustomed to running immediately after getting off the bike. When training for endurance triathlons, I would recommend including at least a short run after every bike ride, even if it is only an easy 10 minute-run.

You will see from my training schedule in the appendix that I sometimes trained every day of the week, rather than the 5 or 6 days that I am now recommending. This was at least partly because of my lack of confidence in my ability to finish that course in Kona. I felt at the time that I needed to squeeze into my schedule as much volume of training as I possibly could in order to get myself up to the level of fitness and endurance that I thought I would need. In retrospect, however, I am inclined to think that a training schedule of 5 or 6 days per week is quite sufficient, provided that you can consistently follow that schedule. That will allow you to include the recommended 9 or 10 workout components each week, which will provide plenty of hard training to build your endurance. It will also allow you to have either one or two full days off, which can be beneficial in terms of rest and recovery. If you do find that you have the energy and the desire to do some type of training on one of your scheduled days off, I would recommend keeping it to an easy active recovery type of workout in order to minimize the risk of overextending yourself.

In the combination workouts, one sport should usually be the primary focus, although some training sessions, such as those that include two tempo workout components on the same day, may involve a relatively balanced focus on both sports. For most recreational athletes, your longest workouts will probably be on the weekends, unless your work schedule happens to allow you to have days off during the week. On Saturdays, for example, I usually used to do a "brick" consisting of a long endurance workout on the bike, followed by either a tempo run or an easy run, depending on how I was feeling. Overall, this was almost invariably my longest, and probably hardest, training session of the week. I usually needed to take a nap for an hour or more on Saturday afternoons.

If your schedule allows you to do one component of your training in the morning and another in the afternoon or evening, that is likely to be so much the better in terms of recovery. On Sunday mornings, for example, I used to like to go for my weekly long endurance run, and then I might go for a tempo swim in the afternoon, by which time I had been able to take at least a short break for recovery and refueling after the long run.

Although most of your training sessions will take the form of combination workouts, you may sometimes want to focus on just one sport alone, particularly if you feel that you need for some reason to put more work into that sport than the other two. This is usually easier to do if you are able to spread your training over 6 days of the week rather than trying to fit everything into 5 days.

A typical week of training during approximately the middle of your training program might be as follows:

Day	Sport	Duration	Intensity	Type of Workout
Sunday:	Run (a.m.)	Long	Low	Endurance
	Swim (p.m.)	Intermediate	Medium	Tempo
Monday:	Off			
Tuesday:	Bike	Short	High	Intensity
	Run	Intermediate	Medium	Tempo
Wednesday:	Swim	Long	Low	Endurance
	Strength			
	(optional)			Strength
Thursday:	Bike	Intermediate	Medium	Tempo
	Run	Short	High	Intensity
Friday:	Swim	Short	High	Intensity
	Run			Easy
	(optional)			
Saturday:	Bike	Long	Low	Endurance
	Run	Shot	Low	Easy

Total weekly workload: Moderate to Hard

    During the early stages of your training program, when the duration of your workouts is still relatively short, your total weekly workload will probably be somewhat easier than it will in the example above. On the other hand, as you get closer to the peak of your program, when the duration of your workouts reaches its highest level, your total weekly workload is likely to be well into the Hard or even the Very Hard range. The good news is that by that time both your body and your mind will have developed enough endurance to get you through that harder workload.

    As I have emphasized above, the endurance workouts, which combine a Long duration and a Low level of intensity, are the most important workouts for the recreational athlete because they are the essential key to building the level of endurance necessary to finish an iron-distance event. In my opinion, they are also critically important psychologically because it is these increasingly long and relatively slow workouts that will allow you to gradually build the confidence that you have the necessary endurance to complete the distances involved in each of the three sports when race day comes around. Consequently, do not miss any of these workouts on your schedule unless you absolutely have to. If you do have to miss a workout, it is better to miss an intensity workout or a tempo workout than an endurance workout. For example, if your energy level is particularly low, you can scale back your intensity workout or tempo workout to an active recovery workout, or even take the day off completely if you really feel that you need the rest more than the workout. Then you will have more energy for those critical endurance workouts that are on the schedule later in the week. As a general rule, it is likely to be more beneficial in the long run to back off rather than push yourself to do a workout that you don't really have the energy for.

By this point, you may be wondering how much time you will need to allocate to your training each week. That brings us to a consideration of volume. Let's assume that each week you plan to include 10 workout components—three in each sport, plus one strength workout, as I have suggested. Let's further assume that you plan to train 6 days per week, with one day off completely. When you get to the peak of your training, you can probably expect to be doing 2 to 3 hours of training per day during 4 days of the week. You can then plan on putting in 4 to 5 hours on the day that includes your endurance run, and 6 to 8 hours on the day that includes your endurance bike workout. That would amount to a total volume of somewhere between 16 and 22 hours of training per week for the typical recreational athlete, although the exact amount of time will certainly vary from person to person depending on the pace that you are able to maintain in each of the three sports. In round numbers, therefore, you can probably plan on about 20 hours of training per week, plus or minus a few hours, at the peak of your training program. The relative amount of time that you devote to each sport will obviously depend to some extent on your ability level in each sport. As a rough guide, if you plan on a total of about 20 hours of training in your peak weeks, then you might allocate about 3 hours to the swim, 6 or 7 hours to the run, and 10 or 11 hours to the bike.

During the earlier stages of your training, the weekly volume will be considerably less than 20 hours per week, gradually increasing to that peak over a period of at least a few months. Obviously, the volume at the start of the training program will vary from person to person depending on your baseline level of fitness. Remember that it is perfectly fine to start at whatever level feels comfortable for you. Just make sure that you allow sufficient time to gradually build to your peak. Don't try to increase your weekly volume too rapidly because it will increase the risk of injury or burnout.

In retrospect, I think that I probably had a tendency to put in a somewhat greater volume of training than I absolutely needed to do in order to accomplish my primary goal of finishing the race. On the other hand, although I allocated as much time to training as I possibly could during that period of time in my life, I probably did not do as much as I would have needed to do if my priority had been to perform to the absolute best of my ability. The fact is that I would have had to retire prematurely in order to do that. I can now say that I'm very comfortable and very satisfied with the amount of training that I did. My training schedule was rigorous and comprehensive enough that it allowed me to go into the race with the confidence that I could achieve my goal, and yet, at the same time, it allowed me to maintain at least a minimal semblance of balance in my life during the process. By consistently following a systematic training plan, you can also find that balance with your schedule.

As you approach the end of your training program, your weekly training volume should reach a peak about three weeks before the race in order to allow sufficient time to taper. By that time, your confidence will be high enough that you can approach the race with a positive attitude and the knowledge that you have done all that you need to do to accomplish your goals. Tapering the volume over the last three weeks will then help to ensure that you have the energy and drive to perform to the best of your ability on race day. Over the course of the first two weeks of the tapering period, your weekly volume can be progressively reduced to about 30% of its peak by the time you get to the weekend prior to the race. During the final days leading up to the race, a few Short duration, Moderate intensity workouts will be quite sufficient as final preparations for the race.

Chapter 24

From Conceptual Framework to Specific Plan

You now have all of the essential conceptual elements that you need to go about developing a training schedule for yourself in a systematic manner. You are ready to start planning the specific details of your training schedule. You know now that your schedule each week will basically include one endurance workout, one intensity workout, and one tempo workout in each of the three sports. Occasionally, you may decide to substitute or add an easy workout for one reason or another. You may also want to include a strength workout if you are able to fit it in. Your weekly schedule will therefore include a total of 9 or 10 workout components, which you will you spread over 5 or 6 days each week, with 1 or 2 days off.

When you are ready to begin your training program, you will also have at least a vague sense of your current comfortable level of endurance in each of the three sports. That will be the basis for your first week of training. If you are not sure what that level is for you, just do a few trial workouts in each sport before you begin your training program. You will soon be able to develop a rough estimate of your starting level. A rough estimate of your endurance is fine, and it is really about the best that any of us can do, anyway. Let's say, for example, that you estimate that your current comfortable endurance levels are approximately 500 meters for the swim, 10 miles for the bike, and 3 miles for the run, around the distances involved in a sprint distance triathlon. The exact distances do not really matter and will, of course, vary from person to person. The important point is that you then know that these initial estimates will be the starting points for your endurance workouts. In addition, you know that in order to finish an iron-distance event, you are going to have to gradually build your endurance from those starting points up to a level at which you are able to swim 2.4 miles, bike 112 miles, and run 26.2 miles by the time race day arrives.

With all that knowledge in mind, the specific details of your training schedule should then flow forth in a fairly straightforward logical progression. Simply keep in mind that first key principle of gradually increasing the volume of training over the course of your program, and you can easily figure out what you need to include in your schedule on a week-by-week basis. I have included the specific details of my Kona training schedule in the two appendices for use as a sample guide, but I would again emphasize that your particular schedule may vary considerably from mine. It will depend on many factors, such as the following: your starting level of fitness, which may be higher or lower than mine was at the start of my program; your particular priorities and goals, which may be rather different than mine; and the time that you have available for training, which may be more or less than I had.

How Long?

One important additional issue that needs to be addressed in a little more detail is the length of your training program. Okay, you can now tell yourself, "I know that I am planning to devote several hours per day, 5 or 6 days per week, to my training." You can now pose the additional question—"How long am I going to have to do that?" The answer, as I have suggested, depends entirely on your starting level of fitness. To be a little more specific, if you are already accustomed to doing some training on a regular basis, and you know or feel that you already have the endurance to do an Olympic distance triathlon, then a 4- to 5-month program similar to the one that I followed during my training for Kona in 2006 should be sufficient. If your endurance is currently at about the level of a sprint distance triathlon, it might be more realistic to plan on a build up of about 6 months. If you have never trained on a regular basis and are just thinking about getting into triathlons, then you might need to take up to a year or possibly even more to build up to the 140.6-mile distance. I have heard of people who have just jumped from virtually nothing into an iron-distance race without doing a whole lot of training at all, but I would definitely not recommend that approach unless you are really into pain and suffering. As a general rule, take as long as you feel that you need for your training program. In addition, keep in mind that, in many ways, the journey is just as important as the destination in making your race the wonderful experience that I believe it can be and should be. Training for any endurance athletic event will inevitably take a considerable investment of time and energy, so make sure the process is rewarding and enjoyable and not simply an ordeal that must be endured.

Another factor that needs to be taken into consideration when you are planning to enter an iron-distance event these days is the rapid growth in popularity of virtually all of such events, both nationally and internationally, in recent years. Entries for the following year's event usually open on the day after the race, and many of the events sell out within a matter of days, or even within a few hours in some cases. A few years ago, you could wait for several months before making a decision to enter some races, but you can't expect to be able to do that any longer. This is certainly the case for most events in the Ironman® series sponsored by the World Triathlon Corporation, as well as for iron-distance events sponsored by other organizations, such as the HITS or Rev3 series. For all practical purposes, what this means is that you will have to decide at least a year in advance if you want to enter a particular event. Once you have made the decision to enter, be ready to go online and sign up as soon as entries open. Depending on the time zone where you live, that could be almost any time of the day or night. One of the benefits of this long term planning is that it does give you a lot of time in which you can gradually build up your endurance. Even if you are completely new to athletics, a year of training will probably be sufficient to allow you to prepare, again provided that you are consistent in implementing your training plan throughout the year. However, if you feel that you need longer than that, by all means take as much time as you need—there are no prizes for rushing it.

Implementing the Plan

There are a multitude of additional topics related to the design and implementation of a training program that could potentially be addressed. As I have said, however, my intention is not to provide comprehensive coverage of all the relevant topics. At this point I want to touch briefly on some of the most basic issues that merit some consideration when it comes to implementing your training plan. A few of the more important issues include *consistency*, *rest and recovery*, *hydration and nutrition*, and *periodization*.

Consistency

You will recall that the second of the two key principles involved in building endurance is to be relentlessly consistent in the implementation of your training plan. I have already touched on this issue a number of times, but it is one of those issues that must be emphasized. In plain language, make a point of actually doing what your plan calls for you to do. This sounds simple enough, but I think most of us know from personal experience, not only in training but also in other areas of our lives, that it is not always as easy as it may sound to put into practice. There are inevitably going to be times when you will have to adjust your schedule because of other responsibilities or unexpected events in your life. If you are forced to miss a workout, make a point of rescheduling it if at all possible, particularly if it is one of your endurance workouts, and try to avoid skipping it completely unless you absolutely have to.

It can sometimes be easy, particularly if you are doing all of training on your own, to blow off a workout because you just don't feel like making the effort for some reason. Maybe you had a particularly hard day at work, for example, or you are running late because you got caught in heavy traffic on your way home. Regardless of whether you will be training alone or with a group, when you make the decision to train for an event as challenging as an iron-distance triathlon, you also have to make a firm commitment to yourself to be consistent and disciplined in your approach to training. The simple fact is that if you skip too many workouts, you will find yourself behind in your training. Inevitably, this will gradually eat away at your confidence and, if you do make it to the race at all, ultimately detract from your performance. Consistency, on the other hand, will lead not only to steadily increasing fitness, but also to steadily increasing confidence that you have what it takes to achieve your goals.

Rest and Recovery

I have also touched on the importance of rest and recovery several times already. I will focus a little more on the topic here because the importance of rest and recovery cannot be overstated. When you are training for an extreme endurance event, it is easy to get carried away with the sheer volume of training, particularly if you have lingering doubts about your ability to finish the race. Under those circumstances, you may end up pushing yourself to do more training than your body can handle and skimping on your rest. Don't do that! You must make sure you get sufficient rest so that your body has a chance to recover from all the work you are going to be putting it through. Remember that it is during the rest periods between workouts that the physiological gains in your fitness are actually made and consolidated.

Training for an endurance triathlon is inevitably going to be demanding in terms of fitting all of the necessary workouts into your schedule. Consequently, the need for rest and recovery is sometimes going to come into conflict with the need for consistency in the implementation of your training plan. Throughout your training program, you will need to find a balance between your commitment to consistency and your need for rest and recovery. The exact nature of that balance will vary from person to person, so ultimately only you can decide what is the right balance for you. At some point, you will no doubt hear someone say that it is better to go into the race 10% undertrained rather than 10% overtrained. I think that is basically good advice, in the sense that you definitely don't want to be fighting fatigue on race day. On the other hand, you certainly don't want to slack off so much that you get to the point where you are overdoing it on the undertraining.

Although consistent implementation of the training program is extremely important, it is equally important to be flexible enough in your schedule to back off and allow additional time for rest and recovery when your body tells you that it needs you to do that. Consequently, it is important to listen to all the messages that your body is sending out to you as you go through your training program. Be just as consistent with your rest and recovery as you are with your training. Make a point of getting sufficient sleep every night, and give yourself permission take a nap on days when you need one. In addition, do not allow yourself to become so obsessively focused on following, without fail, every single detail of the training schedule if the price you pay is to short change yourself on rest and recovery. I would definitely recommend taking at least one day off completely every week, and, as I insinuated above, there is something to be said for taking two days off if it fits with your schedule. Even in the midst of iron-distance training, it is nice to have at least one day a week when I know that I can just go home and relax after work and maybe enjoy a leisurely beer or a glass of wine before dinner instead of having to scramble to get ready for another training session.

Rest and recovery are particularly important after Hard or Very Hard workouts, particularly if you end up having to do these types of workouts on consecutive days. I find that I need to consistently get 7 to 8 hours of sleep per night virtually every night when I am training for an upcoming race, otherwise I will start to feel fatigued after a few days. If you do find yourself feeling excessively fatigued or not sufficiently rested, then by all means take an extra day off. In addition, carefully assess your energy level prior to and throughout each workout, and, if necessary, adjust the duration and/or the intensity of your workout accordingly. Do not hesitate to cut back on the level of intensity, shorten the workout, or even stop the workout completely, if you feel it is necessary to do so. By all means test your limits and do a little extra on those days when you feel capable of doing so, but do not push yourself beyond your limits when you are feeling tired or fatigued. Pushing beyond your limits will not improve your endurance, but it will place your at increased risk for injury, illness, or burnout. Above all, do not allow yourself to feel guilty about cutting back or taking some extra time off if you really feel that you need to do so.

Nutrition and Hydration

Appropriate nutrition and hydration for triathlon training and racing is a topic that is certainly worthy of an entire book in and of itself, particularly for the competitive athlete. I am, however, going to maintain the focus on keeping things simple. Accordingly, apart from a few basic observations, I will not have a great deal to say about these two topics here.

Throughout the entire course of your training program, make sure that you are eating a sufficient amount of food to satisfy your body's needs for all the calories you are making it burn, but don't overdo it. When you feel hungry, don't wait to take something in—your body is telling you that it needs some fuel. Conversely, when you start to feel full, stop eating—you have probably had enough at that point. As much as possible, simply follow the basic general principles of healthy eating—eat regularly; eat moderate sized portions; and eat mostly whole, unprocessed foods, with a healthy balance of carbohydrates, protein, and fats. In my opinion, that is all that is really needed for the recreational athlete.

Some people recommend that you take various kinds of nutritional supplements in order to increase your energy level, enhance your performance, or speed up your recovery. As you probably know, there are a seemingly infinite number of these products on the market now. Maybe I'm a bit too much of a skeptic, but I am not a great believer in supplements. I have tried some of them in the past and I have never found that they make a whole lot of difference for me. If you are not careful, you can end up spending a lot of money on products that come with an awful lot of hype but little, if any, hard research to back up the claims that are made for them. Frankly, I think that some people may often experience a form of placebo effect from taking supplements. Simply put, if you believe they are going to have a positive effect, there is a good chance you will perceive that they actually do have a positive effect. Be aware, though, that there are a multitude of factors that can potentially influence the way that you feel and perform on any given day. Consequently, isolating the specific effect of one particular variable such as a supplement in a meaningful way is extremely difficult, if not impossible, even in a structured research setting, let alone in everyday life. I usually take a multivitamin each day, but that's about it. That has been sufficient for me.

Maintaining appropriate nutrition and hydration during workouts and, most critically, during the race itself is obviously a matter of extreme importance for endurance events. In general, I believe that, if you pay careful attention to how your body feels, it will tell you what it needs, and you can take action accordingly. This general principle worked well for me in Kona, where I felt that my hydration and nutrition were both pretty much spot on. In Western Australia, however, I must admit that I wasn't paying attention as well as I should have been to the messages my body was sending me. Consequently, I found myself somewhat dehydrated toward the end of the bike leg because I had not taken in as much fluid as I needed.

With regard to hydration, it is obviously easy to get dehydrated when you are training or racing for extended periods of time, particularly in hot climates where you are likely to be sweating constantly during both the bike and the run. Make a point of consuming fluids regularly throughout your workouts. Perhaps because I tend to favor simplicity, I often find that water is all I need to stay sufficiently hydrated during shorter workouts, although I do sometimes like to have some type of sports drink available also. There are many brands of sports drinks on the market these days, and you may want to experiment a bit to find which ones work best for you. On those long endurance workouts on the bike and run, I definitely like to maintain a balanced fluid intake of both water and a sports drink. I try to never allow myself to get to the point where I feel excessively thirsty. During races, I make it a point to take advantage of every aid station to replenish my fluids. Perhaps because I have raced almost exclusively in hot climates, the possibility of hyponatremia (excessively low sodium level) resulting from excessive fluid intake has never been a significant concern for me. However, I do realize that it can be an issue for some people in certain situations, particularly if fluid intake is restricted to water only. I have found that a good strategy during races is to alternate between water and a sports drink, in order to get a good mix of fluid, calories, and electrolytes. I have also found that caffeinated beverages can give me a lift toward the end of a long workout or race, but, for various reasons, I'm inclined to think that these types of drinks should be taken in moderation. After a hard workout, I almost always find that I need to keep drinking more than I normally would for the next several hours in order to make sure that my body stays sufficiently hydrated.

In the case of nutrition, sports drinks can also supply some of your caloric needs during long workouts or actual races, but it is important to remember that the longer the workout the more you are likely to need additional sources of fuel to keep you going. As a general rule, if the workout is longer than two hours, plan to take in some extra calories in some form or another. Individual needs may vary somewhat from person to person, but I think it is advisable to take in, on average, at least 200 to 300 calories for every hour that you are going to be out there. That amount usually seems to be about right for me, but some of you may find that you need more than that. Others may find that they do not need that much.

I have usually found that it is much easier for me to take in food, whether liquid or solid, on the bike rather than the run, so during a long brick workout or an actual race, I try to consume the bulk of my calories on the bike. On the other hand, it's probably a good idea to avoid taking in too much food right before you get to T2, so that you don't have too much stuff sitting in your stomach when you start the run. I have also usually found that energy gels or liquid foods are much easier for me to take in than solid foods during a long workout or a race. I particularly like products such as Ensure or Spiz because they are nutritionally well balanced, and you can get as much as 800 calories in a 24-ounce water bottle. It's not fine dining, but a relatively small amount of these products can go a long way. In addition to these types of high calorie products, I also found that a salty liquid, like the chicken soup offered at some of the aid stations on the later part of the run in Kona, was just what my body needed at that point in the race. Vegemite seemed to serve the same purpose for me in the later stages of the race in Western Australia, but I realize that it might not suit everyone's taste.

Although I have in the past tried to eat some solid foods, such as energy bars and bananas, while actually riding or running, I have tended to use them less and less as time has gone by. Just having to make the effort to chew and swallow solid food while I am actively working out often seems to take more energy than it is worth, and the solids are inevitably more difficult to digest than some type of liquid food, particularly at a time when your cardiovascular system is not devoting a great deal of its resources to supplying the needs of your gastrointestinal system. It may make sense to eat something like an energy bar or a banana during a break in the action, particularly in T1 after the swim, but otherwise, I'm now inclined to stick mostly to some form of liquid food for my nutritional needs during long workouts and races. I do, however, try to make a point of eating something like a Clif Bar right after I have finished a workout, followed up by a good solid meal as soon as possible.

Periodization

Many training programs that you will see in books and magazines or online are designed around a concept that has come to be known as *periodization*, which typically includes a number of different phases such as *base, build, peak,* and *taper.* This type of format has been popularized by coaches such as Joe Friel, and it has clearly become an essential way of structuring training programs for competitive athletes who are focused on maximizing speed. It can also be useful for the recreational athlete, although I am inclined to think that, apart from an essential taper period of about three weeks before a big race, following a well-defined sequence of phases is not as critical for the recreational athlete as it is for the competitive athlete. If you are a recreational athlete and your primary goal is just to finish that iron-distance triathlon, I would again be inclined to emphasize simplicity. Accordingly, your main focus should just be on following that first basic principle of gradually and progressively increasing the volume of your training over the course of your training program, so that you eventually reach a peak about three weeks before the race.

It seems to me that the essential principle of periodization programs is the shifting of focus between phases, with the earlier phases generally focusing more on developing the basic building block of endurance, and the later phases focusing more on increasing the level of intensity in order to build speed. As you develop a higher level of endurance, then it certainly does make sense to shift the focus somewhat toward increasing the intensity of some of your workouts to the extent that you are able, particularly the intensity workouts and the tempo workouts. As a recreational athlete, however, this can simply be done on a gradual basis based on your increasing level of fitness rather than by following a clearly defined set of phases.

Once again, keep in mind that the focus of your training as a recreational athlete will primarily be on building the necessary level of endurance and only secondarily on increasing speed through training at higher levels of intensity. Consequently, following a clearly defined periodization program would seem to be of less importance than it is for the competitive athlete. To illustrate this point, consider that an elite triathlete may have ridden over 100 miles on his or her bike hundreds or perhaps even thousands of times during training rides and races. For someone like that, merely doing the distance is no problem, and the focus must be on maximizing speed and competitive edge. In contrast, by the time I started the race in Kona in 2006, I had ridden my bike over 100 miles only six times in my whole life. On race day, my primary concern was having the endurance to bike 112 miles on a highly challenging course in hot and windy weather, immediately after swimming 2.4 miles, and knowing that I still had to run 26.2 miles on a tough course right after I got off the bike. Under those circumstances, I can assure you that maximizing my speed and the intensity of my effort was not at the forefront of my mind on that day. As long as I still had the endurance to keep moving forward, I was satisfied. I suspect that most recreational athletes will have a similar attitude.

Individual or Group Training

Before closing this part of the book, I would like to say a little more about the relative merits of training on an individual basis versus training with a group. As I have already indicated, the bulk of my training since 2002 has been done in a group format. On the other hand, a fairly large portion of my training for Kona in 2006 was, of necessity, a notable exception. There are a great many reasons to recommend joining a training group. For one thing, the group format relieves you of the necessity of planning your own training program when your available time and energy are likely to be at a premium. If you are able to train with a group that is focused specifically on preparing you for a particular event, then much, if not all, of the training schedule will be laid out in detail for you by experienced coaches on a day-by-day and week-by-week basis. All you really have to do is show up at the appointed place and do whatever the schedule calls for. This may be a significant benefit if you just don't have the time or the desire to go about designing your own program.

In my experience, there are also a number of other, more important reasons for choosing to train with a group. In particular, the camaraderie that develops among members of a group who are focused on a common goal provides not only a good deal of support and encouragement but also a level of motivation and inspiration that could sometimes be difficult to sustain over the long haul if you do all of your training alone. In addition, being able to celebrate the achievement of finishing a big event with a group of friends who have all shared the experience of working hard together for several months is a wonderful experience that definitely adds a layer of icing to the cake of personal accomplishment. The relationships with many of the training buddies that I have met while training with Brian Clarke, Boca Hawaii and Teem Marr have evolved into close friendships over the years, to the point that some of these friends have become like members of my extended family in many ways. Not only have we trained and raced together, we have socialized together, we have laughed and had fun, we have traveled together, we have confided in each other, and sometimes we have complained and commiserated about things together. My life, in general, has been greatly enriched by the friendships that have come out of the training groups that I have been involved with.

One other potential benefit of group training is that it may be somewhat easier to maintain your commitment to consistently following your training program if you know that others are expecting you to be there and do what you are scheduled to do. I guess you could call it a simple case of peer pressure. It is harder to make excuses for skipping workouts if you know there are a bunch of your friends who are expecting you to show up and perform, even if it is just another training session. That subtle peer pressure can also help you to push your limits and go beyond your comfort zone during your workouts. For example, after a good group workout, it is not unusual to hear people saying that they know they would not have pushed that hard or gone so far if they had not been with the group. I know I have felt that way many times. On the positive side, therefore, this peer pressure and friendly competition within the group can be beneficial in helping you to improve your level of fitness, and ultimately your performance. On the negative side, however, it can easily draw you into working a lot harder than you originally intended, which can, in turn, potentially lead to overtraining in terms of total workload and/or volume, and ultimately to feeling burned out, if you are not careful. It may also make you more prone to injury of some type. So, if you do decide to join a group, enjoy the benefits of the peer pressure and competition within the group, but don't overdo it, and don't allow yourself to be drawn into pushing yourself beyond your limits.

If you do choose to train with a group, there are, however, also some things to be said for doing at least some of your training alone. There are times when I find that I want or need to take some time for myself, and I can really enjoy the solitude of swimming, biking, or running on my own. It allows me some time to clear my mind and to be alone with my thoughts without having to pay attention to what others around me are doing or saying.

Training alone also provides excellent practice for racing, even if you are not racing as a competitive athlete. Although there are times during a race when you are going to be surrounded by other athletes, some of whom may be close friends, triathlon is ultimately an individual endeavor. At its most basic level, the race is simply the relationship between you and the course. Essentially, the course issues the challenge to every athlete who chooses to participate, and it is then up to you, as an individual, to respond accordingly. It is, therefore, good to have some experience of being out there on your own as you prepare to face that challenge.

Finally, as I hope I have shown in this part of the book, I believe it is well worth taking the time to develop some understanding of the principles behind the training process, so that you know why you are doing what you are doing, regardless of whether you are training alone or with a group. That understanding will enable you to design a simple training program for yourself if you ever choose to do so. I believe that designing and implementing a training program that is specifically tailored to your own individual needs can certainly be a rewarding experience if you have the time and the inclination to do so, or if you find yourself in a situation in which much of your training has to be done alone. Once you have developed a better understanding of the training process, you can still choose to train with a group if you prefer to do so, and the knowledge and experience that you have gained can serve as a basis for making helpful suggestions or providing constructive feedback to the group leaders. In that way, you can potentially contribute more actively to the direction of the group.

Summary

The essential idea that I have tried to communicate in this book is that, with a little determination and perseverance, a recreational athlete of no more than mediocre ability is perfectly capable of successfully taking on the challenge of an iron-distance triathlon. Two of the main themes that I have tried to weave into the book have been mediocrity and simplicity. Accordingly, I have tried to convey two specific messages that I hope can be applicable not only to athletics, but also to our lives more generally. My first message has been "Let us learn to accept and celebrate our inherent mediocrity! It is not only all that we have, but all that we will ever need to achieve our goals." The second message has been "Keep it simple! There is a great deal of joy and satisfaction to be found in simplicity, and not much, if anything, to be gained from making the training process, or life in general, more complicated than it needs to be."

In this final part of the book, I have tried to provide other recreational athletes a simple format for thinking about the process of training for an endurance event, as well as some specific suggestions about how to train for an iron-distance triathlon. These messages are summarized below.

Before making the choice to take on the challenge of training for any endurance event, be clear about why you will be doing it and what your priorities are, so that you know how you are going to approach the training process and the race itself.

When you have chosen the particular challenge that you want to take on, establish a set of specific, realistic goals for yourself.

Once you have made the choice to take on the challenge and set your goals, remember that the primary area of focus for your training is building *endurance*. In essence, this can be done by following two key principles. First, plan to gradually and systematically increase the *volume* of your training over the course of your training program. Second, make a commitment to yourself to be relentlessly consistent in the implementation of your training plan once you have formulated it.

When you are ready to go about setting up a specific training schedule, keep in mind the three basic concepts of *duration*, *intensity*, and *frequency*, which form the parameters of your workouts, and the two additional concepts of *total workload* and *volume*, which provide ways of measuring how much work you are doing. Focus your training program primarily on building a *very high* level of endurance, utilizing a balance of *endurance workouts, intensity workouts* and *tempo workouts*, as well as the occasional *easy workout,* in each of the three sports. Be clear about the purpose of each workout. Work hard when you are supposed to be working hard, but make sure you allow sufficient time for rest and recovery. You know exactly what the challenge of an iron-distance triathlon involves—a 2.4-mile swim, followed by a 112-mile bike ride, followed by a 26.2-mile run. It is a big challenge, no doubt, but basically not a complicated one. All you have to do is keep moving forward until you get to the finish line. With this knowledge and this simple conceptual framework in mind, the details of your training schedule should logically and easily fall into place.

Finally, when you get to race day, make sure that you manage your intensity level appropriately. In other words, pace yourself carefully, so that you don't run out of gas. In addition, make sure that you manage your needs for hydration and nutrition appropriately. Above all, maintain the will to just keep moving forward. It's definitely going to be a long, hard day, but I'm confident that by then you will have what it takes to eventually make it to the finish line.

In the two appendices that that follow, I have included some of the specific details of my training program for the Ford Ironman World Championship in Kona in October 2006. The first appendix is the outline of my week-by-week training schedule covering the period of 20 weeks from early June to mid October. The second appendix is simply a summary of that schedule. Both appendices include an accounting of what I was actually able to complete as opposed to what I had originally planned. Let me reiterate that this schedule is not intended to serve as a model training program that you should follow exactly. Rather, I present it simply as an example, in order to illustrate what I did and what worked for me, in the hope that it can serve as a guide for you. It will probably not fit your needs exactly, and ultimately you will have to determine for yourself what you are willing and able to do during your training.

Good luck with your training. If you are able to acknowledge and accept your mediocrity, take pride in it, and let it shine! Keep it simple and enjoy the journey. I will end by simply reiterating that if I can do it, I have absolutely no doubt that you can too.

APPENDIX A

Kona 2006: Weekly Training Schedule

Week ending: 06/11/06

	Planned	Actual
Monday:	Swim: 1000 meters	Swim: 1000 meters
Tuesday:	Swim: 2000 meters	Swim: 2000 meters
	Run: 1 hour	Run: 1 hour
Wednesday:	Off	Off
Thursday:	Swim: 1000 meters	Swim: 1000 meters
	Turbo: 1 hour	Turbo: 1 hour
Friday:	Off	Off
Saturday:	Bike: 65 miles	Bike: 65 miles
	Run: 2 miles	Run: 2 miles
Sunday:	Run: 13 miles	Run: 13 miles (half marathon)
	Swim: 1000 meters	Swim: 1000 meters

Week ending: 06/18/06

	Planned	Actual
Monday:	Swim: 2000 meters Turbo: 1 hour	Swim: 2000 meters Turbo: 1 hour
Tuesday:	Swim: 2000 meters Run: 1 hour	Swim: 2000 meters Run: 1 hour
Wednesday:	Off	Off
Thursday:	Bike: 2 laps (Tantalus) Run: 1 hour	Bike: 1.5 laps (Tantalus) Run: 50 minutes
Friday:	Off	Off
Saturday:	Bike: 65 miles Run: 2 miles	Bike: 65 miles Run: 2 miles
Sunday:	Run: 1 lap (Tantalus) Swim: 2000 meters	Run: 1 lap (Tantalus) Swim: 2000 meters

Week ending: 06/25/06

	Planned	Actual
Monday:	Swim: 2000 meters Turbo: 1 hour	Swim: 2000 meters Turbo: 1 hour
Tuesday:	Swim: 1000 meters Run: 8 miles	Swim: 1000 meters Run: 8 miles
Wednesday:	Turbo: 1 hour Strength training	Turbo: 1 hour Strength training
Thursday:	Off	Off
Friday:	Run: 14 miles	Run: 14 miles
Saturday:	Swim: 1 mile	Swim: 1 mile
Sunday:	Bike: 65 miles Run: 4 miles	Bike: 65 miles Run: 4 miles

Week ending: 07/02/06

	Planned	Actual
Monday:	Swim: 3000 meters	Swim: 3000 meters
Tuesday:	Run: 1 hour	Run: 1 hour (hill intervals)
	Turbo: 1 hour	Turbo: 75 minutes
Wednesday:	Swim: 2000 meters	Swim: 2000 meters
	Run: 1 hour	Run: 1 hour
Thursday:	Bike: 2 laps (Tantalus)	Bike: 2 laps (Tantalus)
	Run: 1 hour	Run: 1 hour
Friday:	Off	Off
Saturday:	Bike: 75 miles	Bike: 100 miles
	Run: 4 miles	Run: 2 miles
Sunday:	Run: 13 miles	Run: 10 miles
	Swim: 2000 meters	Swim: 1000 meters

Week ending: 07/09/06

	Planned	Actual
Monday:	Turbo: 90 minutes	Turbo: 90 minutes
Tuesday:	Swim: 3000 meters	Swim: 3000 meters
	Run: 1 hour	Run: 1 hour (with intervals)
Wednesday:	Turbo: 1 hour	Off
	Swim: 1 hour	Off
Thursday:	Bike: 2 laps (Tantalus)	Bike: 2 laps (Tantalus)
	Run: 1 hour	Run: 1 hour
Friday:	Run: 13 miles	Off
Saturday:	Swim: 2000 meters	Swim: 2000 meters
Sunday:	Bike: 75 miles	Bike: 75 miles
	Run: 4 miles	Run: 4 miles

Week ending: 07/16/06

	Planned	Actual
Monday:	Run: 12 miles	Run: 12 miles
Tuesday:	Swim: 3000 meters	Swim: 3000 meters
	Turbo: 90 minutes	Turbo: 30 minutes
Wednesday:	Run: 1 hour	Run: 1 hour (hills)
	Swim: 1 hour	Swim: 1 hour
Thursday:	Bike: 2 laps (Tantalus)	Bike: 2 laps (Tantalus)
	Run: 1 hour	Run: 1 hour
Friday:	Off	Off
Saturday:	Bike: 75 miles	Bike: 80 miles
	Run: 5 miles	Run: 5 miles
Sunday:	Run: 13 miles	Run: 12 miles
	Swim: 2000 meters	Swim: 2000 meters

Week ending: 07/23/06

	Planned	Actual
Monday:	Turbo: 90 minutes	Turbo: 90 minutes
	Strength training	Strength training
Tuesday:	Swim: 3000 meters	Swim: 3000 meters
	Run: 1 hour	Run: 1 hour (with intervals)
Wednesday:	Turbo: 1 hour	Turbo: 1 hour
	Swim: 1 hour	Swim: 1 hour
Thursday:	Bike: 2 laps (Tantalus)	Bike: 1 lap (Tantalus)
	Run: 1 hour	Off
Friday:	Run: 13 miles	Run: 13 miles
Saturday:	Swim: 2000 meters	Swim: 2000 meters
Sunday:	Bike: 80 miles	Bike: 80 miles
	Run: 4 miles	Run: 4 miles

Week ending: 07/30/06

	Planned	Actual
Monday:	Strength training	Strength training
Tuesday:	Swim: 3000 meters	Swim: 3000 meters
	Run: 1 hour	Run: 70 minutes (with intervals)
Wednesday:	Turbo: 90 minutes	Turbo: 90 minutes
	Swim: 1 hour	Swim: 1 hour
Thursday:	Bike: 2 laps (Tantalus)	Bike: 2 laps (Tantalus)
	Run: 1 hour	Run: 1 hour
Friday:	Swim: 2000 meters	Swim: 2000 meters
Saturday:	Bike: 80 miles	Bike: 80 miles
	Run: 5 miles	Run: 5 miles
Sunday:	Run: 15 miles	Run: 15 miles
	Swim: 2000 meters	Swim: 1500 meters

Week ending: 08/06/06

	Planned	Actual
Monday:	Strength training	Strength training
Tuesday:	Swim: 3000 meters	Swim: 3000 meters
	Run: 1 hour	Run: 70 minutes (with intervals)
Wednesday:	Turbo: 90 minutes	Turbo: 90 minutes
	Swim: 1 hour	Swim: 1 hour
Thursday:	Bike: 2 laps (Tantalus)	Bike: 1+ lap (Tantalus)
	Run: 1 hour	Run: 90 minutes
Friday:	Off	Off
Saturday:	Swim: 4000 meters	Swim: 4000 meters
Sunday:	Bike: 60 miles	Bike: 60 miles
	Run: 6 miles	Run: 6 miles

Week ending: 08/13/06

	Planned	Actual
Monday:	Strength training	Strength training
	Swim: 1000 meters	Swim: 1000 meters
Tuesday:	Swim: 3000 meters	Swim: 3000 meters
	Run: 75 minutes	Run: 80 minutes (with intervals)
Wednesday:	Turbo: 2 hours	Turbo: 90 minutes
	Swim: 1 hour	Swim: 1 hour
Thursday:	Bike: 2 laps (Tantalus)	Bike: 2 laps (Tantalus)
	Run: 1 hour	Run: 1 hour
Friday:	Off	Off
Saturday:	Bike: 80 miles	Bike: 85 miles
	Run: 10 miles	Run: 10 miles
Sunday:	Run: 15+ miles	Run: 10 miles
	Swim: 2000 meters	Swim: 2000 meter

Week ending: 08/20/06

	Planned	Actual
Monday:	Turbo: 1 hour	Off
	Strength training	Strength training
Tuesday:	Run: 15 miles	Run: 16 miles
Swim:	3000 meters	Swim: 2000 meters
Wednesday:	Turbo: 2 hours	Turbo: 2 hours
	Swim: 1 hour	Swim: 1 hour
Thursday:	Bike: 2 laps (Tantalus)	Bike: 2 laps (Tantalus)
	Run: 1 hour	Run: 1 hour
Friday:	Off	Off
Saturday:	Bike: 90 miles	Bike: 90 miles
	Run: 6 miles	Run: 6 miles
Sunday:	Run: Tamanaha 15K	Off
	Swim: 2000 meters	Off

Week ending: 08/27/06

	Planned	Actual
Monday:	Swim: 3000 meters Strength training	Swim: 4000 meters Strength training
Tuesday:	Run: 15+ miles	Run: 17 miles
Wednesday:	Bike: 2 laps (Tantalus) Swim: 1 hour	Bike: 2 laps (Tantalus) Swim: 1 hour
Thursday:	Turbo: 1 hour	Turbo: 1 hour
Friday (Kona):	Off Run: 1 hour	Swim: 1000 meters Run: 50 minutes
Saturday (Kona):	Swim: 1 hour Bike: 112 miles	Swim: 1000 meters Bike: 108 miles
Sunday (Kona):	Run: 15 miles Swim: 30 minutes	Run: 16 miles Swim: 1000 meters

Week ending: 09/03/06

	Planned	Actual
Monday:	Turbo: 30 minutes Strength training	Turbo: 30 minutes Strength training
Tuesday:	Swim: 4000 meters Run: 80 minutes	Swim: 4000 meters Run: 80 minutes (with intervals)
Wednesday:	Turbo: 2 hours Swim: 1 hour	Off Swim: 1 hour
Thursday:	Bike: 2 laps (Tantalus) Run: 1 hour	Bike: 2 laps (Tantalus) Run: 1 hour
Friday:	Run: 12 miles	Off
Saturday:	Swim: 2000 meters	Swim: 2000 meters
Sunday:	Bike: 112 miles Run: 30 minutes	Bike: 112 miles (Dick Evans) Run: 30 minutes

Week ending: 09/10/06

	Planned	Actual
Monday:	Swim: 2.4 miles	Swim: 2.4 miles (Roughwater)
Tuesday:	Run: 18 miles	Run: 18 miles
Wednesday:	Turbo: 2 hours	Turbo: 1 hour
	Swim: 1 hour	Swim: 1 hour
Thursday:	Bike: 2 laps (Tantalus)	Bike: 2 laps (Tantalus)
	Run: 1 hour	Run: 1 hour
Friday:	Off	Off
Saturday:	Bike: 75 miles	Bike: 75 miles
	Run: 10 miles	Run: 10 miles
Sunday:	Run: 12 miles	Run: 12 miles
	Swim: 2000 meters	Swim: 2000 meters

Week ending: 09/17/06

	Planned	Actual
Monday:	Turbo: 1 hour	Turbo: 1 hour
Tuesday (Las Vegas):	Run: 1 hour	Run: 1 hour
Wednesday (Vegas):	Strength training	Strength training
Thursday (Vegas):	Run: 1 hour	Run: 1 hour
	Swim: 2000 meters	Swim: 2000 meters
Friday:	Off	Off
Saturday:	Bike: 90 miles	Bike: 90 miles
	Run: 25 minutes	Run: 25 minutes
Sunday:	Run: 20 miles	Run: 20 miles

Week ending: 09/24/06

	Planned	Actual
Monday:	Swim: 4000 meters	Swim: 4000 meters
Tuesday:	Turbo: 2 hours	Turbo: 2 hours
	Strength training	Strength training
Wednesday:	Run: 90 minutes	Run: 90 minutes (with hills)
	Swim: 1 hour	Swim: 1 hour
Thursday:	Bike: 2 laps (Tantalus)	Bike: 2 laps (Tantalus)
	Run: 1 hour	Off
Friday:	Swim: 4000 meters	Swim: 4000 meters
Saturday:	Run: 20 miles	Run: 22 miles
Sunday:	Bike: 100 miles	Bike: 100 miles (Century Ride)
	Run: 30 minutes	Run: 30 minutes

Week ending: 10/01/06

	Planned	Actual
Monday:	Swim: 2000 meters	Swim: 2000 meters
	Run: 30 minutes	Run: 30 minutes
Tuesday:	Turbo: 1 hour	Turbo: 1 hour
	Strength training	Strength training
Wednesday:	Off	Off
Thursday:	Swim: 2000 meters	Swim: 4000 meters
	Run: 1 hour	Run: 1 hour (with intervals)
Friday (Kona):	Swim: 2000 meters	Swim: 1000 meters
Saturday (Kona):	Bike: 112 miles	Bike: 115 miles
	Run: 45 minutes	Run: 25 minutes
Sunday (Kona):	Run: 18 miles	Run: 18 miles
	Swim: 2000 meters	Swim: 1000 meters

Week ending: 10/08/06

	Planned	Actual
Monday:	Turbo: 1 hour	Turbo: 1 hour
	Strength training	Strength training
Tuesday:	Swim: 2000 meters	Swim: 2000 meters
	Run: 45 minutes	Run: 45 minutes (with intervals)
Wednesday:	Swim: 1 hour	Swim: 1 hour
Thursday:	Bike: 2 laps (Tantalus)	Bike: 2 laps (Tantalus)
	Run: 1 hour	Run: 1 hour
Friday:	Off	Off
Saturday:	Bike: 70 miles	Bike: 70 miles
	Run: 30 minutes	Run: 40 minutes
Sunday:	Run: 15 miles	Run: 15 miles
	Swim: 2000 meters	Swim: 2000 meters

Week ending: 10/15/06

	Planned	Actual
Monday:	Off	Off
Tuesday:	Swim: 4000 meters	Swim: 4000 meters
	Run: 1 hour	Run: 1 hour (with intervals)
Wednesday:	Bike: 1 hour	Bike: 1 hour
	Strength training	Strength training
Thursday:	Bike: 1 lap (Tantalus)	Bike: 1 lap (Tantalus)
	Run: 30 minutes	Run: 30 minutes
Friday:	Swim: 1000 meters	Swim: 1000 meters
Saturday:	Bike: 30 miles	Bike: 32 miles
	Run: 20 minutes	Run: 20 minutes
Sunday:	Run: 8 miles	Run: 9 miles
	Swim: 2000 meters	Swim: 1000 meters

Week ending: 10/22/06 (Race Week)

	<u>Planned</u>	<u>Actual</u>
Monday:	Off	Off
Tuesday:	Swim: 1000 meters Run: 30 minutes	Swim: 1000 meters Run: 30 minutes
Wednesday (Kona):	Swim: 2000 meters Bike: 1 hour	Swim: 1000 meters Off
Thursday (Kona):	Off	Bike: 1 hour
Friday (Kona):	Swim: 10 minutes Run: 10 minutes Bike: 10 minutes	Swim: 1000 meters Run: 20 minutes Bike: 10 minutes
Saturday (race day):	Swim: 2.4 miles Bike: 112 miles Run: 26.2 miles	Swim: 2.4 miles Bike: 112 miles Run: 26.2 miles
Sunday:	REST!! CELEBRATE!!	

APPENDIX B

Kona 2006: Training Summary

Weekly Goals/Actual

Week ending	Swim		Bike		Run	
	Long	Total	Long	Total	Long	Total
1) 06/11/06	2000	4000	50	100	13	26
Actual:	2000	5000	65	85	13	19
2) 06/18/06	2000	4000	50	100	13	26
Actual:	2000	6000	65	115	10	23
3) 06/25/06	2000	6000	60	120	13	26
Actual:	2000	5500	65	105	14	26
4) 07/02/06	2000	6000	60	120	13	26
Actual:	3000	6000	100	160	10	30

Week ending	Swim		Bike		Run	
	Long	Total	Long	Total	Long	Total
5) 07/09/06	2500	6500	75	150	13	26
Actual:	3000	5000	75	145	7	17
6) 07/16/06	3000	7000	75	150	13	26
Actual:	3000	7000	80	130	12	42
7) 07/23/06	3000	7000	80	160	13	26
Actual:	3000	7000	80	140	14	24
8) 07/30/06	3000	7000	80	160	15	30
Actual:	3000	8000	80	150	15	32
9) 08/06/06	4000	8000	60	120	9	24
Actual:	4000	9000	60	110	9	22
10) 08/13/06	3000	7000	80	160	15	30
Actual:	3000	8000	83	153	10	34
11) 08/20/06	4000	8000	90	170	15	30
Actual:	2000	4000	90	170	16	28
12) 08/27/06	4000	8000	112	180	18	36
Actual:	4000	8000	106	150	17	38

(Kona training weekend)

13) 09/03/06	4000	8000	112	180	12	30
Actual:	4000	8000	112	160	8	17
14) 09/10/06	4000	8000	90	170	18	36
Actual:	4000	8000	75	135	18	42
15) 09/17/06	4000	8000	90	150	18	36
Actual:	2000	2000	90	110	20	34

(Las Vegas trip)

Week ending	Swim		Bike		Run	
	Long	Total	Long	Total	Long	Total
16) 09/24/06	4000	8000	100	180	20	36
Actual:	4000	10000	100	180	22	33
17) 10/01/06	4000	8000	112	170	18	36
Actual:	4000	8500	115	135	20	32
(Kona training weekend)						
18) 10/08/06	4000	8000	70	150	15	30
Actual:	2000	6000	70	130	15	30
19) 10/15/06	4000	7000	30	60	8	15
Actual:	4000	6000	32	64	9	20
20) Race week	2000	3000	20	30	3	5
Actual:	1000	3000	15	18	3	5